ting and Reducing Aggression
.d Violence in Health and Social Care:
A holistic approach

Other Health and Social Care books from M&KPublishing include:

Research Issues in Health and Social Care
ISBN: 978-1-905539-20-8 · 2009

Nurses and Their Patients:
Informing practice through psychodynamic insights
ISBN: 978-1-905539-31-4 · 2009

Perspectives on Death and Dying
ISBN: 978-1-905539-21-5 · 2009

Identification and Treatment of Alcohol Dependency
ISBN: 978-1-905539-16-1 · 2008

Inter-professional Approaches to Young Fathers
ISBN: 978-1-905539-29-1 · 2008

The Clinician's Guide to Chronic Disease Management
for Long Term Conditions: A cognitive-behavioural approach
ISBN: 978-1-905539-15-4 · 2008

The ECG Workbook
ISBN: 978-1-905539-14-7 · 2008

Routine Blood Results Explained (2nd edition)
ISBN: 978-1-905539-38-3 · 2007

Improving Patient Outcomes
ISBN: 978-1-905539-06-2 · 2007

Pre-Teen and Teenage Pregnancy:
A twenty-first century reality
ISBN: 978-1-905539-11-6 · 2007

Issues in Heart Failure Nursing
ISBN: 978-1-905539-00-0 · 2006

Preventing and Reducing Aggression and Violence in Health and Social Care:

A holistic approach

Kelvin Ford

Richard Byrt

James Dooher

Preventing and Reducing Aggression and Violence in Health and Social Care
Kelvin Ford, Richard Byrt and James Dooher

ISBN: 978-1-905539-57-4

First published 2010

British Library Catalogue in Publication Data
A catalogue record for this book is available from the British Library

Notice
Clinical practice and medical knowledge constantly evolve. Standard safety precautions must be followed, but, as knowledge is broadened by research, changes in practice, treatment and drug therapy may become necessary or appropriate. Readers must check the most current product information provided by the manufacturer of each drug to be administered and verify the dosages and correct administration, as well as contraindications. It is the responsibility of the practitioner, utilising the experience and knowledge of the patient, to determine dosages and the best treatment for each individual patient. Any brands mentioned in this book are as examples only and are not endorsed by the publisher. Neither the publisher nor the authors assume any liability for any injury and/or damage to persons or property arising from this publication.

To contact M&K Publishing write to:
M&K Update Ltd · The Old Bakery · St. John's Street
Keswick · Cumbria CA12 5AS
Tel: 01768 773030 · Fax: 01768 781099
publishing@mkupdate.co.uk
www.mkupdate.co.uk

Designed and typeset in 11pt Usherwood Book by Mary Blood
Printed in England by Ferguson Print, Keswick.

Contents

List of figures

List of tables

Acknowledgements

With acknowledgements to clients, students and colleagues, who have taught us so much. Thanks to Fliss Watts, copy editor.

Richard Byrt would like to thank David J. Bowley, Caroline Byrt, Mahesh Chauhan and Sara Le Butt for their support in different ways.

Kevin Ford would like to thank his wife Jane and daughter Rachel for their continuing help and support.

About the authors

Richard Byrt RMN, RNLD, RGN, PhD, BSc (Hons)

Richard is a lecturer-practitioner, nursing, at the School of Nursing and Midwifery, De Montfort University and Arnold Lodge Medium Secure Unit, Nottinghamshire Healthcare NHS Trust. Richard also has experience as a service user and informal carer, and has worked in a wide variety of health and social care settings.

James Dooher RMN, MA, FHE Cert Ed, Dip HCR, CRS, FHEA

James is Principal Lecturer, Academic Lead for Mental Health/Senior Research Fellow, Faculty of Health and Life Sciences, De Montfort University. He has a particular interest in facilitating service users to reach their potential and is actively involved in local networks that promote this. He has worked as a nurse within a range of mental health settings, and for the last 12 years has led Mental Health Nurse education in Leicestershire.

Kelvin Ford Psychol D, MPhil, MSc, MA, BA (Hons), Dip N, Dip Couns, Cert Ed, RMN

Since 1975, Dr. Kelvin Ford has worked as a Mental Health Practitioner, including ten years within a Regional Secure Unit, treating mentally disordered offenders. In 1994 he was appointed Trent Regional Mental Health Fellow, being responsible for Post Graduate Mental Health education for General Practitioners, within Trent Region. He also conducted a major research study identifying mental health educational needs for Primary Health Care Workers. He is currently a Senior Lecturer in Psychology, specialising in mental health care and psychotherapeutic interventions at De Montfort University, Leicester.

Introduction

Welcome to this book, which considers the prevention and reduction of violence and aggression as an aspect of health and social care. It discusses specific skills and interventions in this area, although much of the material has general relevance to professionals working within all fields of health and social care, who may encounter violence or aggression within their working lives.

The book aims to critically explore the common issues and difficulties encountered by professionals, and to provide an insight and understanding which helps the prevention, anticipation, management and evaluation of behaviour that increases threat or risk to the individual and those around them.

The authors argue that:

- All aspects of nursing and multidisciplinary practice are relevant to reducing, and in particular, to preventing, violence and aggression.

- A holistic approach to the individual client is essential, as violence and aggression may be related to a wide range of the individual's needs, problems and strengths, including those that are physical, psychological, spiritual, cultural, social, environmental and related to aspects of diversity.

- All interventions need to be underpinned by:
  - the need to ensure safety and reduce the risk of harm to the individual who is being violent or aggressive and to others who may be affected by that behaviour
  - ethical values, which ensure that interventions do not cause harm and respect the individual
  - evidence related to which interventions are effective and therapeutic for the client, ensure his or her safety and that of others and minimise risk (Byrt and Doyle, 2007).

Violence and aggression and the threat of violence and aggression, be it verbal or physical, are a serious hazard to the health, safety and wellbeing of care workers and their clients. Ideally, no one should face aggression or violence in the workplace, but in reality many people do, and this is becoming increasingly reported where contact with customers, clients, crowds and the general public forms part of a person's job.

For most workers in health and social care, it will be an occasional and infrequent hazard, but for others it can be a daily occurrence. Regardless of the frequency with which incidents arise, it is important to implement safeguards which minimise their likelihood, the risks when they do arise, and the potential negative impact upon staff after the event. Employers are taking their duty of care, and responsibilities for maintaining the health, safety and welfare of employees and service users very seriously, placing the highest value on creating a positive working environment, free from violence, aggression and abuse, and we hope this book contributes to the knowledge base which helps protect all from the effects of violence and aggression.

Chapter 1
A holistic approach

This chapter considers three key themes that will help the health worker understand how to prevent and reduce violence and aggression in relation to other aspects of care. It explores the meanings of 'anger', 'aggression and 'violence', and outlines the differences between assertive, aggressive and other expressions of anger. Understanding these sometimes subtle differences will enable the reader to gain an appreciation of the factors which underlie behaviour that challenges socially accepted patterns, and will give an opportunity for reflection upon personal feelings that will hopefully provide insight to promote a range of alternative patterns of response.

The integration of measures to prevent violence and aggression with other aspects of care

Integration of measures

Our behaviour as professionals is an important part of preventing violence and promoting safety for the people in our care, but this is a complex process, and relies on a range of skills and understanding of the situation to ensure tensions do not escalate into aggression or violence. Kettles *et al.* (2007, p. 3) have argued for the integration of approaches to ensure 'safety of self and others', with the need to relieve distress and have 'respect for the individual and his/her unique needs'. This approach is critical of the separation of interventions to prevent and reduce violence and aggression from other aspects of care. An example would be intensive observation, in which the care workers focus purely on observations in order to reduce risk of harm to others, rather than engaging or interacting with the client, or indeed, providing any holistic assessment or care to meet identified needs (Barker and Buchanan-Barker 2005; Cutcliffe 2009).

A more integrated approach (as shown in Fig. 1.1) is illustrated in the following example. Mr Mahendra Patel (a pseudonym) moved to a crisis house, a type of supported residential accommodation in the community for individuals with mental health problems who are in crisis (Mental Health Foundation and Sainsbury Centre for Mental Health 2002). Mahendra, as he preferred to be called, expressed a preference for moving to the crisis house, rather than to the mental health acute admission ward, where he had been previously admitted when experiencing crises.

Mahendra felt a need for respite and recovery from very distressing experiences, including voices (auditory hallucinations) which called him offensive names. He believed that the voices emanated from other people (for example, the newsagent who sold him his morning paper), and had aggressive thoughts of hitting them. However, no one was actually calling Mahendra offensive names.

Figure 1.1   **Integrated care**

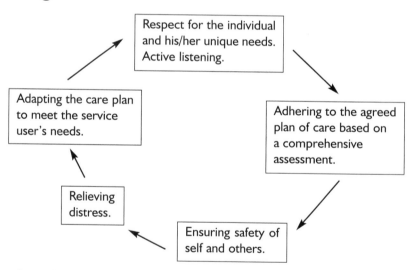

Adapted from Kettles et al., 2007, p. 3
(By kind permission of Quay Books, MA Healthcare, Ltd)

Interventions, carefully planned with Mahendra's involvement, both helped to reduce his distress in response to the abusive voices, and enabled him to find strategies to cope with them better. The latter included talking with a worker he felt he could trust, engaging in a relaxing activity, when required, access to additional ('PRN') medication (prescribed by his psychiatrist), and, in addition, enabling Mr Patel to have quiet periods of meditation. These approaches reduced Mr Patel's distress. They also contributed to other people's safety because he was able to safely ventilate anger related to his voices, find means of distraction, or the meeting of his specific spiritual needs. Various interventions are described later in this book.

What is anger?

What is anger?

Anger consists of both a subjective experience or feeling, which is recognised as 'anger', and accompanying physiological changes and facial expressions. Various authors have argued that anger has emotional, thinking and behavioural components (Gurney, 2009; McKay *et al.*, 2003). The individual experiences him or herself as 'feeling angry' in response to someone or something that engenders frustration or annoyance. Anger is also manifested in thoughts, and sometimes, behaviour, which may be directed towards him or herself or other people or objects (Howells *et al.*, 2008, p. 352; Swaffer and Hollin, 2001, p. 266, citing Novaco 1975 and 1994). Anger involves various changes in hormones and the autonomic nervous system.

What is aggression?

What is aggression?

Only fairly recently, scientists have begun to investigate aspects of the phenomenon of anger, including aggression (Hodgins *et al.* 2009). However, manifestations of anger, including violence and aggression, have been extensively considered by poets, philosophers, theologians and political thinkers, since the times of ancient civilisations (Foakes 2003, Westwood 2002). More recently, insights have been added by a variety of professionals and academics, including nurses (Richter and Whittington 2006), psychiatrists (Simon and Tardiff 2008), neurobiologists (Hodgins *et al.* 2009), psychologists (Flannery *et al.* 2008, Howitt 2009) and sociologists (Collins 2009).

One major concern of those who study aggression is the overabundance of terms used in the research literature. There is considerable overlap in these terms and this is because aggression and violence are difficult concepts to define. 'Scientific usage' of these terms, 'let alone ... popular meanings, [are] unclear' (Farrell and Gray 1992, p. 1). The term 'violence' does not necessarily convey the same meaning to everyone, and it is often used interchangeably with aggression (Rippon 2000). For instance, according to Leiba (1980), individuals described as 'potentially violent' may become aggressive unless they are controlled in some way.

In their comprehensive review of relevant research, Wells and Bowers (2002) found that researchers used a variety of different definitions and types of behaviours in assessing the incidence and likely increases of violence within health services. They state that research studies, up to the time of their paper, had problems of method, definition and clear classifications of types of violence, making it difficult to compare studies to see if there were real increases in violence towards staff. A similar point is made by Howells *et al.* (2008).

This problem may be overcome by NHS Security Management Service requirements that NHS services use a standardised reporting form to document incidents of violence and aggression. The NHS Security Management Service has used this form to measure recent incidences of violence in NHS services (NHS Business Services Authority Security Management Service 2007a).

Possible distinctions between aggression and violence

Some authors make a distinction 'between aggression as the intention to cause harm; violence as actual harm' (Byrt and Doyle 2007, p. 72, citing NICE 2005; Turnbull and Paterson 1999). This distinction has been made by the NHS Business Services Authority Security Management Service (2007a), and is, therefore, of relevance to mental health and learning disability nursing, e.g., in recording, in a standardised way, that particular incidents involve violence or aggression (Gournay *et al.*, 2008). In contrast, 'the definition used by the World Health Organisation associates intentionality with the committing of the act itself, irrespective of the outcome it produces. Excluded from the definition are unintentional incidents – such as most road traffic injuries...' (World Health Organisation 2002, p. 5).

Most recent definitions of violence (including that of NHS Business Services Authority Security Management Service, 2007a) include both physical harm and verbal abuse in their definitions of violence.

Definitions of aggression

The literature includes a wide range of definitions of aggression and violence. Aggression has been defined as:

> 'A disposition, a willingness to inflict harm, regardless of whether this is behaviourally or verbally expressed, and regardless of whether physical harm is sustained' (NICE 2005, p. 5).

> 'Behaviour that is intended to injure another person (physically or verbally) or to destroy property'. The key concept in this definition is "intent", rather than accidentally hurting someone...' (Atkinson *et al.* 2000, p. 406).

The term 'aggression', as used in this book, includes the above definitions.

Some authors have suggested that behavioural definitions of aggression are generally the most precise. For example, Buss (1961, p. 3), defined aggression as a 'response that delivers noxious stimuli to another organism'. This definition is rather narrow and does not include any references to states of 'mind' or 'attitude'. Used in this way, aggression is easy to specify and measure in an experiment.

The term 'aggression' has also been used in referring to more wide-ranging phenomena. This generic sense was well expressed by Stone (1971, p. 1): 'Aggression ranges far in psychoanalytic thought. It may include manifest bodily or verbal action; conscious or unconscious wishes and tensions; a specific qualitative type of psychic energy and the final broad and inclusive idea of the death instinct...' As stated above our use of the term 'aggression' follows the NICE definition incorporating intent to harm.

Definitions of violence

Violence as the illegal or illegitimate use of force

Several definitions of violence include the illegal or illegitimate use of force as a component (NICE 2005, p. 5; Cembrowicz *et al.* 2001, p. 118, Mason and Chandley 1999, World Health Organisation 2002). The Department of Health (2003) and NHS Business Services Authority Security Management Service (2007a, p. 7) define physical assault (a type of violence) as:

Definitions of violence

'The intentional application of force against the person of another without lawful justification, resulting in physical injury or personal discomfort...This definition was designed to apply specifically to the NHS, to replace any other definition previously in use across the NHS and to allow health bodies to be clear about which incidents they need to report.'

Violence as the illegitimate use of power

The World Health Organisation (2002) gives a comprehensive definition of violence that includes the use of force and adds the concept of power. (Power has a number of meanings, but in this context, can be defined as the ability to bring about a desired goal or change (Byrt 2008a; Dooher and Byrt 2005).) World Health Organisation (2002) and Fawcett and Waugh (2008) include a variety of misuses of power as components of violence, including 'threats and intimidation... neglect and all types of physical, sexual and psychological abuse, as well as suicide and other self-abusive acts' (World Health Organisation 2002, p. 5). This source points out that violence can be directed at whole communities and social groups, a point considered later in this book, with the probability of 'injury, death, psychological harm, maldevelopment or deprivation' (World Health Organisation 2002, p. 5).

Physical assault as part of violence

The NHS Business Services Authority Security Management Service's (2007a, p. 13) *Tackling Violence Against Staff* states that physical assault of NHS staff includes:

- 'Physical contact...not just an attempt. Examples include punches, slaps, kicks, head butts, scratches, nips, hair being pulled and strikes by weapons.
- 'Physical contact also means when items (weapons, objects and liquids (including spittle)) thrown hit a member of staff'.

Verbal abuse as part of violence

Some definitions and classifications of violence have been criticised for not considering verbal abuse, including discriminatory language, in addition to physical assaults. We all know the feeling that verbal abuse generates; even what might be considered as mild abuse can leave the recipient feeling injured. Research suggests that, for some staff, verbal abuse may cause as much distress as physical injury (Buckley 2000; Sofield and Salmond 2003).

In relation to this, the Royal College of Nursing (1998) offered the following definition:

> 'Violence is any incident in which a health professional experiences abuse, threat, fear or the application of force arising out of the course of their work whether or not they are on duty'
> (Royal College of Nursing, 1998, quoted in Morgan 2001, p. 107)

The NHS Business Services Authority Security Management Service points out (2007a, p. 13) that 'non-physical assault cases...in some instances, can be more serious than...physical assault'. Non-physical assault is defined in NHS Security Management Service (2004, p. 2) as: 'the use of inappropriate words or behaviour causing distress and/or constituting harassment'.

According to the British Association of Social Workers (1988, p. 1), violence is '...behaviour which produces damaging or hurtful effects, either physical or emotional on other people...' Such a definition recognises that the problem of violence has to do with the feelings of anxiety and fear which are aroused in those on the receiving end, as well as with the more obvious visible results from physical assault.

Examples of non-physical assault

Sometimes non-physical assault is categorised outside of violence. However, the impact upon the recipient may have consequences which are comparable to that of physical assault. Box 1.1 gives a list of forms of non-physical assault, from the NHS Security Management Service (2004, p. 2f).

Box 1.1   **Examples of non-physical assault**

- Offensive language, verbal abuse and swearing which prevents staff from doing their job or makes them feel unsafe.
- Loud and intrusive conversation.
- Unwanted or abusive remarks.
- Negative, malicious or stereotypical comments.
- Invasion of personal space.
- Brandishing of objects or weapons.

- Near misses (i.e., unsuccessful physical assaults).
- Offensive gestures.
- Threats or risk of serious injury to a member of staff, fellow patients or visitors.
- Bullying, victimization or intimidation.
- Stalking.
- Spitting.
- Alcohol or drug fuelled abuse.
- Unreasonable behaviour and non-cooperation, such as repeated disregard of hospital visiting hours…
- Any of the above linked to destruction of or damage to property.

(Quoted from NHS Security Management Service 2004, p. 2f)

Hostility, Hostile and Instrumental Aggression

Hostility

'Anger…needs to be distinguished from hostility, which refers to the negative cognitive evaluation of people or events. Both anger and hostility can give rise to the behavioural expression of aggression, but need not do so' (Howells *et al.* 2008, p. 352). We can distinguish between 'hostile' and 'instrumental' aggression and violence. Instrumental aggression or violence is intended to result in rewards for the individual, and 'the perpetrator does not show emotional arousal (or cognitions) of an angry sort' (Howells *et al.*, 2008, p. 355). Rewards could include avoiding injury by fighting in self-defence or demonstrating power and dominance. In some situations, instrumental aggression could include 'prosocial' aggression, with people in positions of power arguing that they are defending the rights of an underdog (Westwood 2002).

In contrast, in hostile aggression or violence, the sole aim is to inflict injury. The individual experiences the physiological and psychological concomitants of anger, which is usually triggered by something which causes frustration (Howells *et al.*, 2008).

The distinction between hostile and instrumental aggression is not necessarily clear cut. For example, an incident which, on the surface, may look like hostile aggression may serve other ends, e.g., a person who attacks an innocent person may, in turn, be motivated to gain status with other gang members (Paterson and Leadbetter 1999).

Aggressive behaviour can be a result of a wide range of possible motives, for example, power, wealth and status. However, according to Farrell and Gray (1992, p. 6), 'it can be stated with complete confidence that the potential for aggression is present in everyone and that few people are entirely free of angry thoughts and feelings. Most have become aggressive at some time, in response to another's threat, to relieve tension and frustration in pursuit of some goal, or simply to get attention' or positive regard from others. For example, a young man could hope to gain respect from his peers through engaging in violent behaviours to prove that he is an 'OK guy' who can't be 'messed with' (Barker 2005).

'Challenging behaviour'? Or individuals whose specific needs present a 'challenge to services'
(Blunden and Allen 1987, p. 14)

'Challenging behaviour'?

The term 'challenging behaviour' was originally applied to ways that some behaviours of people with learning disabilities challenged services (Blunden and Allen, 1987). More recently, the term has been used to describe individuals with mental health problems and/or learning disabilities.

The problem with a term such as 'challenging behaviour' is that it can become a label, with the individual being seen only as someone whose behaviour causes others difficulty (Emerson 2001; Twist and Montgomery 2005). However:

> The term had been originally used by the North American organization, The Association for Persons with Severe Handicaps. It was designed to stress the fact that difficult behaviours shown by service users should be viewed more appropriately as the product of an interaction between characteristics of the individual and characteristics of their service settings. Hence, 'some behaviours represent challenges to services, rather than problems that individuals with learning disabilities [or mental health problems] somehow carry around with them. If services could rise to the "challenge" of dealing with these behaviours, they would cease to be problems'
> (Allen 2002, p. 3, quoting Blunden and Allen 1987, p. 14)

The term 'challenging behaviour' has been used to describe behaviours injurious to others, as well as to the client, and not in keeping with her/his cultural and social background. Twist and Montgomery's definition emphasises that, in addition to 'significant costs to others' (e.g., from being assaulted), 'challenging behaviour...imposes a significant cost to the person- for example, physical harm to self, social rejection, exclusion from recreational, educational or employment opportunities' (Twist and Montgomery 2005, p. 340, quoting Emerson 2001, p. 3).

Ways of expressing anger: Some questions

Expressing anger

Here are two questions for consideration and discussion:

- Is it appropriate for clients to express anger?
- Is it appropriate for you, as a professional carer, to feel angry with a client?

In answer to these questions, various authors have distinguished between three ways of expressing anger: assertiveness (sometimes referred to as 'assertion'); passivity or non-assertive-ness; and aggression (Duxbury 2000; Linsley 2006; Stuart and Hamolia 2009). The need for care workers to be self-aware in relation to their own feelings and responses to clients' anger, including violence and aggression, has also been emphasised by several authors (Byrt and Doyle 2007; Linsley 2006; Whittington and Balsamo 1998).

'Unfortunately, the words aggression and assertiveness are used synonymously by some people' (Farrell and Gray 1992, p. 3). The client or care worker who expresses anger assertively states his or her concerns, views, rights and needs 'in a clear, confident manner, without denying the rights and needs of others. By implication, an aggressive manner fails to acknowledge the other's rights, and a passive response fails to acknowledge one's own rights'(Farrell and Gray 1992, p. 3), with the individual finding it difficult to express these (Stuart and Hamolia 2009). 'Being assertive is usually preferable to being either aggressive or passive. Passivity, for example, may well serve to reinforce a belief that one is prepared to disregard oneself for the sake of another' (Farrell and Gray 1992, p. 3; see also Stuart and Hamolia, 2009). Passivity can also involve 'bottling up' anger. This is not openly expressed, and may result in depression and/or a build up of anger and resentment, with the individual eventually expressing aggression, verbally or physically, in a sudden, explosive way

(Bowness *et al.* 2008; McKay *et al.* 2003). As an example, two of the authors once worked with an individual ('Fred': a pseudonym) who, understandably, felt very angry about the abuse he had experienced as a child, from adult relatives. 'Fred' felt unable to express his anger towards the abusive relatives, and was usually extremely placid and conforming, rarely expressing his own views and preferences. However, occasionally, when drunk, his aggression was expressed through pub fights, one of which eventually led to his imprisonment and transfer to a medium secure unit. (Details have been changed to ensure the individual's confidentiality and anonymity.)

A factor which is not always considered by the literature on assertive, aggressive and passive ways of expressing anger (e.g., Stuart and Hamolia 2009) is cultural context. For example, what is seen as assertive by individuals in one cultural group may be perceived as either passive or aggressive by other people (Bowness *et al.* 2008; Byrt and Doyle 2007). This needs to be borne in mind when responding to clients, who may, for cultural and other reasons, perceive a care worker's attempt to be assertive in a quite different way to that intended (Arnold 2007b). There is also a danger of making a value judgement that a client is being aggressive when her or his mode of verbal or non-verbal communication is different from that of the worker. Corbett and Westwood (2005) have described how young men may be given a diagnosis of antisocial personality disorder because their values about appropriately 'masculine' behaviour and its expression differ from those of many psychiatrists. Other examples, related to clients' culture, are considered later in this book.

Assertion and aggression are often associated with their functions, for example, in defending something seen as worth preserving, such as 'a principle ... or the pursuit of excellence in sport. Aggression can also have a neutral meaning, as in an "aggressive workout". The above considerations are important when one is assessing or judging another's behaviour'. Whether an individual decides 'that another person is aggressive' or assertive may depend more on his or her own perspective 'than on the characteristics of the act itself' (Farrell and Gray 1992, pp. 2f; see also Bailey 1977).

The relevance of assertive and other expressions of anger to care workers and inter-professional interventions

Relevance of expressions of anger

An understanding of assertive, aggressive and other types of anger has relevance for:

- the ways in which practitioners respond to aggression and violence

- the responses of care workers and other professionals to patients'/clients'/visitors' assertive expressions of anger or concern.

'Research suggests that violence and aggression can be successfully prevented…when practitioners are assertive (e.g., setting clear limits to ensure safety where necessary, but doing so calmly, politely and respecting the patient, client or visitor and his/her rights as an individual' (Byrt and Doyle 2007, p. 74, citing Lowe 1992; McDougall 2000 and Turnbull and Paterson 1999). For example, one young man stopped throwing furniture when asked, by one of the authors, to 'please stop, and tell us what's bothering you'. This individual later said that he was 'gobsmacked because you said "please stop"' (Byrt 1999, p. 44).

In addition, there is evidence that 'both staff aggression in the form of authoritarian (unnecessarily restrictive) attitudes…and failure to make safe limits and structure clear can contribute to, or worsen, violence and aggression' (Byrt and Doyle 2007, p. 74, citing Morrison 1992 and Whittington 2000).

Labelling clients and patients as 'difficult' or 'unpopular'

Labelling clients

Studies suggest that in mental health and learning disability settings, in particular, assertiveness in clients has sometimes been pathologised (seen as 'abnormal', Pilgrim and Rogers 2005). In his pioneering work *Asylums: Essays on the Social Situation of Mental Patients and Other Inmates*, Goffman (1968) describes how assertive complaints are seen only as evidence of mental illness. In addition, in a variety of health services, certain clients have been 'labelled by practitioners as aggressive or "difficult"' (Byrt and Doyle 2007, p. 74). In some instances, these individuals have become 'unpopular patients' (Duxbury 2000; Stockwell 1972), leading to the misinterpretation of assertiveness as aggression.

According to Duxbury (2000, p. 18), clients are particularly likely to be seen as 'difficult' if they:

- question care and treatment
- make choices that are at variance with professionals' views and values
- ask for 'information' in excess of what staff deem to be reasonable.

In contrast, some of the literature on mental health nursing refers to the value of clients' creative anger. For example, Hopton (1995) considers this in relation to the oppression and racism that some clients have experienced in wider society. Individuals' questioning of services and of the discrimination they encounter, has been seen as a necessary and creative aspect of rehabilitation and recovery (Byrt *et al.* 2008; Warner 1992; Watkins 2007).

In conclusion it is useful for the professional to reflect upon the range of factors which might have led to feelings that a service user is being difficult, obstructive or aggressive following an assertive complaint. Following this 'stop and think' process (McMurran 2008), a better understanding may be reached. Clinical supervision will prove very useful in these situations, enabling considered insight, and preventing the health worker from falling into a trap of misinterpretation and any consequent unwarranted negative labelling.

Chapter 2
Violence and aggression in services and the social context

This chapter considers the frequency of violence and aggression in care services, social factors and primary and secondary prevention.

Most clients of health and social services are not violent or aggressive, despite media reporting of particular incidents (Morris 2006; Philo 2001). However, despite problems of method with many studies (Howells *et al.* 2008; Wells and Bowers 2002), there is evidence that a high proportion of health and social care professionals, particularly nurses, are the recipients of physical or verbal violence across a wide range of health services (NHS Business Services Authority Security Management Service 2007b; Healthcare Commission 2006; Upson 2004; Wells and Bowers 2002). During the past three decades, there has been considerable concern regarding the apparent increase in aggressive behaviour by the recipients of health care. Nurses, in particular, have been on the receiving end of aggressive behaviour and violence more than almost any other occupation. This was increasingly identified by the 1990s (Paterson *et al.* 1997; West and Abolins 2001), when studies suggested that at least one in three nurses felt unsafe at work and that not enough was being done to protect them (Ford *et al.* 1997; Porter 1997).

The nature of workers' activity in mental health is the high level of patient or client contact, often coupled with a lack of resources. This makes nurses, in particular, prime targets for aggressive behaviour within the National Health Service (Ford *et al.* 1997, Healthcare Commission 2008; Upson 2004). Traditionally, acts of aggression have, to some extent, been viewed as inevitable, particularly in mental health settings (Whittington and Wykes 1989). More recently, however, concern has grown. Indeed, as more reports are published, it becomes evident that being verbally or physically assaulted is not restricted to particular health settings (Ford *et al.* 1997, Healthcare Commission 2008). Although patient safety has long been a priority within the health service, it is only relatively recently that the safety of health workers has received attention.(NHS Business Authority Security Management Service 2007a).

Chapter 1 included a consideration of the many definitions of violence and aggression in the literature, and the difficulty of comparing studies because of this (Wells and Bowers 2002). NHS Business Services Authority Security Management Service require- ments that NHS services use standardised reporting forms may overcome this problem. The NHS Business Services Authority Security Management Service has used this form to measure recent incidences of violence in NHS services (NHS Business Services Authority Security Management Service 2007a).

Table 2.1 shows 'occupations most at risk of assaults at work'. (At the time of writing, these appear to be the most recent British Crime Survey figures available on occupational violence.)

Table 2.1

Occupations most at risk of assaults at work
2001/02 and 2002/03 British Crime Survey Interviews

Percentage of victims suffering one or more assaults

Protective service occupations, e.g. Prison officers and night club doormen	2.6%
Health and social welfare professionals (including social workers and nurses)	3.3%
Transport and mobile machine drivers and operatives	1.9%
Managers and proprietors in agriculture and services	1.8%
Health professionals (including 'medical and dental practitioners and psychologists')	1.4%
Caring personal service occupations	1.3%
Leisure and other personal service occupations	1.1%
Teaching and research professionals	1.0%

Source: Adapted from Upson 2004. Violence at Work: Findings from the 2002/03 British Crime Survey. Home Office Report 04/04.

Violence and aggression in mental health and other services

Violence in services

Whilst most mental health clients are not violent or aggressive (Morris 2006), within mental health units, 'patient safety incidents involving disruptive and/or aggressive behaviour are the second most frequently reported incident. They account for almost a quarter of incidents' (NHS Patient Safety Agency 2006, p. 34). Several studies have found that the incidence of clients' violence and aggression towards mental health nurses is particularly high, compared with violence and aggression in other health care settings (Foster *et al.* 2007, Lanza *et al.* 2006, Needham 2006, Quanbeck and McDermott, 2008).

High rates of violence and aggression have adverse effects on care workers in many countries and affect 'recruitment and retention' (Jackson *et al.* 2002, p. 13). Research has found that nurses and other professionals are also often the recipients of violence and aggression in other settings, including those listed below:

- Services for individuals with learning disability (Long *et al.* 2007; Lundstrom *et al.* 2007).
- General hospital wards (Lin and Liu 2005; Rowe and Sherlock 2005).
- Accident and emergency departments (Ferns *et al.* 2005).
- Services for older people (Astrom *et al.* 2004; Mullan and Badger 2007).
- Community nursing (Jackson *et al.* 2002; NHS Business Services Authority Security Management Service 2009).
- Social services, including residential homes (Braithwaite 2001).
- Prisons (Cooke 2008; Howells *et al.* 2008; Toch and Kupers 2007). In addition, many prisoners with mental illness are at particular risk of violence from other inmates (Toch and Kupers 2007).

Howells *et al.* (2008, p. 351) report that, within prisons, health care workers and prison officers experience particularly high rates of violence and aggression. A rise in incidents of violence has been reported in prisons in the UK (Padley 2007) and in other countries (Stern 2006). This risk of violence does not necessarily correlate to risks in safety or injury, as many arenas where violence is more likely to take place have embedded measures to minimise the impact, through the training of staff and implementation of policies which are designed to anticipate and extinguish situations that have the potential to escalate.

The NHS Business Authority Security Management Service (2007b) reported that, in 2004–2005, 'a total of 43,301 physical assaults on NHS staff in [mental health and learning disability] environments were reported. This figure is considerably higher than in any other area of patient care'. More recent figures show an increase. From '1 April, 2005 to 31 March, 2006, a total of 58,695 physical assaults were reported' (NHS Business Services Authority Security Management Service 2007b) (see Table 2.2).

Table 2.2

National Physical Assault Data Collection Findings (NHS Security Management Service (2007b), p. 27)

Mental Health Trusts	41345
Acute and Foundation Trusts	11100
Ambulance Trusts	1104
Primary Care Trusts	5145
Special Health Authorities	1

(Source: NHS Business Services Authority Security Management Service 2007b, p. 27)

Healthcare Commission and Royal College of Psychiatrists (2008) figures on violence in mental health units

The former Healthcare Commission asked the Royal College of Psychiatrists to audit the incidence of violence in mental health units (Royal College of Psychiatrists Centre for Quality Improvement 2007a, 2007b). This survey found that over 50 % of mental health nurses, and nearly three in four working with older people with dementias, had been subject to physical violence whilst on duty. Whilst the audit found some increases in provision of 'effective alarms, reporting incidents and... an appropriate mix of skills among the staff team ...improvements were needed, particularly on wards for older people, where physical environments, activities for patients, training and staffing levels were particularly poor' (Healthcare Commission 2008, citing Royal College of Psychiatrists Centre for Quality Improvement, 2007a, 2007b). A Healthcare Commission survey in early 2009 reported that one-fifth of mental health nurses had been physically assaulted on duty in the year before the study. (The reason for percentage differences between the 2007 and 2009 studies appears to relate to differences in questions, with the earlier study apparently asking for details of physical assaults at any time in the past (Healthcare Commission 2009a).) Several other studies report the adverse effects of violence and aggression on both patients (considered later in this chapter) and staff (Richter and Whittington 2006).

NHS Security Management Service requirements for the reporting of incidents and the need for accurate recording

Recording of incidents

In *Tackling Violence Against Staff*, the NHS Security Management Service requires the reporting of incidents of physical assaults, attempted physical assaults and verbal abuse. There is a national 'physical assault reporting system (PARS)…to collate accurate information on the level of violence in the NHS' (NHS Business Services Authority Security Management Service 2007a, p. 7) so that this can be reduced throughout health services. In addition, *Tackling Violence Against Staff*:

- emphasises the need for awareness of aspects of violence and accurate reporting of incidents by all staff
- stresses the importance of support for staff who have been physically assaulted or verbally abused and for them to be aware that they can use the Legal Protection Unit to prosecute 'clients or other people who assault them on NHS premises or in clients' homes' (p. 11)
- outlines the roles of security management directors at local (e.g., Trust) level and local security management specialists.

Past studies have found that incidents of violence and aggression were under-reported in health services (Ferns and Chojnacka 2005; Munro 2002). It is crucial to accurately record occurrences of violence and aggression, not only because of NHS Business Services Authority Security Management Service requirements, but to provide information which can identify the need for resources such as increased staffing to ensure 'the care and safety of patients and visitors' and 'the safety, morale and retention of staff' (Byrt and Doyle 2007, p. 73). Needs for staff education, training and support can also be identified. Accurate recording is also necessary for legal and insurance reasons: e.g., to provide evidence if a client or staff member sued an NHS Trust or other organisation because they were the victim of an assault (Byrt and Doyle 2007).

The wider social context of violence and aggression

The wider social context

The rest of this chapter considers the wider social context of violence and aggression, and its relevance to mental health and social care workers.

Violence in society is often seen as a worsening problem, but there is evidence of considerable violence in the past. For example, Foakes (2003), who studied terrorism, revenge and other violence in Shakespeare's England, comments:

> Human beings, especially males, have been addicted to violence since myths and legends first circulated and recorded history began. Terrorism has long been practiced in many forms, and often in the name of a religious cause…Although Shakespeare's world was very different from that of the present day, and advances in technology have made available weapons he could not imagine, the basic issues remain the same
> (Foakes 2003, pp. 1f)

Just as much contemporary popular entertainment is concerned with violence (e.g., in some computer games and 'video nasties'), there has been a similar emphasis in literature of the past, as in 16th and early 17th century revenge tragedies and other plays (Foakes 2003).

Several authors have commented that the violence and aggression of clients, patients and their visitors may, in part, reflect violence in wider society, and that this needs to be understood (Buckingham 2003; Shepherd 2001b).

In some areas, particularly inner cities, violence is relatively common (Shepherd 2001b). Some of the literature suggests that verbal and physical violence that has started outside care services may be continued by patients and visitors in wards and departments and in their own homes when they are visited by professionals. An example would be the victim of an assault being pursued by his or her attacker into a ward. This might involve domestic violence (Fawcett and Waugh 2008), a gang fight or disinhibited behaviour caused by alcohol or other adverse drug use (Maden 2007). The wider social context is also said to affect community nurses and social workers, for example, in relation to their visits in inner city areas with considerable violence and their geographical isolation, away from colleagues (Beale 1999; Linsley 2006; NHS BSA Security Management Service 2009; Shacklady 1997).

The individual's cultural, family and social background

Cultural background

An understanding of ways that the individual's cultural or social background influence their speech or behaviour can be important in preventing or reducing violence and aggression. For example, a client or patient may appear aggressive to a care worker, but the apparently hostile manner (of the client/patient) may reflect his or her ways of interacting within a particular ethnic, social or peer group (Barker 2005).

'For some individuals, violent offending is an important source of power and positive self-identity' (Byrt 2008b, p. 105, citing Barker 2005 and Gilligan 2001). For example, Barker (2005) found that, in a variety of cultures, the self-respect of many young men, and the respect they received from their peers, was linked with the extent to which they could defend themselves, and the honour of their girlfriends or boyfriends, e.g., through physical assault on individuals who expressed disrespect. The ability to fight was seen as crucial to the individual's masculinity, as perceived by himself and others (Barker 2005). Being able to fight is also important to the self-esteem of some women and older men (Fawcett and Waugh 2008).

It can be noted that the reasons for persistently violent behaviours are many and complex (Flannery *et al.* 2008; Hodgins *et al.* 2009; Richter and Whittington 2006), and involve both environmental and genetic factors (Flannery *et al.* 2008, Viding *et al.* 2009). Research findings suggest that, for some individuals, persistent violence is related to 'multiple sources of disempowerment [and disadvantage] from early childhood' (Byrt 2008b, p. 105). This often involves many areas of deprivation which are inter-linked. Researchers have found that many individuals with 'life-course persistent' (Moffitt 2008, p. 49) violence (i.e., episodes of violent behaviour during childhood, adolescence and adulthood) were affected, before birth, by their mothers' poor nutritional status and ingestion of alcohol and/or other drugs, and in some instances, complications, such as brain injury and anoxia (lack of oxygen) during delivery (Scarpa and Raine 2008).

During childhood, individuals with 'life-course persistent' violence also often experience 'lack of attachment', involving inadequate bonding between parent (or parent figure) and child, and absent or 'inconsistent love, security and discipline' (Byrt 2008b, p. 105). This is sometimes accompanied by neglect and/or emotional, sexual and physical abuse, which may include domestic or intimate partner violence. Multiple material deprivations are also often experienced by individuals with life-course persistent violence. This includes poverty, inadequate or missed education, poor quality accommodation and unemployment (Moffitt 2008, Odgers 2009). These factors are compounded by social exclusion, the negative attitudes of others' and discrimination (lack of life opportunities related to education, employment, income, accommodation and other areas (Watkins 2007)). In addition, compared with most individuals, people with life-course persistent violence experience poorer physical health as children and teenagers, and later in life (Odgers 2009).

Commenting in the *Sunday Times* (Swinford and Dowling 2009) on a story about two boys who battered, tortured and sexually humiliated two innocent children using bricks, lit cigarettes and a noose, Essi Viding, a psychologist at University College London who studies antisocial behaviour in children, said: 'Maltreatment or neglect has a profound impact on a child's brain development. It creates abnormalities in the circuitry which is crucial for interpreting people's emotions'. Swinford and Dowling go on to suggest that there is neurological and obstetric evidence to support this view. The brain develops at its fastest while the baby is in the womb and in the first three years of life. Stressful prenatal environments for both mother and baby can have a profound impact, creating abnormalities in parts of the brain which regulate emotional responses. In dysfunctional children, this can leave them uncommunicative and lacking empathy.

Research findings suggest that, for some individuals, violent behaviours are the main, maybe the only, source of self-esteem and self-worth, and the gaining of respect from others such as peers (Barker 2005; Byrt 2008b). This can be the case particularly for individuals who have experienced the multiple deprivations outlined above, and lack alternative ways of gaining positive satisfactions (Hanlon 2008; Hart 2008).

Some professionals and researchers have proposed, and implemented, early intervention programmes with families whose young children are at risk of lack of attachment, abuse, neglect, poor physical and mental health and various material and other deprivations. There have also been programmes to reduce violence, including bullying, in schools and wider communities, especially in the USA. Some of these have been successful in reducing violence, although there have been problems with the methods used in some studies that have evaluated these programmes (Farrell and Vulin-Reynolds 2008). Dahlberg (2008, p. 480) comments:

> Some of the strategies that offer the strongest evidence of effectiveness are family-based and interventions in early childhood…The most successful programs address the internal dynamics of the family (e.g., cohesion, interaction style), the family's capacity for dealing with external demands, parenting skills and family management practices.

> The earlier these programs are delivered in the child's life, the greater the benefits, although significant benefits have also been demonstrated when delivered to high-risk populations (e.g., youths with substance abuse problems or who have already been arrested for violent or delinquent behavior).
> (Dahlberg 2008, p. 480, citing several sources)

An appreciation of these and other social factors can help care workers and other professionals understand the particular reasons that certain clients (and in inpatient settings, some of their visitors) are verbally or physically violent. In some instances, apparently hostile or rude communication may reflect the individual's usual interactional style with family members or peers, rather than being intentionally aggressive (Barker 2005; Corbett and Westwood 2005) (see Box 2.1).

Box 2.1   **The importance of understanding clients' social context: Some examples**

'Ms Ali Amber' is a young woman with mental health problems and a learning disability who has learned to express her understandable frustration by hitting others, as well as herself. Previous services have not provided Ms Andrews with other ways to express herself (Gates 2007).

'Mr Bart Blue' expresses his fears related to physical abuse by other prisoners, and his concern that he will die of cancer, through rudeness and hostility towards the prison healthcare nurse (Wood 2007).

'Mr Clive Crimson' tends to settle disagreements with other clients by threatening to fight them. His parents and older brothers, and later, his friends, have always settled disagreements in fights. According to social learning theory, Mr Crimson has not learnt, or been exposed to, other ways of resolving disputes (Byrt and Woods 2006). Social learning theory postulates that people learn behaviours within family and social relationships, especially those that occur early in the individual's life (Smith *et al.* 2003).

'Ms Greta Green' is transferred from prison to a mental health unit. In order to survive both prison, and traumatic childhood abuse, Greta has had to present (in her own words) as 'a tough woman who won't be messed with'. This has become an important part of Ms Green's self-identity, as well as, from her point of view, a necessary survival strategy (Aiyegbusi and Clarke-Moore 2009, Gilligan 2001).

Of importance is non-judgmental understanding of these, and other, clients and an appreciation of 'where they are at', and why they behave as they do. These are all crucial components of empathy (Arnold and Boggs 2007) and the forging of a therapeutic alliance, in which client and staff can consider ways to enable people to reduce violence and aggression (Rogers and Vidgen 2006).

An important role of care workers is to enable individuals to choose means, other than violence and aggression, to achieve self-esteem and self-worth. This is particularly important in secure hospitals and prison health services, where many patients have histories of violent offending (Gilligan 2001; National Forensic Nurses' Research and Development Group 2008). For example, at Arnold Lodge medium secure unit (where two of the authors have worked), patients are encouraged to develop self-esteem and find alternative, creative ways to express and channel anger. Besides anger management using cognitive behavioural therapy (Bede *et al.* 2008; Bowness *et al.* 2008), each patient eventually has opportunities to further her or his education, learn a musical instrument and engage in individualised fitness programmes, including access to a gym and multigym (Byrt *et al.* 2005). 'Several studies have found statistically significant correlations between increasing prisoners' education levels and reducing rates of violent reoffending' (Byrt 2008b, p. 105, citing Gilligan, 2001).

Violence as a public health issue

A public health issue

The World Health Organisation (WHO) has declared that violence is a serious public health issue. A Resolution of this body, entitled 'Preventing Violence: a Public Health Priority' (World Health Organisation 2002) recognises that, globally, there are '…serious immediate and future long-term implications for health and social development that violence represents for individuals, families, communities and countries…' (World Health Organisation, 2002, p. XX).

Several aspects of violence in wider society are considered in this WHO report. All of these can impinge on the practice of mental health nurses and other professionals. They include:

- violence of younger people, including bullying at school
- 'child abuse and neglect by parents and other caregivers'
- 'violence by intimate partners' (including some forms of domestic violence)
- abuse of older people and individuals who are vulnerable (vulnerable adults): e.g., many people with learning disabilities and mental health problems
- 'sexual violence'
- 'collective violence', including war, torture and riots
- suicide and self-harm, as internalised forms of violence.

(World Health Organisation, 2002, pp. xix and xxi)

A later report (World Health Organisation 2004) gives guidance on 'implementing the recommendations' in World Health Organisation (2002). More recently, Gavlak and Jamjoum (2009) outline the work of this body in Gaza. The authors describe people's considerable trauma and bereavement from the effects of war and terrorism in this area, and the work of psychologists and other professionals with children and adults affected by the conflict. The effects of such trauma on individuals' expression of anger will be considered later in this book. This is particularly relevant to mental health nursing and other professional disciplines, given the increasing number of people in the UK who are refugees or seeking asylum and who may be users of health and social services (Heptinstall *et al.* 2004; Maddern 2004; Maffia 2008).

Violence within the community: Primary and secondary prevention and the care worker's role

Violence within the community

Since at least the late twentieth century, care workers have been working with other professionals and agencies to reduce the incidence of violence in particular communities (Audit Commission 1999; Riner and Flynn 1999). Fontaine (2009) comments on the role of nurses in primary and secondary prevention of violence and aggression in the community. 'Primary prevention' includes educating the public about the adverse consequences of violence and aggression, and attempting to influence media portrayals of violence (e.g., by meeting with journalists to discuss possible effects on health). Fontaine (2009) refers to the importance of educating parents on the effects on young children of violence between parents. She outlines the care worker's role in helping teenagers to seek help if they experience violence from boyfriends or girlfriends, and in assisting teachers to deal with violence in schools. Fontaine (2009, p. 601) also considers 'secondary prevention', including assessment and interventions with people who have witnessed, or been victims of violence, or who are residents in shelters for people who have been assaulted in domestic (intimate partner) violence.

Rittermeyer (2009, p. 636) considers various aspects of community violence, including violence in the 'workplace...school...street'. She outlines the application of a 'nursing care plan' (Rittermeyer 2009, p. 642) for children and young people who are both the victims and potential perpetrators of violence in a local community. This care plan includes the following:

- 'providing a safe environment'
- 'managing anger'

- 'setting limits'
- 'facilitating self-responsibility'
- 'improving socialization' with the individual's peers and other people
- 'involving the community.'

(Rittermeyer 2009, pp. 642f)

Professionals' work with other agencies to reduce violence in local communities

Working with other agencies

The Department of Health (2008b) have produced *Healthier, Fairer and Safer Communities – Connecting People to Prevent Violence.* This draft document is 'a framework for the early prevention of violence and abuse'. It 'provides information and evidence on preventing violence abuse' for professionals and for 'policy makers and planners' and 'commissioners' of services (Department of Health 2008b, p. 4).

Amongst other topics, this document considers the causative and contributory factors for violence and abuse and 'cycles of violence and abuse' (Department of Health 2008b, p. 9), related to the following:

- Some people who experience abuse in childhood go on to perpetrate violence or abuse later in their lives.
- Violence and abuse may recur in successive generations, with parents abusing their children, who, in turn, abuse their own children, and so on.

It also considers:

- 'Effective interventions', including 'primary...secondary... [and] tertiary prevention' (Department of Health 2008b, p.10). Examples of primary and secondary prevention are given elsewhere in this chapter. 'Tertiary prevention' could include any type of treatment and rehabilitation and recovery process that helps individuals to manage their anger effectively. The use of cognitive behavioural therapy using problem-solving techniques in a medium secure ward (Byrt *et al.* 2005) is an example of tertiary prevention.
- Early interventions with children at risk from abuse and/or of developing violence, and including work with families, 'school-based youth violence prevention programmes' and 'bullying intervention programmes' (Department of Health 2008b, p.11).

- 'Working together for safer communities – connecting professionals' (Department of Health 2008b, p. 11) involves workers of various disciplines and agencies collaborating to reduce violence in specific communities. For example, a nurse in a child and adolescent mental health service (CAMHS) could collaborate with other mental health professionals, a school nurse, teachers, youth workers and police in efforts to reduce bullying and problems related to young people's use of alcohol and other drugs.

Shepherd (2001b) argues that it is important for staff in Accident and Emergency Departments to work closely with 'local communities' and 'local public services' (p. 202), particularly the police, to prevent violence. He states that there are good reasons for Accident and Emergency staff to report violent incidents and information they receive about crimes to the police. Shepherd (2001b) also considers the ethical and legal issues involved.

Throughout England, there are various strategies to reduce violence and ensure safety in local communities. For example, the Government Offices for the East of England (2009) and the East Midlands (2009) outline projects to tackle violent offending and reduce associated problematic drinking and drug taking, e.g., through local services coordinated by the 'Drugs National Treatment Agency Team' (Government Office for the East of England 2009). Local initiatives to reduce violence and enhance safety involve a variety of professionals, volunteers and members of the public. These include people working for the police, youth and community projects and members of 'multi-agency Drug and Alcohol Action Teams' (Government Office for the East Midlands 2009), including nurses, social workers and psychiatrists. As problematic drinking and drug taking is strongly associated with violence and aggression (Kipping 2009), nurses and other professionals involved in this area contribute not only to the health and well-being of individual clients, but also to reducing violence in communities (Fontaine 2009).

Points for consideration and reflection:

- To what extent, if at all, does an understanding of violence in wider society aid your own understanding of violence in your own care setting?

- To what extent do you, or staff that you work with, liaise with other professionals/agencies to effect measures to prevent and/or reduce violence or aggression in the client group with which you are involved?

Domestic (intimate partner) violence

Domestic violence

Domestic violence is sometimes called 'intimate partner violence' (Fawcett and Waugh 2008). 'Domestic violence/intimate partner violence' has been defined as:

> Any violence between current and former partners in an intimate relationship, wherever and whenever the violence occurs. This violence may include physical, sexual, emotional, financial abuse.
> (Stevens 2002, quoted in Dixon 2006, p. 109)

Violence between parents or a parent and another adult can have serious consequences for children living in the same house. Children can be traumatised by watching or hearing domestic violence, and in some instances, may also be subject to violence, which considerably affects 'children's health, welfare, emotional well-being, life chances and safety' (Waugh 2008, p. 109, citing Dowd 2006).

There is increasing recognition of domestic violence of women towards male partners (Carson 2007) and in same sex relationships (Irwin 2008). However, domestic violence in general is often unrecognised as a problem (Dixon 2006) and may be seen as acceptable among some people, particularly men, in certain cultures (Lim and Bell 2008).

The links between domestic violence and violence in children, young people and adults

Sometimes violence, especially in children and young people, reflects violence they have witnessed, or been subject to, in the home. In these circumstances, the individual's violence may be related to either of the following:

- feelings of anger and distress related to physical, sexual or emotional abuse; and difficulty in expressing feelings other than through violence or aggression
- learnt behaviour from adults at home that violence is the way to express feelings or resolve conflicts; and failure to realise

that there are other ways of doing so (Fawcett and Waugh 2008). Social learning theory postulates that people learn to be violent from such early experiences (Linsley 2006).

Multi-disciplinary and inter-agency approaches to reducing domestic violence

Catherine Itzen produced a report for the Home Office, National Institute for Mental Health in England and Department of Health (Home Office *et al.* 2006), entitled *Tackling the Health and Mental Health Effects of Domestic and Sexual Violence and Abuse*. This report indicates the need for mental health nurses and other mental health workers to liaise with other professionals and agencies, including the criminal justice system, in relation to reducing this violence. Such liaison is particularly crucial if the victims of violence are children or young people under 18 or 'vulnerable adults'. If this is the case, the professional would need to report this to her or his manager, who would pass on concerns to the appropriate manager concerned with child protection (Hughes and Owen 2009) or 'safeguarding vulnerable adults' (Mandelstam 2009). Itzen (Home Office *et al.* 2006, p. 12) states that there is need for inter-agency and inter-professional working amongst 'child and adolescent, adult, forensic psychiatry, clinical psychology, counselling, social work, probation, nursing, general practice, accident and emergency and antenatal and paediatric medicine'. The role of voluntary organisations is also stressed.

Bullying and its later effects

Bullying and its effects

There are many and varied definitions of bullying (British Medical Association 2007). According to the Chartered Institute of Personnel and Development (2004):

> Bullying is persistent behaviour against an individual that is intimidating, degrading, offensive or malicious and undermines the confidence and self-esteem of the recipient.
> (Chartered Institute of Personnel and Development 2004, quoted in British Medical Association 2007).

Bullying is of concern to health and social care professionals, firstly because there is evidence that it seriously affects the mental health of the child, young person or adult who is being bullied, both at the time, and in the future. Some young people and adults remain adversely affected by bullying that they experienced as children. 'A quarter of young adults bullied by their peers during childhood report long term harmful effects as a result' (NSPCC Inform 2006, citing Cawson *et al.*, 2000). In addition, there is evidence of bullying, not only in schools (ChildLine 2009), but in mental health wards (Bowers *et al.* 1999; Lawrence 2008) and prisons (Ireland 2002; Leddy and O'Connell 2002; South and Wood 2006).

Violence and bullying in prisons

There is evidence of bullying in both prisons and mental health services (Lawrence 2008; South and Wood 2006). An increasing number of mental health nurses are working in UK prisons (Durcan 2008b), potentially with individuals whose mental illness makes them vulnerable to bullying or violent behaviours (Cooke 2008; Toch and Kupers 2007). The HM Prison Service Violence Reduction Strategy requires all prisons to assess violence and implement strategies to reduce it (HM Prison Service 2009). However, there has recently been wide variation in the extent to which bullying and other forms of violence have been addressed (HM Inspector of Prisons 2009a).

Bullying has been found to be common in prisons (Ireland 2002, Leddy and O'Connell 2002, South and Wood 2006), in relation to the buying and selling of drugs (HM Inspector of Prisons 2009a; Ireland 2002) or the need to maintain status (South and Wood 2006). In South and Wood's study, many prisoners were both victims and perpetrators of bullying.

Bullying in Mental Health Services

There is some evidence that clients with mental health problems may bully each other. For example, Bowers *et al.* (1999) reported that fear of other patients was the most common reason for compulsorily admitted patients to abscond from acute admission wards. Reporting on the Healthcare Commission audit conducted by the Royal College of Psychiatrists Centre for Quality Improvement (2007a), Lawrence (2008) comments that mental health clients 'feel threatened and unsafe, with high levels of drug and alcohol abuse' and limited 'therapeutic activities' for clients and an excessive use of temporary staff. Secure hospitals within at least one NHS Trust have policies on managing and preventing bullying.

Collins and Walford (2008) outline the work of professionals in running courses for older people and individuals with learning disabilities and mental health problems in Wales. Participants were enabled to identify risks, and to take action, including contacting relevant professionals if they experienced violence or other forms of abuse.

An advantage of the approach described by Collins and Walford (2008) is that it actively involves individuals who are or may be vulnerable, in becoming aware of action they can take to prevent abuse and to seek help when it occurs. Many people who are vulnerable would prefer this approach to one where professionals or other carers make all the decisions, without consulting the client or enabling her or him to make decisions (Dooher and Byrt 2005).

Bullying at School

> Being bullied at school, home or online might involve someone pushing you, hitting you, teasing you, talking about you, calling you names. No one has the right to hurt you or make you feel bad...If you are being bullied, you don't have to put up with it, you can talk to someone about it.
> (ChildLine 2009)

Bullying is reported to be a problem for many children at school, with recently, the use of the internet and text messaging in order to intimidate and the filming and texting of violent incidents (Rittermeyer 2009). One study found that '31% of children experienced bullying during childhood, a further 7% were discriminated against and 14% were made to feel different/an outsider. 43% experienced at least one of these things during childhood'(NSPCC Inform 2006, citing Cawson *et al.* 2000).

Children and young people, as well as adults, may be discriminated against on the grounds of gender, disability, cultural or ethnic group, gender identity or perceived sexual orientation. The European Commission (*Daphne Toolkit*) includes an account of efforts by young people with learning disabilities in Scotland, Portugal and Denmark uniting to 'run a campaign against violence and bullying of young people with learning disabilities' through the efforts of voluntary organisations, including 'Enable' in Scotland (European Commission *Daphne Toolkit* 2009). Davis (2006) reported an initiative by the Royal College of Nursing's 'Out' group to reduce homophobic bullying towards children and young people who were, or who were seen as, lesbian, gay, bisexual or transsexual.

Children and Racism was a ChildLine (1998) study of the racism that some children experienced at school.

> Corra, 14, was Irish. She and a black friend were being bullied by a group of six girls. The bullying was racist, they call her IRA and other names. She had been pushed off her bike, and broken her arm. Though her parents had been to the school on three occasions, nothing had been done.
> (ChildLine 1998, p. 22)

CHIPS (ChildLine in Partnerships) provides teaching and other staff with help to set up 'peer support schemes' in schools (ChildLine 2009).

> I used to get bullied, and
> I didn't know what to do.
> I wouldn't want to come to school.
> I'd pretend I had the flu.
>
> But now things are so different,
> School's a better place to be.
> Because of the peer mentors
> And what they did for me
>
> (Natalie Tormey. In ChildLine 2005, p. 2)

The links between underlying distress, and violence/aggression in the form of bullying, are described by Patterson (2006), who reported that depression is experienced by many children and young people who bully their peers. This depression is sometimes associated with the deprivations and family difficulties (Patterson 2005), outlined earlier in this chapter

Reducing violence and aggression in children and young people at school

Reducing violence at school

Reducing violence and aggression amongst children and young people at school may be part of the remit of school nurses and nurses working within child and adolescent mental health services (CAMHS). This could be achieved, in part, through assessments and nursing/multi-professional interventions in relation to the areas in the following list (McDougall 2000; Rutter 2008):

- **Domestic violence**, with provision of appropriate information and counselling, both to children/young people affected by violence between, or from, parents/parents' partners; and within family therapy. Awareness of risks within the school to children and others from violent parents visiting the school.

- **Non-verbal and verbal de-escalation** skills with violent or aggressive children and young people, their parents and other visitors to the school.

- **Alcohol and other drug use and their withdrawal** in children and young people, with appropriate assessments and interventions, and involvement of families (except in specific situations, e.g., where a young person with capacity has asked for his or her family not to be informed (Dimond 2003)).

- **The effects of separation: e.g. death or separation/divorce of parents**, including assessments and interventions for bereaved children/young people who express their grief through violence or aggression.

- **The effects of other sources of stress**, which are overwhelming to the child or young person.

- Issues of **diversity and discrimination**, including racist, sexist and homophobic bullying (ChildLine 1998, Davis 2006).

- Assessment/interventions for children/young people who are violent or aggressive as a result of **delirium** (considered later in this book). For example, a young child could become delirious because of the effects of a sudden very high temperature or as an adverse reaction to some medication, such as steroids.

- A minority of children/young people may become violent or aggressive in response to specific symptoms of **mental illness** or other mental health problems. For example, a child with Asperger's syndrome or other types of autism might become aggressive in response to a sudden, and (for him or her) traumatic change in routine.

(McDougall 2000; Rutter 2008)

Chapter 3
Essential principles and theoretical models

This chapter considers essential principles underpinning the prevention and reduction of violence and aggression, and then reviews causative, contributory and triggering factors, and a number of key explanatory models.

Ethical values underpinning interventions

Ethical values

The following ethical values apply in relation to all multidisciplinary interventions to prevent and reduce violence and aggression:

- The duty of care to ensure the life, health, safety and well-being (beneficence), and prevent harm (non-maleficence) to:
  - the client who is violent
  - other clients
  - any visitors.

- The duty, under Health and Safety legislation, to ensure the life, health and safety of yourself, colleagues and students on placement.

- 'Respect for persons' (Kant 1969, orig. 1785, cited in Thompson *et al.* 2006): to value, and maintain respect for the client who is being violent (regardless of the personal feelings of the professional), respect for other clients and for clients' carers at home, and for colleagues and students.

- Respect for the client's autonomy: placing no more restrictions on the individual's freedom than is warranted by her or his assessed level of risk, and enabling the individual to exercise choice and decision making as much as possible within the parameters of safety.
(Byrt 2008b; Dickenson and Fulford 2000; Thompson *et al.* 2006)

The ethical dilemmas and possible conflicts arising when implementing some of these principles are considered by various authors (Chaloner 2000; Dickenson and Fulford 2000; Paterson 2005).

Providing assessments and interventions that clients and their carers find acceptable and involving their participation as much as possible

'Care workers' assessments and interventions should be acceptable, as far as possible, to clients and their carers' (Byrt and Doyle 2007, p. 72), and should involve their participation, and reflect their experiences and preferences (NICE 2005). In the authors' experience, there is often agreement between client and staff about measures to prevent or reduce violence and aggression. Clients' participation in their care may be possible even during crises involving violence (Byrt 1999).

Ensuring safety and minimisation of risk

Sometimes the needs of the individual conflict with interventions with which she or he does not agree, but which professionals may consider essential to minimise risk to others and ensure safety. Risk refers to the extent that an individual is likely to harm her or himself and others (Morgan and Wetherell 2009; Woods and Kettles 2009a). Ensuring safety involves minimising the risk to the client who is being violent or aggressive, as well as to other people (Byrt and Doyle 2007, p. 71). It includes managerial and staff commitment to care about the safety and well-being of clients, their carers at home and professional colleagues (Cowman 2006, Linsley 2006).

Seclusion, control and restraint and their alternatives

In mental health and learning disability inpatient settings, seclusion and/or control and restraint, against the individual's will, may occasionally, and sadly, be the only way that care workers can fulfil a duty of care to ensure safety and prevent serious physical harm to other people. When seclusion and control and restraint 'cannot be avoided, the skill and humanity with which [they] are implemented should be maximized' (Whittington *et al.* 2006, p. 151). The extent to which such measures are used varies across services and different countries. There is evidence that some services have mostly or wholly replaced seclusion and control and restraint with alternatives, such as opportunities to communicate with staff, and assessing and treating symptoms such as persecutory voices at an early stage (Whittington *et al.* 2006).

Ensuring interventions are in line with Acts of Parliament, codes of professional conduct and good practice guidelines

The prevention and reduction of violence and aggression must be in line with:

- professional codes of staff involved in assessment and interventions, e.g., the Nursing and Midwifery Council (NMC) (2008) Code
- relevant legislation, including 'the Human Rights Act, 1998, the Children Acts of 1989 and 2004 (in relation to children and young people) and the Mental Health Acts for the various countries of the UK' (Byrt and Doyle 2007, p. 71, HM Government 1989, 1998, 2004)
- codes of practice and guidelines related to various legislation, e.g., Department of Health. (2008a), Code of Practice, Mental Health Act, 1983
- guidelines on good practice, e.g., the National Institute of Health and Clinical Excellence (NICE) (2005) *Guideline on Violence* and NHS Business Services Authority Security Management Service (2009 revised), *Not Alone. A Guide for the Better Protection of Lone Workers in the NHS.*

'Reasonable', 'proportionate' and 'least restrictive' interventions

It is important for health professionals to ensure that interventions are 'reasonable', 'proportionate' and offer the least restrictive alternative. For interventions to be justifiable, ethically and in a court of law, any 'force used should be no more than is necessary to accomplish the object' (e.g., to prevent serious risk to others) and be 'in proportion to the harm that is threatened' (Dimond 2008b, p. 307). 'Least restrictive alternatives' also include ensuring that clients are not cared for within levels of security which are unnecessarily high for their assessed levels of risk. However, there is a shortage of facilities, and consequent delays, for example, in transferring secure hospital patients to lower levels of security (Lester and Glasby 2006).

Compassionate and respectful communication

In addition, it is important for health professionals to ensure compassionate and respectful communication and promote the development of an empathetic and professional relationship with the client. This includes a wide range of non-verbal and verbal communication skills, including conveying respect and empathy, with an attempt to understand the individual and the (often stressful and distressing) feelings and experiences related to her or his violence or aggression (Byrt and Doyle 2007; Rogers and Vidgen 2006).

Providing holistic assessment and care

Holistic assessment

It is proposed that violence and aggression cannot be considered in isolation from the needs, strengths and particular problems of the client. Assessment and interventions need to consider the prevention and reduction of violence and aggression in relation to safety, risk, 'biological, psychological, social, spiritual, cultural, psychosexual, economic, legal [and other] factors, and their influence on violence and aggression' (Byrt and Doyle 2007, p. 71). Holistic care includes integrating, rather than separating, risk from other aspects of care; and avoiding only concentrating on restrictive methods and intensive observation, without considering the distress of the client (Kettles *et al.* 2007).

Figure 3.1

Aspects of Holistic Care in Preventing and Reducing Violence and Aggression

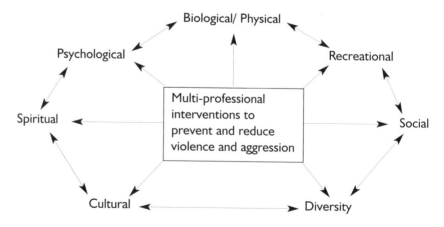

Adapted, with kind permission of Quay Books, MA Health Care Ltd from R. Byrt (2008a)

Ensuring culturally sensitive and culturally competent assessment, care and treatment

Part of holistic care involves assessment, care and treatment that is sensitive to, and meets needs related to the individual's 'culture, ethnic group, religion, gender, age, sexual orientation, gender identity, specific problems, and level of intellectual, cognitive, physical and sensory ability' (Byrt and Doyle 2007, p. 72), in line with the Equality Act, 2006 (HM Government 2006). Culturally sensitive and culturally competent care, in relation to various aspects of diversity, are considered in Chapters 8 and 9.

Providing assessments and care informed by therapeutic interventions and evidence of effectiveness

Providing assessments

The term 'therapeutic intervention' refers to various approaches which are intended to benefit the client, and which are usually based on a body of theory and research evidence. The authors of this book argue that both long-term, and sometimes, short-term measures to prevent and reduce violence and aggression should be informed by one or more therapeutic interventions. This view is based on the authors' practical experience, as well as research evidence that certain interventions are effective in relieving individuals' distress, as well as preventing and reducing violence and aggression (Howells *et al.* 2008; NICE 2005; Rogers and Vidgen 2006). However, Howells *et al.* (2008, p. 368) argue that there is 'insufficient evidence available to determine the effectiveness of [some] programmes'.

Examples of therapeutic interventions, considered in Chapters 12 and 13, include the following:

- psychosocial interventions for people with a mental illness
- antipsychotic and other medication
- behavioural therapy
- cognitive behavioural therapy
- person-centred approaches, including empathic anger management
- therapeutic community principles.

It is suggested that, in relation to clients' violence and aggression, it is good practice always to assess the factors causing, contributing to, or triggering violence and aggression, in order to take measures to ensure safety and assess and manage risk; and to inform 'nursing/multi-professional interventions' (Byrt and Doyle 2007). This is summarised in Figure 3.2.

Figure 3.2

Processes involved in interventions with violent and aggressive clients

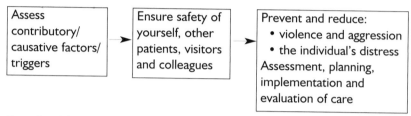

Reproduced from Byrt and Doyle (2007, p. 75), with kind permission of Quay Books

Antecedents, behaviours and consequences

Assessment, including risk assessment, aims to establish:

- causative and contributory factors to, and triggers of, violence and aggression. (antecedents)

- the nature and intensity of the violent or aggressive behaviours

- the consequences or 'consequent events' of the behaviour, that is, the outcome of the behaviour for the client and other people (Emerson 2001).

Assessments concerned with antecedents, the behaviour itself and consequent events are often referred to as ABC assessments (Emerson 2001; Fox and Gamble 2006; Rogers and Vidgen 2006).

Causative and contributory factors and triggers

Byrt and Doyle (2007) suggest that a causative or aetiological factor is anything which appears to be the main cause of violence or aggression in an individual. Cuasative factors can include those which would not result in most other people becoming violent of aggressive. The following are given as examples:

- Ms Greta Green, a retired postal worker, is normally placid and easy-going, but when in hospital with congestive heart failure, she develops delirium (acute confusional state), which lasts a few hours. This is caused by anoxia, a lack of oxygen to the brain. Whilst experiencing delirium, she is temporarily very agitated and attempts to hit a nurse who encourages her to stay in bed.

- Mr Paul Purple, a young man who is a keen supporter of his local football team, is very distressed by command hallucinations, associated with his schizophrenia. He experiences these hallucinations as voices telling him to attack people.

- Ms Rose Red, a young woman who enjoys disco dancing and the 'X Factor', has occasional sudden episodes of violence with little warning. These are related to Prader-Willi syndrome, a condition resulting in learning disability, excessive hunger resulting in obesity, and other symptoms, in which violence and aggression are associated with structural changes to parts of the hypothalamus involved, along with other parts of the brain, in the expression of emotions

(Cassidy and Driscoll 2009).

Most people with delirium, Prader-Willi syndrome and schizophrenia do not engage in violent and aggressive behaviours. Many people's violence and aggression does not have a single cause, but a range of contributory factors, including those related to the individual's physical, psychological, spiritual, economic and other needs. There are various explanatory models of the causes (Byrt and Doyle 2007), outlined in Table 3.1 (page 42).

The term 'trigger' refers to anything which precipitates violence or aggression (Linsley 2006, p. 48; Paterson and Leadbetter 1999), sometimes the last in a series of frustrations or stressors. An example would be 'Ms Paula Pink', an older woman with Alzheimer's disease, who has continued sharing many hobbies with her husband. Following an uncomfortable ride in an ambulance, Ms Pink is admitted to unfamiliar surroundings, and is not welcomed or orientated by nursing staff or given information or explanation. Ms Pink is thirsty, but is not offered a drink. The trigger that sparks off an aggressive response could be an insistence that Ms Pinkundergo a medical examination, without consideration of her perception that this is a gross invasion of her privacy (Goldsmith 1996). Sometimes, as in this instance, the trigger is 'the last straw that broke the camel's back' (Byrt and Doyle 2007, p. 76).

Explanatory models

Explanatory models are bodies of theory which attempt to explain violence and aggression, and in some cases, inform interventions with clients (Flannery *et al.* 2008; Hodgins *et al.* 2009; Linsley 2006; Richter and Whittington 2006). Table 3.1 indicates various

Explanatory models

explanatory models which, in some instances, influence multi-professional interventions.

Table 3.1

Theoretical models seeking to explain violence and aggression and inform professional interventions

Explanatory Model	Aspects of Model/Examples
Risk and safety	Explanations influenced largely by risk and safety considerations
Demographic	Considers relatively fixed characteristics of the individual, e.g., age, gender, ethnic group, occupation
Psychiatric	The association of violence and aggression with types of mental health problem or learning disability
Biological/physical	Physical factors, including those related to: • genetics • damage to brain structure and function • associated physical illness • changes to neurotransmitters • effects of alcohol and other drugs • hormonal changes
Psychological	• Personality variables • Frustration aggression hypothesis • Social learning theory • Interpersonal theories • Psychodynamic theories • Attachment theory
Cultural and diversity	Factors associated with the individual's: • culture (e.g., how this influences the expression of anger) • experiences of discrimination, and ways that this affects professional responses to clients
Spirituality	Individuals' experiences related to spiritual and other belief, hope, meaning and sources of identity that are important to the individual

Organisational/ environmental	The individual's social and physical environment, e.g., relationships between staff and clients, activities available, noise, décor, temperature, crowding and other physical variables
Social/economic	Factors related to the wider social environment, e.g., war, terrorism, domestic violence, physical, sexual and emotional abuse and material deprivations related, e.g., to limited income, poor accommodation, lack of educational and employment opportunity
Sociological and social psychological	Application of sociological and social psychological theories, e.g., those related to critical consideration of: • power • labelling and stigmatisation of clients, and the development of 'moral panics' • self-fulfilling prophecies
Ethical and legal	Application of ethical and legal theories, including those concerned with: • duty of care • 'respect for persons' (Kant 1785) • respect for autonomy • capacity • clients' human rights • use of the least restrictive intervention to ensure safety • proportionality and reasonableness in the use of interventions • other ethical aspects of control and restraint and seclusion

(Flannery *et al.* 2008; Hodgins *et al.* 2009; Linsley 2006; Richter and Whittington 2006; Simon and Tardiff 2008)

Researchers and health professionals increasingly acknowledge that violence and aggression are **multi-factorial**, i.e., that a variety of factors are involved in their cause. This is further considered later in this book. For convenience, in Table 3.1, above various theoretical models are listed separately, but the application of two or more theoretical models is often helpful in understanding the violence and aggression of an individual and in informing her or his assessment, care and treatment (Richter and Whittington 2006).

Some researchers and care professionals have based their studies or interventions on only one or two of the theoretical models, listed in Table 3.1. For example, in the past, many studies of violence and aggression in individuals with mental illness and learning disability studied causative factors and interventions only in relation to diagnosis, without considering issues such as the social and physical care environment or sociological or spiritual factors (Crichton 1995). In the past, at least, discussions about aggression have often resulted in definitions that complement particular theories. Indeed, psychologists have tended to explain aggression within a scheme of psychological causes, and ethologists (scientists who study animal behaviour) tend to advocate a more biological perspective. In an exploration of this issue, Mackintosh (1990) suggested that attempts at explaining aggression are both diverse, and usually influenced by the respective discipline of the protagonist suggesting the explanation. Moreover, he also described a lack of mutually agreed meaning in much of the related terminology. Therefore, discussion is further impaired by semantic difficulties. Mackintosh (1990) also suggested that most of the views held result more from particular authors holding specific views, as opposed to evidence, thereby, implying that most of these theories are mutually exclusive.

A number of authors have criticised such uni-disciplinary approaches (Crichton, 1995). It is now generally considered to be more useful, in practice, to consider a range of different factors in the prevention and reduction of violence and aggression (Flannery *et al.* 2008; Hodgins *et al.* 2009; Richter and Whittington 2006). For example, a number of explanatory models consider the interaction of the following:

- the **characteristics of the individual** with violent or aggressive behaviours
- the **responses of the staff member** (e. g., nurse)
- the **health or social service or other environment**
- The effect of the above on the outcome, e.g., extent of violence or whether this was prevented (Health Services Advisory Committee 1997, Linsley 2006, pp. 11f).

Fig. 3.1 illustrated the integration of a variety of factors in providing assessment, care and treatment for the individual with violent and aggressive behaviours. These factors (safety and risk, biological, psychological, cultural, diversity, spiritual, environmental and others) will be considered in the next chapters.

Chapter 4
Safe, therapeutic environments

Ensuring safety, preventing and reducing risk should be seen as the basis of all therapeutic interventions for individuals with violent and aggressive behaviours. This is confirmed by Appleby (2007, p. 3, cited in Woods and Kettles 2009b), who suggested that 'safety is at the centre of all good healthcare'.

Safety can be defined as freedom from harm – from oneself and from others. Risk refers to the likelihood that an individual will harm herself or himself and/or others and the extent and nature of particular types of harm (Maden 2007; Morgan and Wetherell 2009; Woods and Kettles 2009a).

Several authors have commented on the way in which the UK and other Western societies have become increasingly preoccupied with risk, and the negative consequences of living in a 'risk averse society'. This leads to a focus on the supposed 'risks' posed by various groups of people, including individuals with mental health problems and learning disabilities, resulting in their stigmatisation and a failure to focus on their strengths and needs (Godin 2006; Petersen and Wilkinson 2008). Whilst unnecessary restrictions need to be avoided (Byrt 2008b, Kilshaw 1999), lack of safety can have detrimental effects on both clients and staff, as in the following example known to one of the authors. The unit concerned has been given a pseudonym, and a few details changed, to ensure confidentiality and anonymity.

Safety in 'Aspens'

Admissions to 'Aspens' (a pseudonym) low secure unit were planned, with a prior assessment of prisoners with a mental illness made by a nurse and a consultant psychiatrist (Dr X). On several occasions, the nurse's assessment suggested that, in order to ensure others' safety, the client needed care and treatment in a medium, rather than a low, security setting. However, Dr X disagreed, and admitted several people to Aspens, arguing that they needed help immediately, and that further referral would unnecessarily delay urgent treatment.

Dr X's decision to admit these individuals was motivated by concern, and a wish to help individuals with complex mental health problems. However, as a result of his decisions to admit (without considering the nurse's risk assessment), the number of violent incidents increased, and both patients and nurses felt unsafe. There were a few serious injuries, nurses' sickness rates increased and their morale plummeted. Some patients were eventually transferred to a medium secure unit, resulting in disruption to their care and treatment.

After Dr X left, the multi-professional Clinical Team, including the new consultant psychiatrist, Dr Y, decided that patients would not be admitted to Aspens unless both the assessing nurse and Dr Y agreed that the individual's level of risk warranted a low secure environment, rather than a greater level of security. The result was a much safer and more therapeutic environment within Aspens, with patients and staff feeling that they could relax, and concentrate on treatment and care programmes more effectively.

The professional's responsibility to ensure safety

Responsibility for safety

In Chapter 3, we considered the care worker's responsibility in ensuring her or his own safety; and the safety of the client with violent or aggressive behaviours, as well as other clients, visitors, carers at home and colleagues and students. Ensuring safety and reducing risk is both common sense and required by Health and Safety legislation, which places duties on both employers and employees (Linsley 2006) and is emphasised in some professional codes (see Box 4.1).

Box 4.1

Nursing and Midwifery Council (NMC 2008) requirements in relation to duty of care and managing risk

- 'You must act without delay if you believe that you, a colleague or anyone else may be putting someone at risk.'
- 'You must inform someone in authority if you experience problems that prevent you working within this Code or other nationally agreed standards.'
- 'You must report your concerns in writing if problems in the environment of care are putting people at risk.'

(Nursing and Midwifery Council 2008, p. 06)

The preceding statements about managing risk are relevant to interventions to prevent violence and aggression, including ensuring the safety of clients, yourself and colleagues, although the Nursing and Midwifery Council (2008) Code does not refer to this explicitly.

The relevance of all interventions to ensuring safety

Relevance of intervention

It can be argued that all aspects of care workers' interventions are relevant to the role of professionals in ensuring individual safety and reducing risk. Interventions which contribute to safety, and which are referred to elsewhere in this book, include the skilled use of the social and physical environment, effective use of non-verbal and verbal communication skills and risk assessment/risk management, which may be subdivided into clinical (i.e., in relation to individual clients), and more general health and safety issues. Good observation, including engagement (i.e., the development of a therapeutic relationship and communication with the client) is critical to risk assessment and risk management, and to providing holistic care, to meet physical, psychological, spiritual, cultural and diversity needs. Therapeutic interventions and medication in specific circumstances are useful tools in maintaining safety. Finally, where there is no other way to prevent harm to others (and not as a therapeutic intervention), control and restraint and/or seclusion may be used.

Relational security

Relational security

Relational security includes (Dale and Gardner 2001; Aiyegbusi and Clarke-Moore 2009):

- an holistic assessment, and consequent understanding of the client: an awareness of her/him as an individual with strengths, as well as problems, related to risk and ensuring safety, as well as her/his physical, psychological, cultural, spiritual and other needs.

- establishing and developing a therapeutic alliance: 'the necessary relationship that must exist between a nurse and a patient for positive therapeutic change to take place' (Kirby and Cross 2002, p. 189).

Relational security is intended not only to benefit the client, and relieve her or his distress, but to ensure the safety of the client and others (Dale and Gardner 2001; Aiyegbusi and Clarke-Moore 2009). Dale and Gardner (2001) argue that, in ensuring safety in secure hospitals and units, relational security is as important, in some respects, as aspects of security such as the physical environment (e.g., locked doors, security cameras) and the use of procedures and policies. Much of Dale and Gardner's (2001) chapter can be applied to clients in other settings.

Specific aspects of ensuring safety

Ensuring safety

Specific aspects of ensuring safety include the following:

- The procedure/policy of the organisation should be followed.
- In services where security staff are available, it is important to be aware of the circumstances in which they should be called. This would include instances where an individual is physically violent, and communication and other means are ineffective in preventing harm to other people.
- It is unsafe for staff to be isolated with clients at risk of becoming violent or aggressive, for example in areas at a considerable distance from other professionals.
- If there is risk to a staff member from a client or visitor, she or he should be seen with another colleague or with help near at hand.
- Clients at risk of harming others 'should be cared for in areas where they can be easily observed and engaged with' (Byrt and Doyle 2007, p. 81).
- When seeing clients in a room on your own, where it is likely to be safe to do so:
  - 'Place yourself in a position where you can easily leave via the nearest exit.'
  - 'Avoid having your back to the patient.' This is both for safety reasons and to maintain observation of, and engagement with, the patient.
  - 'Do not put yourself in positions where you could easily be backed into a corner or against a wall' (Byrt and Doyle 2007, p. 81).
- Managers should be told, orally and in writing, about lack of staff or other resources needed to prevent and reduce violence and aggression.

The need for safe space

The provision of a safe space for individuals to express their anger safely and assertively has been described (Barker 2005; Rogers and Vidgen 2006):

> Clearly too few young men – and young women – have places where they can express...frustration...[There is a] need to create cultures of gender and manhood in which young men are encouraged to express their frustration and personal pain in ways that do not include physical violence or substance abuse.
> (Barker 2005, pp. 154f)

Sometimes, violence and aggression can be prevented by providing a room for quiet and/or individual space, separate to the main ward or living area, provided this does not compromise the safety of the client, other clients and staff. Here, the client can receive intensive observation and nursing care from one or more workers (Byrt and Doyle 2007). The safety of the client and staff is a fundamental concern when there is a risk of violent behaviour. Separate rooms should be used to care for individuals with aggressive or violent behaviours, only if it is safe to care for the patient in the room.

Where this is not the case, within health services, clients may be cared for in psychiatric intensive care units (PICUs). These vary considerably in size, from units of four to five beds attached to acute mental health services to large, purpose-built units (Beer *et al.* 2008, p. 7). It is imperative that PICUs are designed in accordance with Department of Health (2002) standards, with (within safety parameters) adequate space and fulfilling activities, and access to a safe, secure outside garden (Beer 2008).

Caring for clients within single rooms

Decisions to provide care for an individual within a single room, and without other clients present, should be based on risk assessment of the following factors:

- The extent to which the client is likely to be aggressive or violent. Evaluation of this needs to be based on continuous risk assessment, as the risk the client poses to others may vary.

- The safety of furnishings and fixtures in the room.
- The assessed needs of the client, including her or his preferences for quiet and solitude and to be with other people.
- The availability of staff to be with the client.
- The extent to which help can easily be summoned from colleagues, e.g., through the use of personal alarms.
- The position of the room, in relation to the proximity of staff. Rooms for individual care should be used only if staff are situated nearby, and are readily available to provide help, if needed.
- The size of the room and facilities available. A very cramped room, uncomfortable furniture or a lack of things to do would be likely to increase the individual's distress, and might potentiate aggression or violence.

(Byrt and Doyle 2007)

The physical environment

The physical environment

Crucial to ensuring safety is attention to all aspects of the physical and social environment of the service or the client's own home (Duxbury *et al.* 2006; NICE 2005; Royal College of Psychiatrists Audit Team 2005; Whittington and Richter 2006). The term 'physical environment' includes all aspects of the individual's material surroundings, including décor, furnishings, space and opportunities for fresh air and exercise (Byrt with James 2007; Campling *et al.* 2004). Measures to ensure therapeutic environments include ensuring not only that the physical environment is safe, but that it is pleasant, attractive and appropriate to clients' cultures. Relevant recommendations are included in standards for specialist services such as psychiatric intensive care units (Beer 2008, Department of Health 2002) and medium secure units (Royal College of Psychiatrists College Centre for Quality Improvement 2007c); and in Bowers *et al.* (2002) and NICE (2005).

In services caring for people with violent and aggressive behaviours, safety may be enhanced by providing windows made of clear materials which will not smash; and chairs and tables which are fixed to the floor, made of unbreakable (but attractive) materials or too heavy to be easily thrown (Dix and Page 2008; Walker 2008). Services also need to avoid ligature points on which items could be tied to harm self or others and reduce items which could be used as weapons. The design of wards and other facilities should enable ready, but unobtrusive, observation, and avoid hidden corners and be well lit. The use of cameras and other forms of surveillance has also been recommended, as has the use of personal alarm systems for all staff members, with a trained response team responding swiftly, but calmly, to emergencies (Bowers *et al.* 2002; Department of Health 2002; Dix and Page 2008; NHS Business Services Authority Security Management Service 2009; Royal College of Psychiatrists College Centre for Quality Improvement 2007c).

However, the extent that these security measures are perceived as unpleasant and restrictive by clients and their carers needs to be considered, especially as there is little research evidence that specific physical security measures necessarily reduce violence and aggression (Cowman 2006). Indeed, in the authors' experience, if clients experience safety measures to be aversive and coercive, this may increase, rather than prevent or reduce, violence and aggression (Byrt 2008b). Aversive environments, in relation to frustration, are considered later in this book.

Safety when visiting clients in the community

Safety when visiting

The following section is based on NHS Business Services Authority Security Management Service (2009) *Not Alone: A Guide for the Better Protection of Lone Workers in the NHS* (page numbers, below, refer to this source). The document considers professionals working in the community and other 'lone workers' who work in isolation in the community or on their own within a health service building. 'Risk assessment' and 'prevention' (pp. 21f) are emphasised, including awareness of objects in the client's home 'that could be used as a weapon'. Guidance is given on identifying the number of staff who should undertake a visit to the client's home or whether it is safe for one nurse to see a client in a room separate from the main day area of a ward.

Professionals are advised to observe for early signs of aggression (e.g., from the use of alcohol or other drugs) and other risks, e.g., from pets in clients' homes. The guidance states that all risks must be documented in a log and in clients' records, and advises that the latter should be marked when clients are at risk of behaving aggressively or violently. This might be necessary to ensure safety, but could stigmatise the client, and affect staff attitudes towards him or her.

Not Alone: A Guide for the Better Protection of Lone Workers in the NHS also states (p. 17):

> Lone Workers should...ensure that...a manager or appropriate colleague is aware of their movements...the addresses of where they will be working...or visiting, telephone numbers and expected arrival and departure times.

The guidance also makes clear that professionals must share information with colleagues about clients with a high risk of violence, 'where legally permissible' (p. 16). It states that staff visiting clients at home on their own should have:

- 'Emergency equipment...[which] might include a torch, map of the local area, telephone numbers for emergencies...first aid kit' (p. 17).

- Personal alarms and 'mobile phones...fully charged' (p. 34). However, 'lone workers should be sensitive to the fact that using a mobile phone could escalate an aggressive situation' (p. 35).

The NHS Business Authority Security Management Service (2009) also emphasises that personal alarms and other equipment need to be supplemented by nurses' skills in communication, risk assessment and risk management and other areas. Guidance is given on assessing and managing risks when escorting clients, e.g., by car, and 'lone workers' are advised to consider parking near the place they are visiting and try to wait for buses in brightly lit areas. 'Post-incident support...action...[and] reviews' (pp. 27f) are considered, as are 'sanctions' against individuals who assault 'lone workers', the latter's 'redress' and deterrence of potential assaults.

Point for discussion/reflection

Besides those mentioned in this chapter, what additional or alternative measures to ensure safety are used in your own practice or placement setting?

Clients' experience of institutional regimes and their possible effect on violence and aggression

The rest of this chapter is concerned with the effects of physical and social environments on violence and aggression.

From the 1950s, there were several research studies of, and government reports on, hospitals for patients admitted for long periods, including older people and individuals with learning disabilities and mental health problems. These reports described institutionalised conditions, where individuals' unique needs were ignored and people were expected to conform to unnecessary rules and restrictions (Gale and Sanchez 2005; Goffman 1968; Martin 1984). Many clients were cut off from the outside world, rarely or never visited by family and friends, and with few possessions and limited personal space (Barton 1966). Often, all aspects of individuals' lives were controlled by the institution. 'Regimes were often custodial and authoritarian, sometimes with rules which were unnecessarily restrictive, in that they were unnecessary to ensure safety or individuals' well-being' (Byrt with James 2007, p. 35, citing Goffman 1968; Pilgrim and Rogers 2005 and Rowden 2002). Similar observations have been made of prisons (Blom-Cooper 2008, HM Inspector of Prisons 2009a; Seddon 2007; Stern 2006). In the worst hospitals and prisons, some vulnerable clients have experienced physical and other forms of abuse, with consequent trauma (Rowden 2002; Sang 2003; Stern 2006; White *et al.* 2003). Individuals' experiences of institutional deprivations and traumas can be related to understandable anger, sometimes expressed as aggression (Weber 2008).

In relation to institutional practices, individuals either withdrew and conformed to the institution, found ways to get round the system, or expressed justifiable anger, which was then pathologised, i.e., perceived to be the result of illness or disability, rather than being seen as a natural, creative and healthy response (Goffman 1968). Thus, an individual's assertive questioning of her or his nursing care could be seen as evidence of 'learning disability', 'dementia', 'mental illness' or being 'difficult' (Duxbury 2000). Clients and their visitors have also been seen as 'difficult' if they failed to conform with task-orientated regimes and rituals (Stockwell 1972; Walsh and Ford 1989). The pathologisation of Randle McMurphy's anger is brilliantly illustrated in *One Flew Over the Cuckoo's Nest* (Kesey 1962).

Kroese and Holmes (2001) state, of individuals with learning disabilities in former large hospitals (p. 71):

> They were at the mercy of strict rules, regulations and routines, whereby other people decided when they were to get up, when to wash, when to eat, what to wear, and who to befriend.

> Living in such deprived, highly controlled environments created severe psychological disturbances for many people. Some...developed very disturbed behaviours, for example...being aggressive to people and property.

The comments of these authors apply, also, to many prisoners and to mental health patients who spent protracted periods in large hospitals. Several other studies report the deprivations from institutionalised life experienced by individuals who lived, often for many years, in large institutions for people with learning disabilities (Atkinson *et al.* 1997; Brechin and Walmsley 1989; Race 2002) or mental health problems (Barton 1966; Newnes *et al.* 1999; Newnes *et al.* 2001). For some clients, especially those who are older, violence and aggression may be associated with justifiable anger and/or response to trauma from multiple deprivations, and in some instances, abuse encountered in institutions, where power resided largely with the staff (Byrt 2008a). Professionals need to understand this in assessment and interventions with these individuals (Weber 2008).

A beneficial physical environment

A beneficial environment

Several authors state that the extent to which health service and other environments are therapeutic is of importance in preventing and reducing violence and aggression, relieving clients' distress and promoting recovery (Byrt with James 2007; Duxbury *et al.* 2006; NICE 2005; Royal College of Psychiatrists Audit Team 2005). This includes clients' experiences of a service as pleasant, homely and welcoming, with attractive furniture and décor, colours and carpets, plants and pictures with safe frames and fixtures (Barlow 2003; Dix and Page 2008;

Lawson and Phiri 2000). Ideally, within budgetary constraints, clients should have some choice related, for example, to the selection of pictures, furnishings and the colour of walls, with clients' artworks on display (Walker 2008). The physical environment should reflect clients' cultural backgrounds. For example, one day centre in an ethnically diverse area had 'drawings of the Caribbean and of famous women from Southern Asia', as well as readily accessible information in several languages (Byrt and Hardie 2007, p. 238). Cleanliness of the service environment; and 'lighting, heating, ventilation and odour' (Byrt with James 2007, p. 34, citing Von Sommaruga 2004 and Whittington 2000) are also seen as important. Clients' needs for fresh air, exercise and access to gardens (with, for some clients, walls that cannot be easily scaled, NICE 2005) have also been emphasised. There has been recognition of people's needs for space, privacy within safe parameters, and the choice of a variety of rooms for quiet, and diverse activities, including individual and group sessions, and 'a space set aside for prayer and quiet reflection' (NICE 2005, p. 14; see also, Dix and Page 2008; Von Sommaruga 2004). The amount of space may also be important (Crowner 2008), but Duxbury *et al.* (2006, p. 285) reported mixed findings in this area, with 'some studies indicating...and others not confirming [a] relationship' with incidences of violence and aggression.

Reduction of noise and activity levels that the individual experiences as distressing and overwhelming can be important for some clients, especially those who experience sensory overload in response to both external noise and persistent voices or obtrusive thoughts (Byrt 2007; Fontaine 2009). Some studies have found increased incidences of violence and aggression at times of greater noise and activity on wards, with consequent sensory overload for some clients, e.g., during meal times in communal dining areas (Hunter and Love 1996, cited in Duxbury *et al.* 2006, p. 284), times when wards are especially busy, and where there is overcrowding, with excessive numbers of patients on wards (Duxbury *et al.* 2006, p. 277). Some studies of mental health acute admission wards have reported overcrowding, as a result of many demands for admission (Firth 2004, Quirk and Lelliott 2001).

Box 4.2

The physical and social environment in a Psychiatric Intensive Care Unit (PICU)

The following account by Walker (2008) outlines ways that the environment in a PICU was made safer and more therapeutic, and indicates certain requirements for furniture that may be needed if clients engage in violent behaviours:

'The team at a…PICU wished to redesign the main social space, which was stark and uninviting…

'The area afforded service users little privacy, as passers-by could see straight through the main door into the social space. The new design has divided the space into distinct zones for eating and seating, and the addition of an internal wall…now obscures the view of the living area from the road.

'Staff and service users were involved in choosing the bespoke leather club chairs which were trialled on the unit before being purchased. They are heavily weighted so that they cannot be thrown, and the manufacture includes toughened seams and non-retractable screws. Heavyweight chairs and tables have been purchased for the dining area, and bright service user artwork now adorns the walls.

'In common with other…PICU projects, improvements to the environment have resulted in a reduction in violent incidents and staff recruitment has also improved.'
(Walker 2008, pp. 15f)

Many aspects of the physical environment are seen as important in guidelines on preventing and reducing violence and aggression (NICE 2005; Royal College of Psychiatrists' Audit Team 2005). Lawson and Phiri (2000) report that, in a comparison of an older and a carefully designed, new mental health ward, there was increased patient satisfaction with the physical environment in the new service. In addition, 'the level of verbal outbursts and of threatening behaviour were…judged to have significantly reduced in the new unit (by 24% and 42%, respectively)' (Lawson and Phiri 2000). Barlow (2003) outlined various improvements in physical environment, including gym equipment and the colour of décor, but the effects on aggression seem inconclusive. In general, there appears to be limited research evidence on the effects on violence and aggression of changing aspects of the physical environment. This is indicated in a review of research in this area to inform the NICE (2005) guideline. In the latter, recommendations on the physical environment are all given a 'D', the lowest of four levels of evidence, although most of these recommendations are seen as indicating a 'good practice point' (NICE 2005, p. 13).

Snoezelen and other multisensory environments

Multisensory environments

Snoezelen and other multisensory environments use a combination of coloured 'light...sound...scent and music' (International Snoezelen Association 2009) which is intended, amongst other aims, to increase relaxation and reduce anxiety. These environments might also reduce aggression, where the latter is associated with anxiety (Bowness *et al.* 2008). Fava and Strauss (2010, p. 160) reported that, amongst individuals with learning disabilities, only those with concurrent autism showed lessening of 'disruptive behaviours' following interventions using Snoezelen. In contrast, Van Weert *et al.* (2005) found that Snoezelen reduced aggression, apathy and depression in older people with dementia. In a systematic review of research, Livingston *et al.* (2005) stated that two randomised controlled trials revealed that Snoezelen resulted in temporary reductions in 'disruptive behaviour', but changes were not maintained in the long term. Experience suggests that, for some people with dementias, Snoezelen and other multisensory environments may worsen confusion and concomitant aggressive behaviours. As with any intervention, the extent to which individuals benefit, and the effects on violence and aggression, need to be carefully monitored (Byrt 2009).

The social environment

The social environment

The social environment of a service is often referred to as the 'milieu' in US texts (Fontaine 2009). It includes the roles and relationships of clients and staff, the communication between them, and associated attitudes. It also involves the culture of the service: the shared values, beliefs and ways of doing things of patients and staff, and the organisational structures of the ward, and its 'regimes, routines, rules and restrictions' and activities (Byrt 2006, p. 193, citing Kilshaw 1999).

The social and physical environments of services, including communication, need to be sensitive to individuals' cultural backgrounds, gender, physical and sensory disabilities and sexualities (Byrt with James 2007; Davenport 2004; Thampy and Bhugra 2004). The NICE (2005, p. 14) *Guideline on Violence* stresses the importance of maintaining clients' 'privacy and dignity' and of providing separate space or facilities for women.

Ward/unit atmosphere'

The 'atmosphere' or 'climate' of services (Schalast *et al.* 2008; Timko and Moos 2004; Wilson *et al.* 2008) is another important part of social environment. There is evidence that some aspects of the social environment are related to the presence or relative absence of violence and aggression. A number of researchers have produced scales to assess the social environment of various services, including, amongst other factors, the degree of 'anger and aggression' (partly related to staff authoritarianism, considered later in this book); 'order and organization' including planned activities; and patients' 'autonomy', involving independence and responsibility, and participation in the day to day social functioning of the service (Timko and Moos 2004; Moos 1974, Schalast *et al.* 2008; Wilson *et al.* 2008, quotations, above, from a scale in Timko and Moos 2004, p. 146). Holmqvist and Fogelstam (1996) stated that the optimum ward environment varies, according to the needs of the individual. Friis and Helldin (1994, p. 343) reported that high levels of aggression in patients were associated with '…high levels of authoritarianism, over-stimulation, a lack of support from staff, a lack of structure and predictability…'. Recent scales to measure ward and other service environments include those by Wilson *et al.* (2008), which, among many areas, evaluates levels of aggression; and the Essen Climate Evaluation Scheme (EssenCES) developed for use in secure hospitals. This measures aspects of therapeutic staff–patient relationships and the extent that social environments are therapeutic and safe, with ' "safety" (versus threat of violence and aggression)' (Schalast *et al.* 2008, p. 49) being an important component of the scale. Jorgensen *et al.* (2009, pp. 118f) found that in their research, 'anger and aggression and staff control were not correlated with patient satisfaction', but add 'other studies have found negative correlations' and 'low levels of this factor are recommended for psychosis wards'.

Expressed emotion

Expressed emotion

Relapse and worsening of some symptoms of schizophrenia have been reported when either carers at home or health professionals display high expressed emotion, characterised by 'hostility, criticism and emotional over-involvement' (Byrt 2007; p. 60, citing Timko and Moos 2004; Watkins 1996). In one study, high staff expressed emotion resulted in increased aggression in hostel residents (Snyder *et al.* 1994). In contrast, Kirby (1997), who evaluated 'ward atmosphere on two wards in a medium secure unit, concluded that nurses did not need to exert custodial control, but used their relationships with patients, and a relaxed ward environment, to prevent and reduce aggression' (Byrt 2007, p. 63). Study findings suggest that, not surprisingly, mental health clients' stress levels increase in response to the violent behaviours of their peers (Bowers *et al.* 1999). On acute admission wards and some other services, this is sometimes related to the effects of alcohol and other drugs (Atakan 2008; Burbach 2008).

Point for discussion/reflection

In your practice or placement setting, are there any changes to the physical and social environment that could be made so that they are safer and more therapeutic?

Amounts of structure and activities

Structure and activities

Research suggests that a lack of structure and clear leadership is associated with increased violence (Quanbeck and McDermott 2008). Structure includes opportunities for meaningful, fulfilling activities. Boredom and long periods of inactivity with nothing to do (sometimes associated with long waiting times, e.g., in Accident and Emergency departments) have been found to be associated with violence and aggression in a variety of health settings, including mental health and learning disability units (NICE 2005; Richter and Whittington 2006; Royal College of Psychiatrists 1998; Royal College of Psychiatrists Audit Team 2005) and Accident and Emergency departments (Britten and Shaw 1994; Health Services Advisory Committee 1997; Shepherd 2001b). The Health Services Advisory Committee(1997) recommended measures to reduce boredom and frustration in Accident and Emergency departments by providing information about waiting times, 'reading material... [and] a.television' (Health Services Advisory Committee 1997, p. 14). Torphy and Hall (1993, p. 539) report that, in a medium secure unit, there was 'virtually no violence in areas designed for occupation or therapy or in public spaces out of doors'. In contrast, several studies found high levels of boredom in mental health acute admission wards (Royal College of Psychiatrists Audit Team 2005; Sainsbury Centre for

Mental Health 2006; Walton 2000). 'Structured days' have been introduced, with the appointment of staff to coordinate a variety of activities (Bose 2009) and 'protected therapeutic time' spent with patients and reductions in nurses' time spent on paperwork (NHS Institute for Innovation and Improvement 2009). Some authors refer to the importance of individually tailored activities which meet the needs of the individual, and take into account both her or his particular aptitudes and preferences and the avoidance of both under-stimulation and expectations that the individual cannot cope with (Byrt 2007; Gamble *et al.* 2009; Siddle and Everitt 2002).

Some clients living in the community may experience boredom, for example, because of restrictions in mobility, e.g., as a result of a stroke (Squires and Hastings 2002) or because of factors associated with limited motivation or energy or depression (Gamble *et al.* 2009) and/or social exclusion, e.g., lack of access to educational or leisure activities (Tew 2005; Watkins 2007). In addition, it has been suggested that boredom is one factor associated with bullying in children and young people, with a need to ensure that school and other activities are interesting (Rigby 2002), since some bullying may be associated with a need for excitement. Where this is the case, channeling and diversionary activities might be of use.

The NICE (2005) *Guideline on Violence* recommends:

> Services should be able to accommodate service users' needs for engaging in activities and individual choice – there should be an activity room and a dayroom with a television, as boredom can lead to disturbed/violent behaviour.
> (NICE 2005, p. 14)

Feeley and Jones (2008) and McCue (2000) describe the use of activities enjoyed by individuals with learning disabilities to enable the gradual introduction of other activities, essential to their well-being, but which they found stressful. This can result in reductions in aggression in response to stress. Byrt and Doyle (2007) outline the use of writing and drawing to divert an individual from aggressive thoughts about another client.

The use of activities for diversion and channelling to prevent violence: an example from practice

Feeley and Jones (2008) outline the use of diversion with a child of 3 years, 10 months with Down Syndrome and so-called 'challenging behaviour'. The child, 'Cody' (a pseudonym) engaged in behaviours such as 'ignoring [carers'] requests and dropping to the floor'. Although Cody is not described as being violent or aggressive, the diversion techniques outlined by Feeley and Jones (2008) could equally apply to violence or aggression and could also be used with young people and adults with learning disabilities. This 'intervention ... involves offering the child a preferred item to distract him/her from the aversiveness of the request' (Feeley and Jones 2009, p. 5 of online version).

Aversiveness included Cody's dislike of moving to different parts of the classroom, possibly because he found it difficult to cope with sudden changes in his environment. So, at times when it was necessary for Cody to move to another part of the room 'Cody's teacher asked him to carry supplies...or blow the class whistle in order to gain [other children's] attention' (Feeley and Jones 2009, p. 5 of online version). These were activities that Cody enjoyed doing – described by Feeley and Jones as 'preferred items/activities'.

Activities in a psychiatric high-dependency unit

Thomas *et al.* (2006) outline the use of a structured activity programme in an Australian psychiatric high dependency unit. Their research found that, following the introduction of this programme, there was a 'statistically significant' reduction in 'the number of PRN [i.e.when required] medications dispensed' (Thomas *et al.* 2006, p. 266) and in associated violent and aggressive behaviours.

Point for consideration/reflection

In relation to the service where you work, consider the role of activities in preventing and reducing violence and aggression.

Prison environments

Surveys of individuals in prison and young offenders institutions have found that large proportions have mental health problems, sometimes associated with violent offending (Durcan 2008a). Senior (2005) estimated that, in one men's prison, 'at any one time, 27 % of the population of the prison would require intervention...for mental health problems' (Senior and Shaw 2008, p. 184). In a major study, Singleton *et al.* (1998) found that, of

Prison environments

sentenced prisoners, half of the men, and nearly two-thirds of the women had a diagnosis of personality disorder; and about a third of both women and men were dependent on drugs. 6% of the men and 13% of the women had 'schizophrenic or delusional disorder' and 7% and 16%, respectively, had attempted suicide in the year before the study (Singleton *et al.* 1998, cited in Durcan 2008a, p. 294).

Preventing violence may be difficult in some penal institutions because of environments which perpetuate it and because security and containment may be accorded higher priority than other aims (HM Inspector of Prisons 2009a; Ramsbotham 2005; Stern 2006). Maeve and Vaughan (2001) refer to the difficulty of providing adequate nursing care to individual prisoners when the total prison environment is unhealthy and stressful for them. Besides a lack of physical space, and prolonged periods in cells experienced by many individuals who are prisoners (HM Inspector of Prisons 2009a, 2009b), some of them do not have access to 'regular showers, changes of clothes…Increasingly, two prisoners share a cell meant for one, with a common toilet in full view (and often providing the only place where one of them can sit)' (HM Inspector of Prisons 2009b).

These environmental factors may contribute to violence and aggression in prisoners with mental health problems or learning disabilities, as may limited time to associate with other prisoners or engage in meaningful activity. This increases isolation and boredom and reduces opportunities for support from peers or staff. All these factors may make violence and aggression and self-harm more likely (Blom-Cooper 2008; Durcan 2008a, 2008b; HM Inspector of Prisons 2009a, 2009b; Stern 2006). People with mental illness are more likely to be bullied by other prisoners (Toch and Kupers 2007). In Durcan and Knowles's (2006) study, many individuals reported that other prisoners' bullying was a problem.

Activities and boredom in prisons

Torphy and Hall's (1993) finding of lowered rates of violence when clients were involved in activities in a medium secure unit, is likely to have some relevance to prisons, including prison health services. Despite increases in some prisons in health service, educational and occupational provision, HM Inspector of Prisons has referred to effects of overcrowding adversely affecting 'safety, respect, purposeful activity and resettlement' (HM Inspector of

Prisons 2009a), with many individuals remaining in cells 'up to 23 hours a day' (HM Inspector of Prisons 2009b). Research findings suggest that such prolonged isolation could result in sensory deprivation (Meehan *et al.* 2000); and engender frustration, thus making violence and aggression more likely, particularly in individuals who find it difficult to manage frustration in other ways (Bjorkly 2006).

Wood (2007) describes the use of activities in a prison therapeutic community for young people, partly as an alternative means of expression to offending. She outlines the role of professionals in persevering with encouraging the young people to engage in creative activities, and to contain aggressive behaviours through establishing therapeutic relationships and communication: 'The challenge for staff is to draw the boundary for creative expression, in such a way that enthusiasm and spontaneity are encouraged, but behaviour remains contained, and the overall task is maintained' (Wood 2007, p. 157).

The role of education in prisons has also been considered. In his review of research on preventing violent offending, Gillam (2001) reported many US studies which found that when prisoners progressed in their education, they were less likely to commit violent crimes.

Can pets reduce violence?

Can pets reduce violence?

Finally, pets have been used therapeutically with individuals with learning disabilities and mental health problems, and with older people in a variety of services (Scholl *et al.* 2008). Ormerod (2008) describes the therapeutic use of pets with prisoners, some of whom had committed violent offences. The pets helped to reduce individuals' tension and aggression. One man said:

> This wee cat saved my sanity. It was the first thing I showed affection…in seven years. The cat has brought me through some very difficult times. If you have lost that concern for other people, and you get a cat to care for, I think that's where caring begins in a place like this.

> I was a violent man and used to find it difficult to communicate with other people. But 'Puss' really helped me, and because of her, my behaviour has improved.
> (Ormerod 2008, pp. 287 and 288)

One of the current authors worked with an individual who reported similar benefits from two rabbits which she kept near the ward. 'Millie' (a pseudonym) said that initially, it was easier to relate to the rabbits than towards other individuals, about whom she sometimes had violent fantasies. The rabbits appeared to enable 'Millie' to begin to gradually relate to, and feel that she could communicate with people. Two years after being discharged from the ward, 'Millie' said she was living happily at home with various pets, and no longer engaged in violent fantasies or behaviours.

The next chapter will consider de-escalation, with particular reference to communication, another important aspect of clients' social environments.

Chapter 5
De-escalation: reducing arousal and aggression

This chapter will consider de-escalation or ways of reducing violence and aggression, with reference to the individual's experience of psychological and physiological arousal and effective non-verbal and verbal communication.

De-escalation

De-escalation

The term de-escalation refers to the methods used by staff to reduce violence and aggression, particularly non-verbal and verbal communication skills, and specific interventions, including distraction and channelling aggression. It can also include the values of an organisation and its 'culture...policies and procedures' (Paterson and Leadbetter 1999, p. 95, quoted in Byrt and Doyle 2007, p. 86).

De-escalation may include interventions based on specific therapeutic approaches: for example, enabling a client to use cognitive behavioural techniques. This might include the use of learnt problem-solving approaches, with, for example, the client temporarily withdrawing from the situation which has triggered anger or using relaxation techniques (Bede *et al.* 2008; Bowness *et al.* 2008). The use of therapeutic interventions is considered in Chapters 12 and 13. These de-escalation techniques, especially those based on specific therapeutic interventions, may be most successful in the earlier stages of developing anger/aggression (Paterson and Leadbetter 1999), a point which is further considered later in this chapter.

Although de-escalation methods are generally seen as good practice (NICE 2005; Quanbeck and McDermott 2008; Richter and Whittington 2006), there are mixed findings from research on the effects of staff training in de-escalation, in relation to the number of incidents of aggression. One randomised controlled trial found 'no reduction in the number of violent incidents', following staff training in de-escalation, but 'a decrease in the use of coercive measures' (Richter *et al.* 2006, p. 215) such as restraint and seclusion.

Physiological and psychological arousal in relation to violence and aggression

Physiological and psychological arousal

An aim of de-escalation is to reduce arousal and this is likely to lessen the risk of violence and ensure safety, as well as reduce the individual's distress and discomfort from the psychological and physiological effects of aggression (Paterson and Leadbetter 1999; Richter 2006). In order to reduce arousal, it is necessary to understand some of these effects.

The term arousal refers both to how a person experiences anger or other emotions (what it feels like), and to specific changes in the body (Morrison and Bennett 2009). When the individual encounters a stressor (e.g., a trigger leading to an aggressive response), this results in various physiological processes involving several parts of the brain, endocrine glands and the autonomic nervous system. The latter includes sympathetic and parasympathetic nervous systems, which are 'sets of nerves arising in an area in the brainstem known as the medulla oblongata' (Morrison and Bennett 2009, p. 223), which is towards the base of the cerebrum, the main part of the brain. Nerves in both the sympathetic and parasympathetic nervous systems are linked to many organs in the body. It is mostly the sympathetic nervous system that is activated during arousal, and which results in the physical changes (described later in this chapter) experienced by the individual who feels aggressive. Similar physical changes occur if she or he experiences sexual arousal or emotions such as fear or joy (Fontaine 2009; Morrison and Bennett 2009).

Physiological processes accompanying feelings of aggression, anger and fear have been referred to as 'the fight or flight reaction' (Paterson and Leadbetter 1999, p. 100, quoted in Byrt and Doyle 2007, p. 84) or 'stress response' (McKay *et al.* 2003, p. 20). In response to the stressor (e.g., something triggering anger), several parts of the brain are activated. These include, in particular, the limbic system and the pre-frontal lobes (Morrison and Bennett 2009).

The limbic system and its role in aggression

The limbic system refers to various parts of the brain, which are interconnected and concerned with preserving the life of the individual and the human species by regulating 'autonomic and endocrine function, particularly in relation to emotional stimuli' (Swenson 2006), including triggers for aggression and other forms of anger, and consequent arousal. The limbic system includes parts 'of the frontal, parietal and temporal lobes that form a continuous band of cortex in a ringlike formation around the top of the brain stem' (Fontaine 2009, p. 103), as well as many structures 'in the core context of the [cerebrum], just above the brainstem' (Fitzgerald undated). According to some authorities, the limbic system includes 'the thalamus, amygdala, hippocampus and hypothalamus' (Fontaine 2009, p. 103). However, there is some disagreement amongst researchers about which parts of the brain comprise the limbic system (Buckley 2003). The amygdala and hypothalamus are particularly involved in experiences of anger and responses to triggers precipitating this emotion.

Amongst other functions, the amygdala enables 'social learning', whereby the individual is socialised and learns 'to avoid actions that will harm others' (Hill *et al.* 2009, p. 102, citing Blair 2006), including aggressive or violent speech or actions. The amygdala is also involved in the recognition of other people's facial expressions, e.g., their fear in response to an individual's aggression. Accurate recognition of this would help the individual to control her or his anger. Conversely, damage to the amygdala can make it harder for clients to learn to modify their aggression or to recognise others' responses towards it (Blair 2009).

The limbic system is connected, via neurotransmitters, to the pre-frontal lobes at the front of the cerebrum (Morrison and Bennett 2009). Neurotransmitters are chemical messages that travel between neurons (cells in the brain, Richards *et al.* 2007, pp. 2f).

The pre-frontal lobe, autonomic nervous system and relevant hormones

The pre-frontal lobe enables the individual to interpret the stimuli that provoke aggression, to make judgements about it and to think about, and decide on a response (Fontaine 2009). For example,

'Roy's' feelings of anger and the accompanying physical changes would be largely related to the functioning of his limbic system, particularly the hypothalamus and the amygdala (described below). However, when Roy says to a care assistant: 'I feel really pissed off. I feel like hitting Raj, but can I talk to you, instead?', this would indicate pre-frontal lobe functioning (de Brito and Hodgins 2009). This involves Roy making a judgement about the disadvantages of hitting Raj and the benefits of talking to the care assistant. Complex mental activity such as thinking, interpreting, planning and making judgements, involving the pre-frontal lobes, are known as 'executive functions' (de Brito and Hodgins 2009). Damage to the frontal lobes makes it harder for the individual to carry out these executive functions.

When Roy experiences aggression or other forms of anger, his hypothalamus produces a hormone called corticotrophin-releasing factor. This causes Roy's pituitary gland (situated near the hypothalamus) to secrete adrenocorticotrophic hormone, which, in turn, stimulates the adrenal cortex, the outer part of the adrenal glands, which are above each of Roy's kidneys. The adrenal cortex produces various hormones, including cortisol, which mobilises fats and other sources of energy to various organs in Roy's body, so that he can more readily fight or run away from the situation that is provoking his anger (Fontaine 2009, p. 106; Morrison and Bennett 2009, p. 225).

When Roy is angry, his hypothalamus, with other parts of the brain, also stimulates his autonomic nervous system, especially his sympathetic nervous system, which conveys messages via neurotransmitters (including acetylcholine and noradrenaline) from the hypothalamus to several organs in Roy's body. The autonomic nervous system acts directly on the muscles and organs to stimulate some of the physical changes characteristic of anger and other emotions (Morrison and Bennett 2009). In addition, the central parts of the adrenal glands (the adrenal medulla) are activated, and they also produce noradrenaline, as well as adrenaline. The hormones are circulated, from both the hypothalamus and the adrenal medulla, via Roy's bloodstream to the organs in his body (Morrison and Bennett 2009, p. 225) to prepare him for 'fight or flight', a mechanism first recognised by Cannon (1932), theories of which were modified by Selye (1974) and later researchers (Morrison and Bennett 2009).

Physical changes in the individual's experience of aggression and other forms of anger

The physiological mechanisms, outlined above, explain the physical changes experienced when the individual is angry. These changes are likely to be particularly marked when she or he is aggressive. The heart beats faster, blood pressure rises, and an increasing amount of blood, containing glucose from the liver, is pumped away from the stomach and intestines and towards muscles, causing feelings of tension, and possible 'shaking with anger'. The individual breathes faster, often with shallow, rather than deep breaths. The skin may be flushed, or otherwise change colour. The individual starts to sweat more, and may experience pressure to pass urine or empty his or her bowels. The mouth may feel very dry and appetite for food is likely to diminish (Morrison and Bennett 2009, p. 224). Ways to relieve these unpleasant effects of arousal are described later in this chapter. The physiological changes were adaptive for our pre-historic ancestors, for example, in enabling them to fight or run away from predators. However, arguably, the features of arousal may not have evolved sufficiently to help individuals to adapt and respond effectively to sources of anger in early 21st century post-industrial societies (Morrison and Bennett 2009).

Assessment for signs of aggression

Crucial to ensuring safety, and enabling de-escalation, is careful observation of the client for signs of increasing aggression. These vary with the individual, and may include those outlined in the NICE (2005) *Guideline on Violence* (Box 5.1), as well as 'shouting, swearing, clenching fists' (Le Butt and Chauhan undated). Increased muttering, pacing up and down, and the use of particular swear words may indicate that the individual is becoming increasingly aggressive. If the individual responds in this way to auditory hallucinations, signs that she or he is experiencing these voices, with impending aggression, may include staring at a part of the room and muttering. (However, only a minority of people experiencing voices are aggressive.) Sometimes, signs of imminent aggression are very specific to the individual, and may include, for example, the wearing of a particular item of clothing or a sudden and unusual decision to avoid particular people. Of course, such behaviours may not have any significance, and should not be 'pathologised' (see p 55); risk assessment can establish particular signs of impending aggression for an individual client (Maden 2007; Woods and Kettles 2009a). Relational security (including the extent to which a particular worker knows the client well) will enable risk assessment, the identification of impending aggression and the implementation of de-escalation and other interventions (Dale and Gardner 2001).

Box 5.1

Warning Signs of Violent Behaviours: NICE (2005) *Guideline on Violence*

The National Institute for Clinical Excellence (NICE) (2005, pp. 18f) *Guideline on Violence* lists 'warning signs to indicate that a service user may be escalating towards physically violent behaviour'. These include the following:

- 'Facial expressions tense and angry.'
- 'Increased or prolonged restlessness, body tension, pacing.'
- 'General over-arousal of body systems (increased breathing and heart rate, muscle twitching, dilating pupils).'
- 'Increased volume of speech, erratic movements.'
- 'Prolonged eye contact.'
- '…Replicating, or behaviour similar to that which preceded earlier…violent episodes.'
- 'Reporting…violent feelings.'
- 'Blocking escape routes.'

Reducing the unpleasant effects of arousal as part of de-escalation

Reducing the effects

Research findings suggest that some people find their aggression and violence exciting. This is the case with individuals with 'sensation seeking' behaviours, including some people with antisocial personality disorder, who may become easily bored and indulge in violence and aggression for 'kicks' (van Goozen and Fairchild 2009). (However, these individuals may, nevertheless, also experience considerable distress in response to other situations, National Forensic Nurses' Research and Development Group 2006.) Individuals with instrumental aggression may behave violently, not in response to feelings of anger, but for specific rewards such as gaining excitement and relieving boredom (Howells *et al.* 2008). However, clients who are aggressive or violent in response to frustration or other adverse environmental stimuli are more likely to experience psychological and physical arousal, and possibly, to experience this as distressing. They may also be experiencing anxiety and other unpleasant feelings, with any of the accompanying uncomfortable physical sensations, as outlined above. This needs to be borne in mind during nursing/multidisciplinary interventions (Richter and Whittington 2006; Turnbull and Paterson 1999). An important aim of de-escalation is to reduce the client's arousal and enable her or him to feel less distressed and more comfortable, as well as less aggressive. In order to do this effectively, the worker needs to be self-aware, particularly of her or his own level of arousal, caused by understandable anxiety in the face of a stressful situation. Unless recognised, staff members' levels of arousal may result in their rushing in, fuelled by adrenaline, to unnecessarily restrain a client, instead of safely enabling her or him to express concerns. High arousal in staff may, in addition, result in their saying things which unintentionally trigger further aggression (Byrt and Doyle 2007; Paterson and Leadbetter 1999; Whittington and Balsamo 1998).

Box 5.2 includes examples of interventions which may help to reduce arousal, and thus diminish aggression.

Box 5.2

Reducing physiological and psychological arousal:
From Byrt and Doyle 2007, p. 86

- 'An opportunity to sit down, with the [professional] also doing so (if this is safe).'
- 'An opportunity for the individual to talk, and be listened to (provided, again, this is safe). In some (though not all) circumstances, this may help the individual to "get things off his or her chest", with a consequent reduction in physical, as well as psychological, tension. '
- 'Use of...non-verbal and verbal communication skills'
- 'Offer of a hot or cold drink...In addition to [reducing a dry mouth], the drink can indicate the [worker's] caring', and perhaps, have a social function.'
- 'In some circumstances, making food available, particularly if the individual has not eaten for a while, and has a low blood sugar level.'
- 'Providing diversion, channelling and safe means to communicate feelings' (Byrt and Doyle 2007, p. 86).
- Providing a variety of non-verbal means of expression would be important for some individuals who find it hard to express themselves orally, e.g., certain individuals with learning disabilities (Gates 2007) or

acquired brain damage or dementias (Squires and Hastings 2002).

- For some clients, relaxation techniques may help to reduce aspects of physical arousal. These could include enabling the individual to take slow, deep breaths, and relaxing groups of muscles to reduce tension. Guided imagery might also be used to enable the client to focus on relaxing and peaceful thoughts and images (Monk-Steel undated; Muir-Cochrane 2009).

The 'assault cycle' (Kaplan and Wheeler 1983) and its implications for professional practice, including the preservation of safety

The 'assault cycle'

Reducing arousal is likely to be most easily achieved in the early stages of aggression (Richter 2006). It has been argued that interventions need to take account of the extent to which an individual is violent or aggressive (Leadbetter and Paterson 1999; Linsley 2006, p. 48). Kaplan and Wheeler (1983) described five phases of the 'assault cycle'. Subsequent authors have modified this model (Paterson and Leadbetter 1999; CALM 2008). Kaplan and Wheeler (1983) outlined the following phases (Paterson and Leadbetter 1999, p. 103, citing Kaplan and Wheeler 1983):

- 'the triggering phase'
- 'the escalation phase'
- 'the crisis phase'
- 'the recovery phase'
- 'the depression phase' (following the immediate crisis).

Implications for professional practice

Paterson and Leadbetter (1999) and Linsley (2006) suggest that an awareness of the phases of the 'assault cycle' reached by an individual has implications for interventions to ensure the safety of the potentially or actually aggressive or violent individual, other clients/visitors and staff, and to relieve the client's arousal, and reduce her or his level of distress.

Paterson and Leadbetter (1999) outline their 'CALM (Crisis Aggression Limitation and Management)' model, based on the model of Kaplan and Wheeler (1983). Paterson and Leadbetter's (1999) model involves seven phases which are associated with specific interventions, as follows:

'Phase 1: The onset of arousal responding to increased anxiety'
(Paterson and Leadbetter 1999, p. 111)

In this initial phase, Paterson and Leadbetter (1999) recommend assessment of the client, dealing effectively with the client's concerns, reducing anxiety and building rapport. Suggested 'strategies' include many of the non-verbal and verbal communication skills considered later in this book. Of particular importance is the authors' advice to 'avoid behaviour that might be interpreted as authoritarian or patronising' (Paterson and Leadbetter 1999, p. 112).

'Phase 2: Dealing with increasingly angry behaviour'
(Paterson and Leadbetter 1999, p. 112)

In this phase, 'calming and/or de-escalation' (Paterson and Leadbetter 1999, p. 112) is recommended, as is the need for the worker to adapt her or his response to the client's main emotion at the time.

'Phase 3: Dealing with the onset of aggressive behaviour'
(Paterson and Leadbetter 1999, p. 113)

Here, professionals are advised to 'prevent further escalation, reduce...arousal' and enable the client to deflect thought from their aggression. Amongst many 'strategies', calmness, negotiation, safe limit setting, without being confrontational, and speaking clearly are proposed. If de-escalation does not occur, it is recommended that the worker unobtrusively get help, administer 'medication if prescribed' and discreetly ensure that the client cannot access items that could serve as weapons. Sensitivity to the client's need for space and avoidance of 'threats' and 'unrealistic expectations' is also suggested (Paterson and Leadbetter 1999, p. 114).

The current authors recommend that it would be safer for workers to obtain help during Phase 1 or Phase 2 for some clients, e.g., those whose risk assessment indicates a rapid escalation of violence.

'Phase 4. Dealing with physically violent behaviour'
(Paterson and Leadbetter 1999, p. 114)

During this phase, ensuring 'safety of staff and clients' is the main aim. Strategies include techniques to ensure staff safety, 'restraint, medication, seclusion' and 'escape', presumably, staff leaving the situation, although the implications of this are not made clear.

Paterson and Leadbetter (1999, p. 115) wisely warn against 'over-reacting, especially the use of excessive force, panic' and being punitive. They state that the 'unacceptability' of the client's behaviour should be communicated to her or him. This is not considered in relation to whether it would be judgemental or might escalate further violence, or in the context of the extent to which the client is able to be responsible for her or his behaviour (Mandelstam 2009; Richards and Mughal 2009). However, Turnbull and Paterson (1999) (in which Paterson and Leadbetter 1999 occurs) does include other chapters where these factors are considered.

Other aspects of non-verbal and verbal communication are not considered by Paterson and Leadbetter (1999) in relation to their phase 4 ('dealing with physically violent behaviour'), despite the general commitment to communication in the CALM approach (CALM 2008; Paterson and Leadbetter 1999). However, in the experience of the current authors:

- non-verbal communication, which endeavours to convey calm, and concern and respect for the individual should continue, as much as possible, whilst the individual is being physically violent;

- whilst verbal communication may be difficult with individuals who are violent, this is not always impossible, and may depend partly on the nature of the worker – client relationship and previous communication (Aiyegbusi and Clarke-Moore, 2009).

'Phase 5: Dealing with aggression once the person is no longer physically violent' (Paterson and Leadbetter 1999, p. 116)

Aims at this phase relate to reducing risk and re-establishing a therapeutic relationship and communication with the client. Interventions include 'a gradual relaxation of restraint' (Paterson and Leadbetter 1999, p. 116), in accordance with the client's diminishing violence, giving any 'first aid' needed, seeking 'medical advice', and administering medication as necessary. Involving 'senior management or security staff' is also recommended. Paterson and Leadbetter (1999) also suggest avoiding premature discussion of the violent behaviour, as the individual will not be ready to consider this during phase 5, and there might be a further escalation of aggression and violence.

'Phase 6: 'Dealing with lessening but persistent arousal' (Paterson and Leadbetter 1999, p. 116)

'Problem-solving' is introduced at this phase, with the individual being encouraged to identify possible triggers, and consider other ways of expressing frustration and anger, in relation to 'the organisation's rules and expectations' (Paterson and Leadbetter 1999, p. 116). (In addition, the current authors suggest that clients' views about the organisation should be listened to, and any appropriate action taken.) Paterson and Leadbetter (1999) suggest providing 'space' and a drink for the client and staff member. This could reduce arousal, but care needs to be taken not to trigger further violence, act in a punishing way or cease careful observation of the client. In addition, judgement would need to be exercised with hot drinks if the client is likely to throw them.

In relation to triggers, Woodward *et al.* (2004) comment:

> We all have a baseline of behaviour which, for most people, is non-aggressive. When a behaviour changes, it emerges from that baseline to the trigger phase...This is a particularly high risk time. In this phase, anything other than careful intervention by the practitioner can cause considerable escalation, possibly to actual aggression...

> The trigger can be any action or statement that could be perceived by the client as provocative...Staff need to have a good assessment of their individual clients and the factors likely to trigger any one individual.
>
> (Woodward *et al.* 2004, p. 138)

'Phase 7: 'Helping an aggressor to learn from an incident' (Paterson and Leadbetter 1999, p. 117)

Paterson and Leadbetter (1999) state that, in this final phase, the aim is 'debriefing', involving helping the individual to learn and develop personally from examining the incident. These authors comment that this approach contrasts with punitive reactions on the part of staff. It also varies from reactive approaches, where people are secluded or restrained, with no opportunities to discuss the consequent trauma to them, or to consider other ways to manage distressing feelings manifest as violence or aggression (Norton and Dolan 1995). Several other authors also emphasise the importance of staff debriefing to discuss their feelings and experiences after violent incidents (Linsley 2006; Needham 2006; Paterson and Leadbetter 1999).

The practical application of models related to 'assault cycles'

Further research appears to be needed on the extent to which clients actually demonstrate the phases in Kaplan and Wheeler's (1983) assault cycle and in the CALM Model (Paterson and Leadbetter 1999). Practical experience suggests that some individuals' aggression gradually increases (e.g., in response to frustration, Richter 2006). However, clients with instrumental aggression may plan a violent action, for example, to exert power over another person, or for revenge reasons. In these circumstances, physical violence may be very sudden, and without earlier 'warning signs' that a client is about to engage in violent behaviours (Howells *et al.* 2008). In addition, research could establish the extent to which specific interventions, including those outlined by Paterson and Leadbetter (1999), are effective in de-escalating aggression during its different phases. Paterson and Leadbetter (1999) point out: '...The [CALM] model is attractive both theoretically and ideologically, but it may potentially depend on whether staff can reliably discern where a client is in the assault cycle, which is not yet established. It is presently subject to evaluative research...' (p. 110).

McKenzie *et al.* (2003) researched 'the impact of staff awareness of the assault cycle on staff working in learning disability services' (p. 15). McKenzie *et al.* (2003) found that many staff were unaware of the implications of the phases of the assault cycle on specific interventions. A possible criticism of the study is the apparent assumption of the authors that interventions at particular points in the assault cycle are always appropriate or inappropriate.

The paper refers to research on the influence of 'environmental factors and staff variables such as the interactional styles and practices of immediate caregivers' (p. 15). These areas are considered in Chapters 4 and 9.

Point for reflection/discussion

a) One test of the usefulness of any model is how effectively it can be applied in professional practice. In practice, how easy would you and your colleagues find it to assess 'where a client is in the assault cycle'?

b) Does this assessment affect your decisions concerning:

- client and staff safety
- other aspects of professional interventions?

Conclusion

This chapter has considered de-escalation; the nature of arousal, with reference to relevant physical changes; ways to reduce arousal, and interventions at various phases of a cycle of violence and aggression, in relation to the 'CALM (Crisis Aggression Limitation and Management)' model, outlined by Paterson and Leadbetter (1999), and based on the model of Kaplan and Wheeler (1983). The next chapter will consider non-verbal and verbal communication used in de-escalation.

Chapter 6
Non-verbal and verbal communication

Communication is an important aspect of de-escalation (defined at the beginning of Chapter 5), and any worker is well advised to consider the impact of what they say, how they say it and the gestures they use as part of the delivery very carefully. According to Finnegan (2004, p. 10), communication:

> ...is not confined to linguistic or cognitive messages, but also includes experience, emotion and the unspoken. Communication is envisaged as creative human process...It encompasses the many modes of human interacting and living, both near and distant...

O'Carroll and Park (2007, p. 106) define interpersonal communication as:

> The process by which information, meanings and feelings are shared by people through the exchange of verbal and non-verbal messages.

Verbal communication includes what is said (the speech content), the tone, pitch and volume of voice. Also of relevance is whether client and worker speak the same language (see Chapter 8) and the use or absence of unnecessary jargon (Boggs 2007; Fontaine 2009; O'Carroll and Park 2007). Using jargon can alienate those who are not familiar with it, emphasising a power difference (Dooher and Byrt 2005). Non-verbal communication includes listening and 'facial expression' (O'Carroll and Park 2007, p. 116) and the use of silence, gestures such as nods of the head, posture when sitting or standing, the amount of space between client and worker, eye contact and touch (Boggs 2007; Fontaine 2009; O'Carroll and Park 2007).

Key components of therapeutic communication and worker-client relationship are related to verbal, and, in particular, non-verbal communication. In relation to the client, these include respect, establishing trust, being non-judgemental (Aiyegbusi and Clarke-Moore 2009; Freeth 2007); and Carl Rogers' core conditions of 'congruence, unconditional positive regard and empathy' (Freeth 2007, p. 127; see also, Rogers 1967; Rogers 1990).

Tables 6.1 and 6.2 summarise some of these aspects of communication, in relation to approaches likely to be effective and ineffective in preventing and reducing violence and aggression.

Table 6.1

Aspects of worker verbal communication and its likely effect on violence and aggression

(Boggs 2007; O'Carroll and Park 2007; Richter 2006; Willis and Gillett 2003)

Aspect of communication	Likely to prevent or reduce violence and aggression	Unlikely to prevent or reduce violence and aggression/may increase them
Content of speech	Conveying respect and concern for the client Taking what she or he says seriously Offering apology/ explanation, as necessary	Conveying disrespect and lack of concern for the client Dismissing what she or he says Not offering apology or explanation when needed
Tone of speech	Sounds interested and respectful	Sounds bored, uninterested and disrespectful
Pitch of speech	Speaks clearly, but not too loudly Sounds pleasantly assertive, but not authoritarian	Raises voice, perhaps shouts Sounds authoritarian
Verbal limit setting	Sets limits clearly in order to ensure safety, but does so in a polite, respectful manner	Sets limits in an authoritarian way, which results in the client feeling 'put down' and disrespected

Availability of client choices	Offers client safe alternatives Negotiates with the client where possible	Not prepared to offer alternatives or negotiate with the client in situations where it would be safe to do so
Adaptation of communication to clients' needs	Adapts communication to client's needs, without being patronising Takes into account client's abilities and problems in using verbal and other communication	Does not adapt communication to client's needs or assess whether communication is understood by her/him
Technical language/ jargon	Avoids using technical language/jargon and tries to use language shared with the client	Uses technical language/ jargon Does not attempt to use shared language with the client
Assessment of language needs and provision of interpreter	With colleagues, assesses language needs and provides interpreter and materials in first language, as needed	No assessment and provision related to interpreters

Table 6.2

Aspects of worker non-verbal communication and its likely effect on violence and aggression

(Boggs 2007; O'Carroll and Park 2007; Paterson and Leadbetter 1999; Richter 2006; Willis and Gillett 2003)

Aspect of communication	Likely to prevent or reduce violence and aggression	Unlikely to prevent or reduce violence and aggression/may increase them
Active listening	Active, attentive listening of both verbal and non-verbal communication, conveying interest in the client, and avoiding interrupting her/him	Failure to listen Frequently interrupts the client Does not convey interest in the client
The use of silence	Able to assess whether the client needs periods of silence Enables this, as necessary	Does not assess the client's possible need for silence Says things to the client because of worker's own discomfort with silence

Facial expression	Conveys interest and concern Mirrors client's emotion (apart from aggression)	Does not convey interest and concern Not congruent with client's emotion (e.g., smiling when client is expressing sad thoughts)
Gestures such as nods of the head	Conveys interest and understanding, but not excessive Avoidance of aggressive gestures, such as finger-pointing at the client	Irritating over-use of gestures, such as head nodding Use of aggressive gestures
Posture when sitting	Open, relaxed posture, perhaps leaning forward slightly, demonstrating that the worker 'is receptive to the [client's] communication' (O'Carroll and Park 2007, p. 113)	Closed posture, e.g., 'folding arms...crossing...legs' (O'Carroll and Park 2007, p. 113), which might suggest a lack of receptiveness to the client
Posture when standing	Open, relaxed posture, standing at a slight angle (45 degrees to the client), rather than directly facing her/him, and 'hands held [with] palms open' (Paterson and Leadbetter 1999, p. 104).	Closed posture: e.g., 'hands on hips like a cowboy in a Western' (Byrt and Doyle 2007, p. 87) Standing directly in front of the client
Space	Sensitivity to the client's needs for space: bearing in mind any cultural needs Avoidance of invasion of client's space	Standing too close to client Insensitivity to her/his need for space Cultural needs not considered
Eye contact	Maintaining eye contact in a non-threatening way to convey interest and enhance communication	Staring at the client or making eye contact that she or he finds uncomfortable
Touch	Awareness that touch may be misinterpreted or seen as in-appropriate by the client, e.g., because of culture or gender Use of therapeutic touch only when the worker is sure that this will benefit the client	Use of touch when this could trigger or worsen aggression (e.g., if the client sees it as a threat or as culturally inappropriate)

Specific aspects of non-verbal and verbal communication

Verbal and non-verbal communi-cation

The authors' practical experience, and much of the literature, including national guidelines, suggest that a range of non-verbal and verbal communication skills is crucial in preventing and de-escalating (reducing) violence and aggression (Linsley 2006; NHS Business Services Authority Security Management Service 2005, 2009; NICE 2005; Richter and Whittington 2006). Indeed, the NHS Security Management Service (2005) emphasises communication in its mandatory syllabus for all mental health and learning disability care workers. However, research on the effectiveness of some of these communication skills appears to be lacking (Richter 2006), although several studies indicate the importance to clients of therapeutic communication and relationships, including their application to preventing and de-escalating violence and aggression (Chandler-Oatts and Nelstrop 2008; Duxbury and Whittington 2005; Meehan *et al.* 2006; Secker *et al.* 2004). This is considered further in Chapter 8.

As long ago as 1888, Eva Luckes referred to the importance of good worker communication with clients, including those described as 'irritable':

> It is especially when your patients are weak and helpless and irritable, that you need to be gentle and considerate towards them; they are so completely in your power, and they may so easily be made to suffer more than they need do, by your having a sharp way of speaking, a rough touch, or a grumbling manner of attending to them. (Luckes 1888, p. 14)

Point for reflection/discussion

In relation to your own area of work, or your practice placement, are there any areas of communication you consider:

● are examples of good practice in relation to interventions with individuals who are aggressive or violent?

● could be improved, in order to more effectively prevent or reduce aggression and violence?

Congruence

Congruence

Some communication skills are related to Carl Rogers' core conditions of client-centred therapy (sometimes called person-centred or humanistic therapy, Freeth 2007; Parker-Hall 2009).

These core conditions, 'congruence, unconditional positive regard and empathy' (Freeth 2007, p. 127), are described in detail in Rogers (1967) and Rogers (1990).

Each of the core conditions requires self-awareness (see Box 6.1). Congruence includes authenticity: the worker's 'awareness of [her/his] feelings and reactions' (Byrt and Doyle 2007, p. 86, citing Burnard 1999) in response to the client and her or his aggressive or violent behaviour. It also involves the worker's decision about whether to disclose her or his feelings and responses to the client (Parker-Hall 2009). This would be influenced largely by safety issues, and whether the worker's disclosure (as with all therapeutic self-disclosure) was in the client's best interests (Stuart 2009). This would not be the case if the client is becoming increasingly aggressive or is engaging in violent behaviours, as he or she could perceive feedback from workers as judgemental and negatively critical, with possible escalation of aggression or violence (Paterson and Leadbetter 1999). However, in some therapeutic interventions, clients may receive constructive feedback from staff and other clients about how their aggression affects others. This may occur in cognitive behavioural therapy (Bede *et al.* 2008; Bowness *et al.* 2008), mentalisation based therapies (Bateman and Fonagy 2004), and therapeutic communities (Byrt 2006; Winship, 2009; see Chapters 12 and 13 below). Within these therapeutic interventions, feedback from staff would be in the context of a supportive, caring worker – client relationship (Byrt 2006).

Other aspects of congruence include being sincere, instead of, for example, pretending interest (Keen and Lakeman 2009). The latter would be manifest in a worker stating to a client that she is interested in his account of aggressive feelings, whilst fidgeting and looking out of the window, longing for the shift to end. This could possibly result in an increase in the client's aggression (Paterson and Leadbetter 1999). Congruence also involves not being defensive, e.g., if an aggressive client complains about the worker, a congruent response would be to listen carefully to the client, and offer an apology, if necessary (Arnold and Boggs 2007).

Empathy

Empathy consists of an attempt to accurately understand and appreciate the views, perspectives and experiences of the client and to clearly convey this understanding to her or him (Freeth

Empathy

2007; Parker-Hall 2009; Stuart 2009). In addition, Kunyk and Olson (2001) argued that empathy must also include taking practical action in relation to the client's expressed concerns. In relation to a client ('Kay') who is expressing a complaint in a verbally aggressive manner, a worker's empathy would include an attempt to appreciate 'Kay's' perspective through active listening: 'a participatory process in which the [worker] listens not only for facts, but also for the underlying meaning of the communication, with its attached values, attitudes, and feelings' (Arnold 2007a, p. 235). Part of the worker's empathetic response would be to seek clarification if she or he was not sure what Kay meant, or ask for more precise details, e.g., related to the nature of the complaint. The 'taking practical action' aspect of empathy could be offering an apology, giving information about the service's complaints procedure and responding by remedying a situation about which the client is concerned (Evans and Byrt 2002). In some situations and with some clients, it may be appropriate to see empathy as a developing process, which improves as the worker gets to know the client better. Like congruence, empathy involves self-awareness, including the worker's cognisance of gaps in her or his understanding of the client, and an acceptance that this may take time to develop (Aiyegbusi and Clarke-Moore, 2009). Aggressive anger may be defused through the demonstration of empathy, and in some situations by paraphrasing 'the content of what is being said' to ensure that this has been understood, and by 'reflecting feelings' (Ford and Rigby 2000, p. 10) of the client.

Whilst the use of touch has sometimes been described in relation to demonstrating empathy, with people who are violent or aggressive it should be used very cautiously, and only if the worker is sure that the client will see it as of benefit (Ford and Rigby 2000; Paterson and Leadbetter 1999).

Unconditional positive regard

Unconditional positive regard

Unconditional positive regard, another of Carl Rogers' core conditions (Rogers 1967; Rogers 1990) includes respecting and valuing the client, as a unique individual, regardless of her or his behaviour. Congruence requires that the worker is honest about her or his feelings about the client's behaviour, with unconditional positive regard involving a determination to work consistently with the individual, despite the difficulties, and within safety parameters (Prins 2005). In his research on nurses working with individuals with antisocial and other personality disorders in high security hospitals, Bowers (2002) found that some nurses felt able to maintain therapeutic relationships with these people, partly because they were able to see 'the whole person', and be prepared to understand the reasons for their aggressive behaviours. Carr-Walker *et al.* (2004) also found that many prison officers were able to maintain positive attitudes towards these individuals. In contrast, Mercer *et al.* (1999) described how other nurses in a high security hospital were unable to progress beyond seeing clients with antisocial personality disorder as 'evil', and saw them only as people who had committed violence offences.

Box 6.1

The need for self-awareness: an example from practice, 'Mr. Les Black' (a pseudonym) and the linen cupboard

The following account, based on the experience of one of the authors earlier in his career, illustrates the importance of self-awareness and other important principles in the prevention of violence and aggression. Details have been changed to ensure anonymity.

One afternoon, I arrived for work, slightly late, and in a bad mood, as I had had a hectic morning dealing with personal matters. Immediately after handover, 'Mr. Les Black' asked if we could go to the Unit's linen cupboard to collect sheets for the ward. Patients were involved in this activity, as part of their rehabilitation.

When we got to the linen cupboard, Les put all the sheets and pillow cases on to the trolley. I suggested that we should leave some linen for other wards. When Les disagreed, I said nothing, but with an authoritarian manner, firmly put some of the sheets back on the shelf.

Les started shouting at me, and when we returned to the ward, attempted to hit me. At an appropriate time, when Les was calm, we sat down to discuss the incident, with another staff member. I apologised for my reaction, and both Les and I agreed that it would have been better to have returned to the ward with all the sheets, and negotiated the return of some of the linen later in the day.

Les said that he had also learned from the incident, and that it illustrated for him his tendency to have a 'short fuse'. Over the ensuing months, Les was enabled to examine ways to express his anger creatively and assertively, rather than aggressively. I resolved to be more self-aware in future.

The following points are raised by this incident:
* The importance of self-awareness. I should have been more aware, at the start of the shift, that I was in a bad mood. Acknowledging this to

myself would, in my experience, have enabled me to ensure that my feelings did not adversely affect my communication and response to Les.

- The need to be more aware of risk factors (considered in Chapter 4). I should have been more observant, and recognised signs that Les could become aggressive or violent. For example, he sounded irritable, and was pacing restlessly before we went to the linen cupboard. Les had previously shown such behaviours before becoming aggressive or violent.

- Based on this assessment, I should have realised that it was unsafe to have gone with Len to the linen cupboard, which was some distance from other staff.

- It was important that I apologised, and admitted that I was wrong. Appropriate apologies can sometimes prevent further aggression or violence (Paterson and Leadbetter 1999). Furthermore, organisational climates where the patients are always seen as 'wrong', and the staff as 'right' are disempowering.

- The timing was also important in relation to attempts to enable Les to examine, and learn from, the incident. It was also important for a neutral staff member, who had not been involved in the incident, to be present.

- It was also important that I reflected on the incident and learned from my mistake.

- Finally, some aspects of interventions were influenced by the therapeutic framework: a modified therapeutic community with principles of open communication to enable residents to discuss, understand and resolve problems.

Point for reflection/discussion

Reflect on an incident where a client was violent or aggressive.

1. Consider the extent to which your own or colleagues' self-awareness was important in your response to the client.

2. What went well?

3. What could have been improved?

Active listening

Carl Rogers' (1967, 1990) core conditions provide a basis for other non-verbal and verbal communication skills, including active listening, with the worker expressing interest and concern in what the client is saying. This is conveyed through close attention to what is being said, without interruption, as well as to the client's non-verbal communication, such as angry or sad facial expressions (Arnold and Boggs 2007). The use of prompts, such as 'would you like to tell me more?' can also indicate interest and a readiness to listen, as can the listener's tone of voice and appropriate eye contact (Arnold and Boggs 2007; Ford and Rigby 2000; Stuart, 2009).

> Give eye contact, as with a normal conversation, and demonstrate that you are actively listening...Prolonged direct eye contact (i.e., staring) should be avoided, as it is likely to be interpreted as provocative and threatening.
>
> (Ford and Rigby 2000, p. 10)

An example of active listening in practice

'Ira' (a pseudonym) was a young woman who was frequently troubled by voices which sometimes told her to assault other people. (Such voices are called 'command hallucinations' (Maden 2007, see Chapter 12, page 173.) One of the authors noted that 'Ira's' distress and thoughts of harming other people were often alleviated by providing active listening, with an opportunity for her to talk about her voices and thoughts to a staff member who maintained clearly expressed interest and concern. It was important to assess, with Ira (as with other clients) whether active listening relieved her distress and accompanying aggressive thoughts (Gamble and Brennan 2006a). This was usually the case, and Ira often said that she felt 'much better' after opportunities to talk to, and be heard by, a worker.

However, some clients may find other approaches, such as a distracting activity, are more likely to reduce both anxiety and aggression (Byrt and Doyle 2007). 'Re-direction' may be a helpful approach. Ford and Rigby (2000, p. 10) suggest:

During escalation, try to break the momentum by changing the situation in some way. Perhaps introduce yourself if you do not know the person, or suggest that they sit down. This is a useful technique, sometimes referred to as 'redirection', the aim of which is to momentarily redirect the focus of their anger and to return to the issue when they feel a little calmer.

Reducing physiological arousal is outlined in Chapter 5. This can include encouraging the client to be seated, provided this is safe, with the worker also taking a seat (Byrt and Doyle 2007). Workers should 'adjust [their] position as the [client] adjusts theirs. If sitting, avoid sitting on chairs that directly face each other...An angle of about 45 degrees...is less threatening' (Ford and Rigby 2000, p. 10). However, the exact position of the chairs depends on the needs of the client and what she or he feels comfortable with. Ford and Rigby (2000, p. 10) suggest that it should be ensured that staff and client 'are on seats of the same height', avoiding 'standing over a sitting client. This can make an individual feel very "crowded"'. If the client declines to sit, the worker would also remain standing in a relaxed, open posture (as outlined in Table 6.2), as this is likely to be safer and to facilitate communication (Paterson and Leadbetter 1999; Willis and Gillett 2003).

Sensitivity to the client's need for space is also important: 'Angry and aroused individuals have a particular need for personal space... [Staff] have been known to provoke incidents by not respecting this, or by unwittingly adopting a confrontational stance' (Ford and Rigby 2000, p. 10). Needs for space may be influenced, in part, by the client's cultural background and personal preferences (Arnold 2007b) and how well she or he knows and trusts the worker, and people in general. Some individuals with schizophrenia have particular needs for space because of suspicion of others. This may be because of the way other people are behaving towards them, but can also be related to paranoid delusions, i.e., specific types of belief that other people are persecuting or harming them in some way (Maden 2007). In addition, some clients may need to withdraw from others because of sensory overload or other sources of stress (Gamble and Brennan 2006a).

Talking 'quietly but clearly' (Byrt and Doyle 2007, p. 86) enables communication in a non-threatening way. A raised voice, particularly shouting, may increase aggression (Paterson and Leadbetter 1999; Morrison 1992), but the individual also needs to be able to hear important information. When a young man ('Gus') threw an armchair, soon after his admission to a mental health service, and was about to hurl another, it was crucial that a staff member said, distinctly and assertively: 'Please can you stop what you're doing, and tell us what's bothering you.' Gus did so, partly, he said later, because he was so surprised to be asked this politely and quietly. He also stated that he would have fought back if he had been confronted in an authoritarian way (Byrt 1999). The literature suggests that a crucial aspect of de-escalation is avoidance of arguing with the client or saying or doing anything that could be seen as provocative, patronising or judgemental.

Examples of statements that could be seen in this way include: 'There's no need to behave like that' and 'You don't need to be angry' (Paterson and Leadbetter 1999). It is also preferable to avoid phrases such as 'you must do this...' (Ford and Rigby 2000, p. 10). This can entrap the worker and the client. 'If you are trying to sell a course of action to a [client], try to offer more than one option, if possible, which would be satisfactory from your point of view' (Ford and Rigby 2000, p. 10).

'Timing of interventions' (Byrt and Doyle 2007, p. 86) is also critical, with, for example, avoidance of detailed consideration with a client of the reasons for her or his behaviours during or soon after a violent incident (Paterson and Leadbetter 1999, see Chapter 5).

'Remaining calm, mirroring and mood matching'

'Remaining calm...'

Workers can 'attempt to read the mood of the client by observing their non-verbal behaviour and be aware of the ways in which [workers'] own body language may be interpreted by the client' (Ford and Rigby 2000, p. 10). Whilst workers need always to maintain calm, if this is demonstrated as nonchalance, condescension or lack of concern or interest, this may fuel aggression or violence (Paterson and Leadbetter 1999; Linsley 2006; Richter 2006).

Mirroring and mood matching are responses that demonstrate concern, interest and involvement, and are intended to decrease aggressive and violent behaviours (Ford and Rigby 2000; Linsley 2006; Paterson and Leadbetter 1999). The term 'mirroring' has been used to describe the worker's adapting her or his physical posture to reflect that of the client, without slavishly copying her or him. For example, if the client sits back, it would probably be more appropriate for the worker to do so, rather than sitting on the edge of the chair (Linsley 2006). In Paterson and Leadbetter (1999), 'mirroring' partly refers to the worker's presentation of a low level of emotional arousal, with the aim of enabling the client to reduce her or his arousal level.

Mood matching involves empathetic responses to what the client is experiencing or feeling at the time; for example, the worker's expression of concern, and avoidance of inappropriate smiling if a client is expressing feelings of sadness. However, Ford and Rigby (2000) point out that mood matching does not involve displaying anger to the client in response to her or his aggressive behaviour. Rather, the aim is to 'match the aggressor's aggression with concern, involvement and interest' (Ford and Rigby 2000, p. 10). Workers need to be aware of their own levels of physiological arousal and develop techniques to decrease this, as high levels of staff arousal may result in over-reaction to aggressive incidents (Richter 2006).

Frustration and other forms of 'aversive stimulation'

'Aversive stimulation'

It is also important to be aware that other feelings may underpin or accompany aggression, e.g., bereavement or loss or anxiety, as was the case with 'Ira' in relation to her voices (described earlier in this chapter). Anxiety and aggression may be a response to frustration, for example, because of not being able to have needs or requests met when these are important to the individual. Whittington and Richter (2006, pp. 51f, citing Whittington and Wykes 1996) outline 'three types of aversive stimulation (frustration, activity demand and intrusion)' which often precede aggression and violence. 'Activity demand' appears to refer to expectations that the client engage in activities when she or he does not wish to do so, and 'intrusion' to unwanted contact with others (Whittington and Richter 2006). The links between aversive stimulation and aggression suggest the importance of assessment of environmental factors that the client finds unpleasant or distressing, and of minimising these factors as much as possible (Royal College of Psychiatrists *et al.* 2007). Examples are outlined in Chapter 13.

Authoritarian attitudes are a form of 'aversive stimulation'. Research suggests that staff attitudes are crucial in the prevention and reduction of aggression and violence. Morrison (1992) found that on certain mental health wards in her study, there was:

> ...a tradition of toughness...in which staff described their jobs in terms of controlling patients and enforcing rules...The underlying philosophy of control led to a rigid set of staff behaviours that ultimately provoked patients into behaving aggressively...Physical methods of control were emphasised, at the expense of verbal safety...

(Morrison 1992, p. 23)

Establishing 'common ground'

Establishing 'common ground'

In contrast, an important component of de-escalation is to endeavour to work with, rather than against, the client, and to establish 'common ground' or shared agreements and understandings as much as possible (Lowe 1992; Byrt and Doyle 2007). However, as indicated in Box 6.2, this does not necessarily involve expressing agreement with the client.

Box 6.2

Working with the client

'If a health professional is defending a particular rule [or] policy...(e.g. no smoking policy), he/she should ensure that the client realises that. In other words, it is important not to make a no smoking rule a personal issue. Alternatively, it is important to personalise yourself' (Institute of Psychiatry Health Services Research Department 2002, p. 24).

'If it appears that, as a [worker], you are receiving abuse simply because of your role...indicate your name. Moreover, try to use the client's name in the conversation, as this can help with establishing a rapport.

'Some words, such as "we", may have a more calming effect and suggest a feeling of [a wish to work with the client]. Alternatively, [other words] such as "no" or "why", may do the opposite. Phrases such as: ..."the situation we are in" ...utilise the "togetherness" effect of "we"' (Ford and Rigby 2000, p. 10).

'Negotiation' and a 'working alliance'

Negotiation

Research findings suggest that some clients perceive aggressive confrontations with staff as situations which they have to 'win' (Lowe 1992; McDougall 2000). In such circumstances, including those resulting in 'aversive stimulation' (Whittington and Richter 2006), there is evidence that, provided it is safe to do so, violence and aggression can be prevented or reduced through negotiation of safe alternatives, and enabling the individual not to 'lose face' (Lowe 1992; McDougall 2000). In relation to 'Gus' (described earlier in this chapter), this was achieved by offering him, at the appropriate time, an opportunity to discuss the problems underlying his initially violent behaviour, and by taking his concerns seriously (Byrt 1999).

There need to be reasonable explanations for the setting of limits to ensure safety, with emphasis on collaboration and the forging of a 'working alliance', to indicate staff's wish to work together with the client towards a solution to difficulties (Friis and Helldin 1994; Harris and Morrison 1995; Richter 2006). Harris and Morrison (1995) suggest that negotiation and collaboration with clients may enable them to effectively modify aggressive behaviours, in contrast to authoritarian responses, which may reinforce them. Working with the client (rather than against her or him) may involve the commencement of 'problem solving and [attempting] to work with the client to generate solutions to the specified problem and act to remedy the problem, if this is possible' (Ford and Rigby 2000, p.10).

Conclusion

Several authors emphasise the importance of respect for clients as individuals, based on therapeutic staff – patient relationships and communication, as crucial in defusing aggression (Dooher 2006; Paterson and Leadbetter 1999; Richter 2006; West and Abolins 2001). Whilst there will be real differences in power between client and staff, which should be acknowledged, it is generally agreed in the literature that efforts should be made to work with the client in reaching solutions to prevent and defuse aggression (NICE 2005; Richter 2006). This may generate 'a process of mutual thought and consideration of the options available, and ultimately attempting to empower the patient as much as possible' (West and Abolins 2001, p. 63). The next chapter will consider biological explanations of violence and aggression.

Learning Resources
Centre

Chapter 7
Biological explanations of violence and aggression

This chapter is concerned with biological explanations for violence and aggression, including the effects of changes in brain structure and functioning and related interventions. Violence and aggression can result when the pre-frontal lobe and other parts of the frontal lobe, amygdala and hypothalamus, in particular, are damaged. Damage to the frontal lobe can affect, not only violent and aggressive feelings and behaviours, but also judgement. If judgement is affected, this might influence the individual's decision to express violence and aggression, and/or result in misinterpretation of other people, which, in turn, could influence violent and aggressive feelings and behaviours (Liu and Wuerker 2005).

> Cognitive processes directed by the prefrontal cortex are vital in the expression of human emotions. For example, whether an individual reacts with fear or aggression to a noxious stimulus … is largely a product of the individual's memory, reasoning, and decision making processes, which are controlled by the pre-frontal cortex [the outer part of the pre-frontal lobe].
> (Wilson 2003, pp. 388f)

Several authors have argued for multi-factorial approaches in attempts to understand the causes of violence and aggression and related interventions. In relation to this, Liu and Wuerker (2005) state that, whilst psychological and social factors should be considered, there has been a bias in nursing against biological explanations to inform preventative and other interventions. They argue that 'nursing is ideally placed to develop a new body of knowledge based on a biological perspective that can lead to more effective prevention programmes for violence' (Liu and Wuerker 2005, p. 229).

Equally, other professional disciplines may be biased towards particular explanatory theories (Okasha 2002) and interventions that accord with their specific studies and professional socialisation. These factors may influence how workers explain and understand clients' aggressive and other behaviours and the interventions they decide to use (Emerson 2001).

Complications in pregnancy and childbirth

Complications in pregnancy and childbirth

Liu and Wuerker (2005, pp. 231f) provide a comprehensive overview of 'birth complications' and 'prenatal factors' (before birth), including the effects of nicotine and other drugs during pregnancy and of expectant mothers' diets that are deficient in protein, cholesterol, iron and zinc. Scarpa and Raine (2008) review many studies in this area, which suggest that, during pregnancy, the development of the brain (including the pre-frontal lobe, amygdala and hypothalamus, areas involved in violence and aggression) of the unborn or newly born infant may be affected by the following (Scarpa and Raine 2008, pp. 156f):

- 'Birth complications', including being born prematurely, delivered by forceps, 'caesarian section ... lack of oxygen during delivery and pre-eclampsia in the mother'. (The latter includes high blood pressure and other symptoms.)
- Minor, or more major, disorders of the developing brain.
- 'Prenatal nicotine exposure'.
- 'Malnutrition' in pregnancy.
- Excessive ingestion of alcohol, leading to 'foetal alcohol syndrome'.

Scarpa and Raine (2008) point out the 'implications for prevention and intervention' (p. 162) to prevent and reduce both physical and mental ill health in the child and the mother and violence and aggression, not only in childhood, but in teen years and adulthood. These authors also consider how both biological and social factors contribute to violence and aggression. Social factors can include, for example, unemployment leading to poverty and consequent malnutrition in pregnancy. Parents' levels of education may also be relevant, and affect knowledge of adverse effects of smoking, heavy drinking or inadequate diet during pregnancy (Liu and Wuerker 2005; Scarpa and Raine 2008).

The links between 'life-course persistent' violent behaviours and physical ill health

Odgers (2009, pp. 23f) reviews research which has found a link between 'life-course persistent' violence and physical ill health. The term 'life-course persistent' refers to violence which starts in early childhood and persists into adolescence and up to at least middle age (Odgers 2009). This author reviews several longitudinal studies, in which individuals have been studied from, or soon after, birth up to early or middle adulthood. The study found that small children who develop life-course persistent violence are at greater risk of injuries, including those sustained from parental physical abuse and poor physical and mental health. In turn, injuries and poor health are often associated with poverty and multiple sources of deprivation.

Most teenagers take risks, but during adolescence, individuals with life-course persistent violence, compared with their peers, 'are more likely, to engage in a range of risk-taking and health-compromising behaviours'. These include drinking alcohol and/or using drugs and other substances from an early age, 'dangerous driving' (with consequent increased risk of injury) and 'risky sexual behaviours.' Within penal institutions, teenagers with life-course persistent violence may lack 'the basic prerequisites of healthy development, including a lack of proper nutrition, exercise and medical care' (Odgers 2009, p. 31). This author comments that, for these individuals, unhealthy childhood and adolescent lifestyles may persist into adulthood, with increased risk of many diseases, including heart disease, diabetes and other illnesses associated with obesity. Odgers (2009) outlines the need for interventions in early childhood, not only to reduce violence and aggression in both childhood and later life, but to improve individuals' physical and mental health. She argues (p. 36):

> Innovative and cross-disciplinary approaches that cut across psychology, criminology, neuroscience, biology and medicine [and, one might add, health and social care] are required to advance our understanding of the developmental course of both antisocial [including violent and aggressive] behavior and physical health problems.

> Findings ... suggest that the prevention of early behavioral problems may provide an opportunity to reduce not only

future crime and violence, but may also [improve] adult health ...

The next part of this chapter will consider changes in the structure and functioning of the brain, and the implications for workers' interventions with clients.

Changes in structure and functioning of parts of the cerebrum

Changes in the cerebrum

Chapter 5 considered parts of the brain concerned with violent and aggressive feelings and behaviours include the following parts of the cerebrum and the links between them and other parts of the brain:

- the pre-frontal lobe in the frontal lobe
- the amygdala in the temporal lobe
- the hypothalamus at the base of the cerebrum (main part of the brain).

Further details are given in Box 17.1.

Box 7.1

The 'emotional circuit': Links between the hypothalamus, amygdala and pre-frontal cortex in the frontal lobe

'Harper-Jaques and Reimer (1998) propose the term "emotional circuit" to describe the interrelationship between the emotional processes of the limbic system [including the amygdala and the hypothalamus] and the neuro-cognitive processes of the frontal lobe and other parts of the cerebral cortex' (Linsley 2006, p. 15).

'The functioning of this system is hypothesised to determine the meaning a person gives to a particular situation. Thus, meaning is influenced by physiological capacity to:

- perceive incoming messages
- prioritise among competing stimuli
- ... interpret [messages and stimuli] in relation to stored ideas, beliefs and memories

and subsequently to respond' (Linsley 2006, pp. 15f).

For example, 'Ada' perceives someone ('Bob') looking in her direction. Because she is alert to the possibility that people behave aggressively towards her (based on her previous experiences), Ada prioritises this, i.e., sees Bob's glance in her direction as more important than other things around her. She interprets (actually, misinterprets) this as: 'Bob is staring at me'. Her response is to hit Bob and shout: 'Why are you staring at me?' All this has involved Ada's 'emotional circuit' (Harper-Jaques and Reimer 1998), linking her hypothalamus and amygdala with her pre-frontal lobe, which results in the 'meaning' that she attributes to Bob glancing in her direction.

(About.Com: Biology (undated); Flannery *et al.* 2008; Hodgins *et al.* 2009; Taylor and Laraia, 2009)

Causes of brain damage contributing to violence and aggression

Causes of brain damage

Damage to the pre-frontal cortex, amygdala, and hypothalamus can be caused by the following (Liu and Wuerker 2005):

- cerebral tumours in these areas (Richards *et al.* 2007)
- types of dementia, such as Alzheimer's disease, vascular dementia and Huntington's disease (Richards *et al.* 2007)
- syndromes resulting in learning disability: e.g., Prader-Willi syndrome, which results from damage to the hypothalamus from birth (Richards *et al.* 2007) and Brunner's syndrome (outlined later in this chapter)
- acquired brain injury resulting from acute conditions of sudden onset. These include stroke and trauma from, e.g., a serious road traffic accident or a fall onto the head, lack of oxygen to the brain, untreated and serious hypoglycaemia (low blood sugar) and encephalitis and meningitis (infection of the brain, or the meninges) (British Society of Rehabilitation Medicine and Royal College of Physicians 2003). (The meninges are 'membranes around the brain and spinal cord' (Richards *et al.* 2007, p. 352)).

Interventions in the rehabilitation of people with acquired brain injury

Interventions

If acquired brain injury involves damage to the hypothalamus, amygdala or pre-frontal lobe, violent or aggressive behaviours may result. This is especially common in children following a severe head injury, with greater likelihood of 'conduct disorders' (Scarpa and Raine 2008, p. 154). In addition, 'approximately 70% of patients with brain lesions due to head injury show aggression and increased irritability. Men who batter their spouses are significantly more likely to have suffered head trauma in the past, compared to other men' (Wilson 2003, p. 389).

The British Society of Rehabilitation Medicine and Royal College of Physicians (2003) indicate that interventions to reduce violent or aggressive behaviours need to be delivered within the context of clients' other needs, related, for example, to incontinence, disturbances in movement, vision, communication and hearing and problems with activities of daily living. All these difficulties may compound the individual's frustration and loss of self-esteem. These factors, besides damage to the pre-frontal area, amygdala or hypothalamus, may contribute to aggression or violence. Fairclough (2002, p. 50) considers the understandable 'anger, frustration and resentment' that individuals with acquired brain injury may experience. Professional interventions would include thorough assessment of the individual's strengths and needs, understanding, and empathising with the individual's problems and resulting anger and other feelings and implementing practical measures to reduce incontinence and where possible, improve movement, and provide speech therapy and aids to hearing and rehabilitation. Interventions to prevent and reduce violence and aggression would need to take account of any memory problems, which might make it difficult for the individual to remember techniques for managing anger.

In 'complex partial seizures (previously called temporal lobe epilepsy)' (Turnbull 1999, pp. 32f), seizures may take the form of episodes of aggression in an altered state of consciousness (Wilson 2003). This author describes a man with complex partial (temporal lobe) seizures whose violence completely diminished following surgery on the amygdala.

Causative factors in individuals with psychopathy: The role of the amygdala

The role of the amygdala

Research, reported by Blair (2009), has found that the amygdala in the temporal lobe functions differently in people with psychopathy (sometimes called psychopathic disorder or sociopathy). These individuals have very high incidences of violent behaviours, are impulsive, easily bored, seek considerable stimulation and excitement, and find it hard to feel empathy for others or remorse. They also experience difficulty in learning from experience or from therapies which seek to reward or reinforce positive behaviours (Hare and Neumann 2008; Neumann *et al.* 2007). Some individuals with antisocial personality disorder also have traits of psychopathy (Woods 2006).

People with psychopathy may have explosive episodes of violence, as well as planned instrumental violence, in the absence of frustration and anger (Blair 2009, National Forensic Nurses' Research and Development Group 2006). People with traits of psychopathy can be of most levels of intelligence, including moderate or mild learning disability. The following section details relevant research findings, in relation to the functions of the amygdala and individuals with psychopathy.

The amygdala, learning from experience, empathy and attachment to others

The amygdala helps us to learn to respond to aversive (unpleasant) stimuli. Research has found that individuals with psychopathy react very slowly to such stimuli, e.g., when told that 'a stimulus is associated with shock' (Blair 2009, p. 128). This appears to make it harder for such people to learn from experience, whether this is from others in their everyday environment, or attempts to change behaviours (e.g., through cognitive behavioural therapy) or rewards or punishments in a prison environment, what Blair (2009, p. 131) refers to as 'stimulus-punishment and stimulus-reward associations':

> Stimulus-reinforcing learning is crucial for socialization, for learning that some things are bad to do, and individuals with psychopathy fail to take advantage of standard socialization techniques. As such, they are more likely to use antisocial strategies to achieve their goals.
> (Blair 2009, p. 131, citing Wootton *et al.* 1997)

The amygdala helps us to recognise other people's facial expressions. Most of us modulate our behaviours in response to this, for example, we recognise that a client has a facial expression of fear or anger, and modulate our response accordingly. Individuals with psychopathy find it difficult to attend to, or to recognise expressions of fear. This may affect their ability to be empathetic towards other people and what they are experiencing and thus, make violence more likely (Blair 2009).

Individuals with psychopathy also find it difficult to maintain continuous, positive relationships, both in their personal lives, and with professionals (National Forensic Nurses' Research and Development Group 2006). This is partly because, compared with most people, they find it hard to feel attachment to others, that is, a sense of desiring a consistent and continued relationship with them. This has implications for the development of consistent, therapeutic professional–client relationships and a preparedness to work with the client, and value her or him as an individual (Bowers 2002; Prins 2005). 'Individuals with psychopathy may find their caregivers less rewarding stimuli, and be less motivated to maintain contact with them' (Blair 2009, p. 131).

Blair (2009) also reports research findings that individuals with psychopathy have dysfunction of part of the frontal lobe, 'the ventromedial prefrontal cortex'. This dysfunction results in 'impairment in decision making' (Blair 2009, pp. 123 and 129), which can affect learning from experience and reinforcement.

Executive functions and implications for interventions with individuals with frontal lobe damage

Frontal lobe damage

De Brito and Hodgins (2009) refer to executive functions. These involve both the frontal lobe and its connections with other parts of the brain. Brain damage which results in changes to executive functions may result in violence and/or aggression, for the reasons outlined below. It is essential for the worker to base interventions on an understanding of the difficulties that individuals with frontal lobe damage experience in controlling their aggression (Gates *et al.* 2000; Royal College of Psychiatrists *et al.* (2007); Stokes 2000; Stokes 2002).

The central features of executive functions, as applied to violence and aggression, are as follows:

- 1. 'Executive control is necessary to deal with novel tasks that require us to formulate a goal'(Rabbitt 1997, p. 3, quoted in De Brito and Hodgins 2009, p. 171). If the structure and/or functioning of the frontal lobe is affected, frustration and possible aggression could result because the person finds carrying out a task particularly difficult. Aggression might be reduced by ensuring that clients are not expected to engage in tasks that they find too difficult, and by offering help when it is needed (Gates *et al.* 2000).

  In addition, the individual might find it easier to react explosively and aggressively when angry, than to adopt more complex expressions of anger which require considerable thought, e.g., deciding not to say something until she or he feels calmer (De Brito and Hodgins 2009).

- 2. Executive functions enable us to remember. For example, an individual might be violent because of the frustration of not being able to remember or because she or he forgets creative strategies in expressing anger (e.g., to count to ten or to not immediately respond to someone who appears annoying). It is important that workers recognise when clients have difficulties with memory and avoid unrealistic expectations, which could worsen their frustration and aggression (Stokes 2000; Stokes 2002).

- 3. Executive functions enable us to start 'new sequences of behaviour and the interruption of ongoing sequences' and 'also control the allocation of attention, especially in complex tasks' (De Brito and Hodgins 2009, p. 171). This would mean, for example, that an individual whose frontal lobe functioning was affected, and who, in the past, normally avoided immediate expressions of rage, could be more prone to sudden explosive outbursts and would find it less easy to focus attention on other, creative ways to express anger. Assessment of the antecedents (items that trigger) aggression (see Chapter 3), and attempting to reduce their presence or their effects could be helpful. For example, the individual might respond aggressively to loud noise. Provision of a quieter environment might be helpful (Gates et al. 2000).

- 4. 'Executive functions are essential to avoid responses that are inappropriate to the context' (De Brito and Hodgins 2009, p. 171). For example, an individual with frontal lobe damage might shout with frustration in a public place such as a shopping centre, when most people's norms and values require quieter ways of expressing anger, an example of the relationship between biological and social factors. Gently and quietly reminding the individual of the context, or distraction might be helpful. So might an assessment of problems that the client has with coping with particular environments, and either modifying the latter to reduce stress, or enabling her/him to access less stressful environments (Royal College of Psychiatrists, et al., 2007).

- 5. 'Executive functions allow the strategic allocation of

attention and synchronization of responses in dual-task performance' (De Brito and Hodgins 2009, p. 171) (i.e., doing two things at once). This could mean that an individual becomes frustrated, and possibly, aggressive because he cannot manage to attend to what a worker is saying and at the same time, to put on an item of clothing. It is, therefore, helpful to enable the client to finish one task at a time, and if possible, communicate only when she or he is not engaged in another activity. In addition, as suggested in Chapter 10, giving brief chunks of communication or information may be better understood and less frustrating than long, complicated sentences (Arnold and Ryan 2007; Bryan and Maxim 2006).

- 6. 'Executive functions have a monitoring role on performance: detecting and correcting errors; altering plans deemed to be unsuccessful; identifying opportunities for new goals; formulating, selecting, and executing new plans' (De Brito and Hodgins 2009, p. 171). All of these executive functions could be affected in an individual with changes in frontal lobe functioning. Her or his difficulties in these areas would need to be considered in interventions to prevent and reduce violence and aggression, with a recognition that, without skilled and consistent help, the individual might find it very difficult to find alternative, more creative ways of expressing anger.

- 7. '...Executive functions enable the attention to be sustained continuously over long periods' (De Brito and Hodgins 2009, p. 171). This would need to be borne in mind when considering the length of interventions to relieve distress, enhance the individual's quality of life and prevent or reduce violence and aggression. Short periods of time on particular activities, with immediate rewards and benefits, would be necessary (De Brito and Hodgins 2009; Gates *et al.* 2000; Royal College of Psychiatrists *et al.* 2007; Stokes 2000; Stokes 2002).

Low autonomic arousal in some individuals with violent behaviours

Arousal

In Chapter 5, we considered the physiological and psychological arousal which are experienced by most clients with violent or aggressive behaviours, and by professionals in their responses.

Low levels of psychological arousal in response to fear have been found in relation to 'criminal and violent behaviour in both children and adults' (Scarpa and Raine 2008, p. 152), including people with psychopathy (described earlier in this chapter). This low level of arousal 'represents an underlying risk factor for antisocial behavior, mainly because chronic understimulation promotes a need for thrill- and sensation-seeking' (Patrick and Verona 2008, p. 113). For example, some individuals (including adults with psychopathy and antisocial personality disorder) might engage in violence mainly for 'kicks', because they enjoyed the excitement. This might be especially likely if the individual found it particularly difficult to gain excitement in other ways. This has implications for collaborating with clients in seeking safe, creative activities that they find sufficiently exciting and stimulating, and which relieve boredom (Wood 2007), e.g., the provision of frequent opportunities for exercise (Adams 2002; Biddle and Mutrie 2008). Exercise is considered in Chapter 11.

Neurotransmitters involved in violence and aggression

Neuro-transmitters

Neurotransmitters are chemical messages that travel between neurons (cells in the brain; Richards *et al.* 2007, pp. 2f). In relation to specific neurotransmitters, research findings indicate a probable association between 'low levels of … Serotonin' and high levels of 'Dopamine, Norepinephrine and Acetylcholine and the amino acid gamma-aminobutyric acid (GABA)' (Stuart and Hamolia 2009, p. 578) with violent and aggressive behaviours. (Norepinephrine is also known as noradrenaline, Morrison and Bennett 2009). Linsley (2006, p. 15) concludes that neurotransmitters 'do not cause aggression on their own', but that 'they may contribute to the severity of the aggressive episode'.

Liu and Wuerker (2005) argue that diets during pregnancy that are low in 'the amino acid, Tryptophan' may contribute to the child's eventual violence and aggression: 'Because Tryptophan is the dietary building block of [the neurotransmitter] Serotonin, diets low in Tryptophan could contribute to the low levels of Serotonin found in impulsive violent offenders' (Liu and Wuerker 2005, p. 232, citing Virkkunen *et al.* 1995 and Werbach 1995). Low levels of Serotonin have been found in individuals with antisocial personality disorder (Gelder *et al.* 2001). In addition, people who use the recreational drug ecstasy have been found to experience relatively high levels of aggression and raised levels of norepinephrine (noradrenaline) (Wilson 2003). Levels of this neurotransmitter are also raised when individuals experience extreme arousal, and this may result in rapid and excessive reactions to insignificant threats (Linsley 2006).

Excessive amounts of dopamine have been found in individuals with schizophrenia. Antipsychotic medication which reduces dopamine may result in diminished violence and aggression in the minority of clients with schizophrenia with such behaviours. This is partly because of the effects of antipsychotics in reducing symptoms, such as delusions and hallucinations, which may result in violence or aggression (Citrome 2008). (A delusion is an individual's belief associated with a mental illness, and which is not held by other people in her or his cultural, spiritual and social groups. An hallucination is a perception of any of the five senses (hearing, vision, touch, taste and smell) which is associated with a mental illness, and which is not shared by other people in her or his cultural, spiritual and social groups. Other people usually see the belief or perception as 'odd' and it cannot be explained solely as an innovation or breakthrough in spirituality, thought or experience (Barker 2009).)

Hormones of significance in violence and aggression

Hormones of significance

In Chapter 5, we considered hormonal changes that occur when the individual experiences arousal. Cortisol has been found to be of particular importance in violence and aggression. It is a hormone secreted by the adrenal cortex (the outer part of the adrenal gland) in response to stress (Morrison and Bennett 2009; van Goozen and Fairchild 2009), as part of the 'fight or flight response'. Research has found that that in adults, low cortisol levels are associated with increased propensities to violence and aggression, but this has not always been found in teenagers and children with aggressive behaviours (van Goozen and Fairchild 2009, p. 209, citing several studies). In adults, at least, it is hypothesised that if individuals have low amounts of cortisol, this may mean that hurting or attacking others, or the fear of other people's reactions or of punishment, does not cause them to feel particularly stressed. Some researchers have argued that this could make violent and aggressive behaviours more likely in individuals with low cortisol levels (van Goozen and Fairchild 2009).

In men, testosterone levels are at a peak in the late teens, when violent offending is commonest. However, other variables are likely to contribute to violence and aggression in young men (Flannery *et al.* 2008). Contrary to popular belief, research findings indicate that high testosterone levels have, in general, little effect on violence and aggression (van Goozen and Fairchild 2009), unless they are combined with low levels of the neurotransmitter, serotonin (Liu and Wuerker 2005) or the presence of a genetic defect occurring in Brunner's syndrome, a condition resulting in learning disability, and which affects neurotransmitters (Buckholtz and Meyer-Lindenburg 2009).

Some research has found a link between pre-menstrual syndrome and violence and aggression. Pre-menstrual syndrome has been used as a 'legal defence' by some women convicted of murder (Niehoff 1999). Bullock and Mackenzie (2003, p. 35) comment, in a text on learning disability nursing practice, that: 'clinical experience has shown that [women] with menopausal syndrome increasingly suffer from difficult to manage behaviour that has correlated each month with their menstrual cycle'. However, feminists have criticised research in this area, and have argued that the findings indicate the biased assumptions of (predominantly male, and possibly, sexist) scientists (Byrt *et al.* 2001; Dixon 2006).

Genetic factors and the importance of considering the client's environment

Genetic factors

Finally, from a detailed review of twin studies, Viding *et al.* (2009) concluded that both 'genetic and environmental factors interact' in potentiating violence and aggression. The latter are associated with a few genetic conditions (De Brito and Hodgins 2009; Liu and Wuerker 2005). Violent or aggressive behaviours have been described, for example, in some people with certain types of learning disability (Niehoff 1999) and in individuals with Huntington's disease, a condition in which neurons die in large numbers, usually in younger and middle aged people (De Brito and Hodgins 2009; Richards *et al.* 2007). Individuals with Brunner's syndrome have learning disabilities and 'episodic aggressive outbursts', besides other symptoms (Niehoff 1999, p. 234).

However, other factors are likely to be contributory. We suggest that it should never be assumed that an individual's aggressive behaviours are 'only' caused by genetic factors, especially in view of research findings of the interconnections between genes and environment (Viding *et al.* 2009); and on causes of 'challenging behaviour' in individuals with learning disabilities and dementias, which suggests that environmental and other factors, including communication, are likely to contribute to aggressive behaviours and their prevention and reduction (Emerson 2001; Jansen *et al.* 2005; Royal College of Psychiatrists *et al.* 2007). For this reason, and to reduce individuals' stress and frustration, it is crucial to provide environments which are beneficial and therapeutic, as outlined in earlier chapters of this book. The next chapter considers aspects of the worker–client relationship and communication in relation to clients' views and specific needs, and aspects of culture and diversity.

Chapter 8
Culture, diversity and communication

The last chapter considered the importance of working with the client in preventing and reducing violence and aggression. This chapter considers the participation of clients and their carers at home and clients' perspectives related to their culture and diversity and specific communication needs.

The importance of service users' and carers' perspectives

Some authors argue that it is essential to consider the perspectives of clients, and where appropriate, carers at home, in interventions to prevent and reduce violence and aggression (Dooher and Byrt 2003; Meehan *et al.* 2006; NICE 2005; Royal College of Psychiatrists *et al.* 2007):

> Attempts to adequately address aggressive behaviours may be misguided in the absence of patient input, because recent research has identified clear distinctions between the perceptions of staff and patients... Capturing the insights of [clients] should provide better understanding of the inter-personal and contextual factors that contribute to aggressive behaviour.
> (Meehan *et al.* 2006, p. 20)

Several key documents emphasise the importance of service user perspectives in considering ways to prevent and reduce violence and aggression. Relevant documents include the following:

- Royal College of Psychiatrists *et al.* (2007) stress the importance of considering, and incorporating, the views of individuals with learning disabilities with 'challenging behaviours' and their carers at home.

- The Royal College of Psychiatrists Audit Team (2005) asked learning disability and mental health service users their views about preventing and reducing violence and aggression.

- The National Institute for Clinical Effectiveness (NICE) (2005) *Guideline on Violence* emphasises 'working with service users' (pp. 26f) and respecting their rights and preferences. (An example of clients' involvement in developing this guideline is given later in this chapter.)

- In *Every School Should Have One. How Peer support Schemes Make Schools Better*, the voluntary organisation, ChildLine (2005), describes how the views of children and young people can be used to reduce bullying. Some children have been involved in supporting peers who have been bullied (ChildLine 2009).

- *The Independent Inquiry into the Death of David Bennett* considers the perspectives of David Bennett, particularly in relation to cultural issues and his specific needs (Blofeld 2003). This inquiry was initiated by Dr Joanna Bennett, Mr Bennett's sister, who did much to campaign for an independent inquiry (Andalo and agencies 2004).

The importance to clients of workers' communication skills

Workers' communication skills

Research on the views of clients in relation to how nursing and other staff respond to violence and aggression include Duxbury and Whittington (2005), Meehan *et al.* (2006), Secker *et al.* (2004) and various other studies summarised in Abderhalden *et al.* (2006). Although these research projects concern mental health clients in hospital, it can be argued that the findings have relevance to other clients in various settings. Researchers (Abderhalden *et al.* 2006; Duxbury and Whittington 2005; Meehan *et al.* 2006; Secker *et al.* 2004) found that clients:

- consider communication skills to be particularly important in preventing and reducing violence and aggression

- report a lack of communication from care workers

- state that mental health nurses over rely on seclusion and control and restraint.

Studies of staff views have also found that many nurses stress the importance of communication skills in preventing and reducing aggression (Finnema *et al.* 1994; Lowe 1992; McDougall 2000; Stokes 2002). Clients in a study by Duxbury (2002) reported an over-emphasis on 'reactive' measures, such as control and restraint and seclusion, in situations when the use of communication skills could have been effective. Duxbury (2002, p. 172) reported a 'lack of staff engagement with clients' before, during and after incidents of violence and aggression. This and other studies have identified 'staff–client relationships', 'powerlessness', environmental factors and 'the organisation of care' (Duxbury 2002, p. 173) as contributory factors in causing, or preventing, violence and aggression. Ryan and Bowers (2005) reported the use of 'coercive manoeuvres', such as preventing clients from walking to areas which were unsafe for them to enter. Whilst such measures were sometimes necessary to ensure safety, their use could have been prevented through the use of communication skills (Ryan and Bowers 2005). Alexander (2004, cited in Ryan and Bowers 2005) found that clients experienced 'coercive manoeuvres' (Ryan and Bowers 2005, p. 701) as unpleasant and humiliating. These authors conclude that such measures may result in some clients not trusting, or wishing to engage with, staff.

Secker *et al.* (2004) make the following comment on a mental health acute admissions unit. Their observations, based on their own research, have clear implications for the prevention of violence and aggression:

> ...There was little evidence of the staff...simply spending time with, and thus being available to clients before the reported incidents [of violence and aggression] took place, and no evidence at all of anyone spending time with the clients who later became involved in the incidents...

> ...The description of the clients' behaviour suggests that they were frightened, distressed people for whom reassurance was...important...

> ...Had the staff on duty been able to respond to clients' agitation or distress, this might have avoided what appeared to be an inevitable escalation, culminating in the management of all but one patient by control and restraint, followed by the administration of intramuscular medication...

Staff accounts of what happened ...revealed little attempt to reflect on, and learn from, the incidents, either with the clients involved, or as a staff team...

In those cases where some discussion with the client was described, the overriding aim appeared to have been to correct the client's behaviour, rather than exploring what happened from the client's perspective or considering together how it might have been avoided...'
(Secker *et al.* 2004, pp. 174f.)

Questions for reflection/discussion

Consider the following conversation reported by a nurse in the study by Secker *et al.* (2004), in relation to the questions below:

I...told him that 'Look here, you are quite a good guy [but] whatever somebody says, you become angry'...From that time on, he started swearing...and I told him: 'Look here, this emphasizes what I've been telling you'. Then he started becoming quite threatening again...
(Secker *et al.* 2004, p. 176)

1. To what extent was the care worker's intervention likely to de-escalate the client's aggression?

2. What other non-verbal and verbal communication could the care worker have used with the client?

Equality, diversity and culture

Communication and a consideration of clients' perspectives also need to be related to clients' culture and diversity. This is considered in the next part of this chapter and in Chapter 9.

The term 'equality' has a number of meanings, including the idea that all individuals are entitled to the same life opportunities, and the same quality of service. 'Diversity' has been defined as 'social variety across and within groups of people' (Thompson 2003, p. 10, quoted in Byrt *et al.* 2007, p. 219). Equality also involves the principle that no individual or group of people should be discriminated against, for example, in relation to aspects of diversity, including their ethnic group, culture, religion, sexual orientation, gender, gender identity; or because of mental health problems or learning, physical or sensory disabilities (Addo and Smith 2008; Thompson 2003). 'Culture has been defined ... as the values and beliefs shared by a group of people; and the sense of how individuals do and view things in their group' (Henley and Schott 1999).

Respect for individuals' equality, diversity and culture is included in professional codes of conduct. For example, the Nursing and Midwifery (NMC 2008, p. 02) Code states: 'You must not discriminate in any way against those in your care'.

The relationship of experiences of violence and aggression to discrimination

Violence and discrimination

In relation to violence and aggression, several studies have found that the extent to which clients are satisfied with health and social services is partly related to professionals' sensitivity to, and attempts to meet needs related to aspects of diversity considered above (Byrt *et al.* 2007; Sewell 2009). The current authors suggest that dissatisfaction with services which fail to be sensitive to the individual's needs, may be associated with understandable frustration and assertive or aggressive anger.

Some writers on discrimination have argued that, as members of oppressed groups recognise discrimination in wider society and in health services, they become creatively angry, challenging oppression, instead of internalising others' negative attitudes. This process is often experienced as an empowering 'raising of consciousness' by the oppressed individual (Barnes and Mercer 2003; Byrt 2008a). Nurses and other professionals may recognise such anger as creative, justified and assertive (Freire 1996; Hopton 1995) – or deny or 'pathologise' it (i.e., wrongly perceive it to be a sign of the individual's mental health problem or learning disability (Pilgrim and Rogers 2005). (See Chapter 4.)

Research suggests that attitudes held by nurses and other professionals have sometimes mirrored those in wider society, e.g.:

- 'Women clients should not be assertive'
- 'Young black patients tend to be dangerous' (Blom-Cooper 1992; Prins 1993).

Certain forms of cultural expression or communication have sometimes been misinterpreted by professionals as 'aggressive' or 'rude', when this is not intended by the client (Arnold 2007b).

It is suggested that the above findings can help the worker to reflect on her or his attitudes, and those of colleagues, in relation to the prevention and reduction of violence and aggression.

Evidence of discrimination

Research has found that individuals facing discrimination in wider society sometimes experience this in health and social services and prisons (HM Inspector of Prisons 2009a; Sewell 2009). This can take the form of both overt (deliberate) discrimination and institutional discrimination, where a service fails to be sensitive to, or meet needs related to the individual's culture and diversity (Blofeld 2003; Secker and Harding 2002; Sewell 2009).

> There has been evidence of discrimination in some mental health services in relation to individuals from black and minority ethnic groups (Blofeld, 2003, Blom-Cooper, 1992, Prins, 1993, Secker and Harding, 2002); women (Byrt *et al.*, 2001, Parry-Crooke, 2000, Jeffcote and Watson, 2004); and individuals who are gay, lesbian, bisexual or transsexual (Aiyegbusi and Byrt, 2006, Blom-Cooper, 1992, King *et al.*, 2004).
> (Byrt *et al.* 2007, p. 221. See also Sewell 2009)

There have been many examples of institutionalised racism in services, with, for example, black people and individuals from minority ethnic groups being over-represented amongst individuals who are secluded, transferred to secure hospitals, or admitted compulsorily under the Mental Health Act, 1983 (Sewell 2009). The Independent Inquiry into the Death of David Bennett, during restraint in a medium secure unit, concluded that Mr Bennett's needs related to culture and spirituality had not been met and that his complaints of another client's racism had not been taken seriously or investigated (Blofeld 2003).

The Equality Act 2006 (HM Government 2006, p. 1) set up a Commission for Equality and Human Rights to replace separate commissions on 'racial equality', 'equal opportunities' for women and men, and 'disability rights'. The Act covers these areas, as well as religion, sexual orientation and gender identity, in relation to public services (HM Government 2006). This Act makes it illegal for professionals, managers or staff in public services to behave in an overtly discriminatory way (e.g., through expressed attitudes, language or actions) towards an individual or group of individuals. An example might be to assume that individuals who are black are more likely to be violent than other clients, as was found in one government inquiry (Prins 1993).

In addition, an organisation is in breach of the Equality Act, if it provides services or interventions (e.g., related to the prevention and reduction of violence and aggression) which fail to be culturally sensitive or culturally competent. This relates to a person's ethnic group, age, gender, disability (physical, learning or sensory), sexual orientation and gender identity.

Examples of institutional discrimination in relation to the Equality Act 2006

Institutional discrimination

Examples of institutional discrimination which could be illegal under the Equality Act (HM Government 2006) include the following:

- Failing to allow an individual, subject to intensive observation, opportunities for prayer or quiet reflection, in accordance with her/his beliefs (unless there were important safety reasons for doing so).

- Women being restrained by men, except possibly, in emergencies, with a failure to appreciate the impact this has on women in relation to cultural taboos, and their past experiences related to sexual and physical abuse by men (Fontaine 2009).

Public services evaluate the extent to which they meet the requirements of the Equality Act 2006. For example, the Department of Health assesses this through a 'single equality schedule' (Department of Health 2009). However, despite this, and the findings of the David Bennett Inquiry (Blofeld 2003) and Delivering Race Equality initiatives (Department of Health 2005, 2009), 'the Healthcare Commission's [2009] audit of mental health and learning disability services...showed that there had been no improvement in the experiences of service users from black and minority ethnic backgrounds since its first such survey in 2005' (Parish 2009, p. 3, citing Heathcare Commission 2009b, p. 9). The relative dissatisfaction with services of black and minority ethnic clients needs to be borne in mind in planning interventions, including those to prevent and reduce violence and aggression.

Comments by service users in the development of the NICE (2005) *Guideline on Violence*

Chandler-Oatts and Nelstrop (2008, p. 33) outline ways that the participation of black service users was facilitated, through 'focus groups', so that their views could be included in the NICE (2005) *Guideline on Violence*. Amongst the many comments of black service users were the following:

> The perception that goes along with being black is that they're violent and they are aggressive, and the misconception that necessarily, because we might gesticulate quite a lot or we might talk loudly, we might laugh loudly, yeah, the perception that's linked with that is of a violent and aggressive nature.

Service users stated that control and restraint and seclusion were particularly overused on black people: 'Most of the time, if you're black, you're going to get bent and twisted up and carried into seclusion' (Chandler-Oatts and Nelstrop 2008, pp. 36f).

Women, their needs, and experience of violence

Dixon (2006) provides a very useful overview of issues concerning women and violence. 'Several authors outline the importance of understanding women's self-harming and [violent and aggressive] behaviours in relation to their experiences of oppression in society, and within family and other relationships, in particular' (Byrt *et al.* 2007, citing several authors).

- In some health services, notably mental health, assertive behaviour has been seen as less acceptable in women, and has sometimes been wrongly interpreted as 'aggressive' by professionals (Byrt *et al.* 2001; Dixon 2006).
- Some women experience 'flashbacks' of sexual and physical abuse during some interventions, especially if they are restrained. For this reason, it has been argued that male staff should never be involved in restraining women patients (Gallop 1999, cited in Byrt *et al.* 2001).
- Many women clients of mental health services have experienced physical and/or sexual abuse (Dixon 2006).
- Domestic violence (also known as intimate partner violence) is a problem for many women and some men (Dixon 2006). (See Chapter 3.)

- Women with violent and aggressive behaviours have been found to have, overall, very different needs, and different reasons for violence and aggression to those of men. For these and other reasons, it has been concluded that they need different services to men (Jeffcote and Travers 2004).

Individuals who are lesbian, gay, bisexual and transsexual

Sexual orientation

Research suggests that, although there are some areas of good practice, nurses and other health professionals are not always sensitive to the needs of lesbians, gay men, bisexual and transsexual individuals and their partners (Department of Health 2007). Services which fail to take account of these needs are likely to result in clients' understandable frustration and anger, and contribute to violence and aggression in a minority of individuals. The following are amongst the main findings of research:

- There are some lesbian- and gay-friendly services (Davies and Neal 1996, Fish 2006; Fitzgerald 2003), although many lesbians and gays encounter negative attitudes, including homophobia, from health professionals, and in the past, unhelpful and often harmful psychiatric 'treatments' (Godfrey 2003; Golding 1997; King *et al.* 2004; Smith *et al.* 2004).

  'We are as diverse as anyone else, but we need high quality, non-judgmental counselling and sensitivity. We need to describe our experiences and need validation and support – not silence or embarrassment…'
  (gay respondent in study by Golding 1997, p. 41).

- Research findings suggest that care workers fail to recognise the importance to lesbians, gay, bisexual and transsexual clients of their partners and friends and their wish for them to be involved in their care (including interventions to prevent or reduce violence and aggression), be given information in relation to this, and contacted in an emergency (Godfrey 2003; Unison and RCN 2004).

- Research has found that many assessment procedures assume that all clients are heterosexual and, in relation to transsexualism, have an unchanging gender identity (Godfrey 2003; Unison and RCN 2004).

● Gay affirmative therapy, where the individual and her or his identity and sexual orientation is validated and affirmed, has been found helpful (Davies and Neil 1996).

Cultural sensitivity and competence

Cultural sensitivity and competence

In relation to the topic of this book, equality involves, for example, not making unwarranted assumptions that clients of particular ethnic groups are more likely to be aggressive than others (Blofeld 2003; Prins 1993) or labelling certain clients as 'always manipulative' or 'never worth communicating with'. Equality also means that all clients likely to benefit from an intervention, such as cognitive behavioural therapy, have equal access to this, regardless of their background or where they live (Thompson 2003). Cultural sensitivity to clients' diversity means that assessments and interventions take account of individuals' varied needs. Successful implementation of these assessments is known as cultural competence (Andrews and Boyle 2008).

Box 8.1

NICE (2005) *Guideline on Violence*:
Recommendations Concerning People with Diverse Backgrounds and Needs, Including Individuals of Black and Minority Ethnic Groups

The National Institute for Clinical Excellence (NICE) (2005) *Guideline on Violence* states:

'Staff should be encouraged to [communicate with] service users from diverse backgrounds, including those with special needs, about their experiences, and to offer them support and understanding, especially if their experience has been negative'

'Services must identify a board member [e.g., a member of an NHS Trust Board] to take specific responsibility for all matters relating to equality and diversity. Responsibilities must include the nature and adequacy of service provision in relation to the short-term management of disturbed/violent behaviour, training on all matters relating to equality and diversity, monitoring service usage by ethnicity, and consultation with local Black and minority ethnic groups'.

'Individual care plans should detail staff responsibilities for de-escalation with service users who have disabilities, including those with physical impairment and/or other communication difficulties.'

(NICE 2005, pp. 92f)

Cultural sensitivity as openness to clients' different understandings

Cultural sensitivity can include the worker's understanding that the client may not view her or his violent and aggressive behaviours as problematic. What the worker sees as 'aggression' may be perceived by the client as a problem in living or related to a spiritual crisis, or 'normal behaviour: what all my mates do' (Byrt *et al.* 2007, citing Mason and Chandley 1990; Schafer 2002). In some instances, workers' constructions of violence and aggression as a health or social problem may contradict clients' understandings, based on cultural or spiritual beliefs. For example, Khalifa and Hardie (2005) found that some Muslim clients and their families attributed various behaviours to jinn (a type of spirit), rather than to Western psychiatric views of mental illness. From these and other examples (Byrt *et al.* 2007), it can be concluded that workers need to be aware of individuals' cultures and spiritualities and how these may affect clients' perceptions of violent and aggressive behaviours. Khalifa and Hardie (2005) stress the importance of professionals respecting and collaborating with healers from other cultures; and involving them in the care or treatment of the client if she or he wishes this.

One of the authors worked with a woman ('Sally') who was bewildered by therapeutic groups where residents discussed the management of their anger. 'I've never done that before', she said. 'Me and my mates and my family have always had a good punch up if we don't see eye to eye.' Once Sally had got used to being a resident in a modified therapeutic community, she responded well to interventions to reduce her aggression, and occasional violence.

The example of Sally illustrates the need for us, as workers, to be aware that client and staff may perceive violence and aggression very differently. The client's perceptions, and the extent to which she or he sees violence and aggression need to be assessed thoroughly (Parker-Hall 2009), as does her or his level of motivation to change. A useful aid to understanding this is Prochaska and DiClemente's (1982) 'stages of change' model. This consists of the following stages, which have implications for assessment and implementation of interventions, particularly of the longer-term therapies.

At the 'pre-contemplation stage' (O'Carroll and Park 2007, p. 185, citing Prochaska and DiClemente 1982), 'Sally' does not see aggressive behaviours as problematic, and is bewildered by staff suggestions that this is the case. Workers need to be aware, at this stage, that this is how Sally perceives the situation. Interventions would be directed at ensuring the safety of Sally and other people, developing therapeutic worker–client communication and relationships, and listening attentively to Sally. (See Chapter 6.) Once good rapport is established, the worker might tentatively ask questions or make suggestions which might help Sally to begin to consider aggressive behaviours.

In the 'contemplation stage' (O'Carroll and Park 2007, p. 185, citing Prochaska and DiClemente 1982), Sally is aware that there could be a problem, and is starting to think about doing something about it. Sally might think: 'Rani isn't too bad for a member of staff, and perhaps I could join the problem solving group she suggested. I like to have a good fight in the pub, but my temper lost me those two jobs, so perhaps it's a problem sometimes.'

When she reaches the 'commitment stage' (O'Carroll and Park 2007, p. 185, citing Prochaska and DiClemente 1982), Sally decides she will take up the offer of the problem solving group. She agrees with Bob, the staff member running the group, that she will look at events triggering her anger, and see how she can apply the problem-solving techniques (involving cognitive behavioural therapy principles) that she learns in the group (Bede *et al.* 2008; Bowness *et al.* 2008). However, understandably, Sally has initial difficulty in applying these techniques, and sometimes forgets to use them in the heat of the moment.

In the 'action stage' (O'Carroll and Park 2007, p. 185, citing Prochaska and DiClemente 1982), Sally is able to apply what she has learnt in the problem solving groups: for example, if she is feeling aggressive, counting to ten before responding to another client, or withdrawing from a difficult situation in a non-provocative way (Bowness *et al.* 2008).

At the 'maintenance stage' (O'Carroll and Park 2007, p. 185, citing Prochaska and DiClemente 2007, p. 186), Bob, the facilitator, and the other clients in the problem solving group offer continued encouragement (e.g., feedback on progress) in relation to Sally's successes in expressing anger assertively, rather than aggressively. Sally is also enabled to learn from the occasions when she was aggressive, and to learn about the particular 'triggers' of her own aggression.

Next is the 'exit stage' (O'Carroll and Park 2007, p. 186, citing Prochaska and DiClemente 1982). Here, Sally is usually managing her anger effectively, and has completed the problem-solving group.

Six months after she has left the service, Sally experiences a 'relapse stage' (O'Carroll and Park 2007, p. 186, citing Prochaska and DiClemente 1982). She responds with verbal aggression to provocation from others a few times in pubs, and nearly gets into a fight. She meets with Rani and Bob, staff members, a few times, and is able to recognise that her aggression was a response to various stressors, including the break up with her girlfriend, and moving into a new flat. Following this relapse, her progress in managing her anger is maintained.

Examples of cultural sensitivity and cultural competence

Examples of sensitivity and competence

Examples of cultural sensitivity and cultural competence include the following (as usual, pseudonyms have been used):

- Workers appreciate that 'Mr Ali Khan' needs space to pray throughout Ramadan at specific times during the day, and does not like to be disturbed at these times. This space for prayer is essential to Ali's spiritual well-being (Narayanasamy 2001) and, besides other functions and benefits, provides him with a means to cope effectively with his feelings of anger.

- 'Ms Amy Klee' needs workers to recognise that the most important person in her life, and the one to contact in an emergency, is her partner, 'Mary'. Amy has periodic outbursts of aggression as a manifestation of distress about abuse when she was a child. At such times, Mary is the person she finds most helpful. Amy is also helped by workers' appreciation that she needs to be 'out' as a lesbian (Aiyegbusi and Byrt 2006).

- 'Mr Ady King' expresses concern that, in a previous service, he was treated in a racist way, with staff making assumptions that he would be violent because he is a young black man. Ady is relieved that, in the service to which he is admitted, staff take his concerns seriously, and demonstrate respect for him as an individual. 'Such an approach, which respects each individual and his or her unique needs is relevant to the care of all [clients]' (Byrt *et al.* 2007, p. 219, citing Addo 2006).

- 'Ms Ada Kane' has recently been admitted to 'Eastvale', a residential home for older people with dementia. The day after her admission, she gets up at 4.00 am, and attempts to hit the care assistant who tries to persuade her to return to bed. The following day, the manager of 'Eastvale' asks Ms Kane's husband her preferred time for getting up, as Ms Kane cannot give this information herself. Mr Kane explains that his wife used to be a postal worker who always arose at 4.00 am during the week to start an early shift. Following this information, Ms Kane is enabled to get up when she wishes, and no longer attempts to hit staff (Goldsmith 1996).

Stigma, negative discrimination and social exclusion

Stigma and exclusion

Finally, an individual's violent and aggressive behaviours, as well as other people's devaluing her or him because of culture, ethnic group, religion, gender, sexual orientation, age or disability, (Sewell 2009; Thomas and Woods 2003) may:

- result in his or her stigmatisation, negative discrimination and social exclusion. Indeed, some definitions of 'challenging behaviour', particularly related to individuals with learning disabilities, include their social exclusion as a result of the behaviour (Emerson 2001; Mansell *et al.* 2008; Royal College of Psychiatrists *et al.* 2007).

- be worsened by stigmatisation, negative discrimination and social exclusion, all of which can engender understandable frustration and anger. The latter could be expressed either creatively and assertively (Hopton 1995) or aggressively.

Stigmatisation refers to seeing someone only in terms of an attribute which is discredited in wider society: e.g., perceiving an individual only as 'a schizophrenic' or 'a case of Prader-Willi syndrome', without regard for other identities, such as son, lover, good cook or keen football fan.

Social exclusion refers both to other individuals' 'discriminatory and stigmatising attitudes' and a 'lack of opportunities, choices and life chances available to most people' (Byrt *et al.* 2007, p. 220). These include: opportunities for friendships, loving family life, close, loving relationships and sexual fulfilment, employment; education and training, other meaningful activity, accommodation of a reasonable standard, adequate income and avoidance of poverty and its effects, including malnutrition, leisure activities, relaxation and holidays, and freedom from harassment and crime victimisation (Sewell 2009; Watkins 2007). If a client is socially excluded in relation to any of these, this could result in understand-able frustration and anger. In a minority of clients, this might be manifest in violence and aggression. Workers need to ask themselves whether social exclusion is a relevant contributory factor. It can be argued, in relation to recovery principles, that all interventions and services must contribute to clients' social inclusion, including the various life opportunities listed above (Sewell 2009; Thomas and Woods 2003; Watkins 2007). This has been emphasised by various authors in relation to individuals with 'challenging behaviours' (Emerson 2001; Mansell *et al.* 2008; Royal College of Psychiatrists *et al.* 2007).

It can be argued that the prevention and reduction of violence and aggression is unlikely to be successful unless there are attempts to increase individuals' social inclusion (National Institute for Mental Health in England 2004). Research has found that aspects of social exclusion (e.g., in deprived inner city areas) are associated with violence and aggression in communities (Flannery *et al.* 2008; Hodgins *et al.* 2009; see Chapter 3).

Questions for reflection/discussion

1. To what extent do you think that the violence or aggression in specific client(s) is associated with: a) a lack of understanding of, or difficulty in meeting, needs related to their diversity? b) their social exclusion?

2. With reference to the prevention and reduction of violence and aggression, identify examples of good practice and possible changes or improvements in this area.

Conclusion

This chapter has explored aspects of clients' participation, culture, equality and diversity, and their relevance for preventing and reducing violence and aggression. The next chapter will explore these topics further, in relation to individuals with specific communication needs.

Chapter 9
Individuals with specific communication needs

The next two chapters explore individuals' specific communication needs, related to interventions to reduce violence and aggression and to aspects of culture, equality and diversity. This chapter will consider this with reference to individuals whose first language is not English, individuals who are refugees or seeking asylum, people in prisons and detention centres, and individuals with learning disability. Bereavement and grief are also briefly considered.

Some violence and aggression can be understood as a way to communicate, particularly in individuals who find it difficult to communicate through speech or in other ways. This includes a minority of individuals with learning disability, including those who also have so-called 'challenging behaviours' (Addo and Smith 2008; Royal College of Psychiatrists *et al.* 2007), and some people with diagnoses of schizophrenia, personality disorder and other mental health problems (Rogers and Vidgen 2006). Changes in brain function and/or anatomy occasionally result in violent and aggressive behaviours, as a result of stroke, head injury, dementia, some types of learning disability and cerebral tumour (Richards *et al.* 2007).

When communication by professionals is ineffective, it may be seen as poor practice. For example, when:

- they do not see communication with clients as important, or have limited time to do so, e.g., because of a lack of staff and excessive paperwork (Meehan *et al.* 2006);
- '[c]oercive measures, such as control and restraint and seclusion' are sometimes used unnecessarily, with little recourse to communication and other means to prevent and reduce violence and aggression (Meehan *et al.* 2006);

- professionals do not communicate with particular clients because, for example, the latter do not use verbal communication, speak in a language other than English or engender discomfort in staff because of specific problems or needs that they find hard to meet (Jahoda and Wanless 2005; Tribe and Raval 2003);

- professionals' communication is not geared to the client's specific communication needs (Addo and Smith 2008; Bryan and Maxim 2006);

- clients' efforts to communicate are not taken seriously, e.g., because they are seen only as evidence of 'challenging behaviour', 'dementia' or 'personality disorder' (Byrt *et al.* 2006) – 'Take no notice. It's just her Asperger's syndrome/Alzheimer's/borderline personality disorder';

- clients' needs for hearing or visual aids are not recognised so that they feel isolated and unable to communicate their needs (Arnold and Ryan 2007).

These points are considered in this chapter and in Chapter 10.

Questions for reflection/discussion

1. Are you involved in the care of clients with specific communication difficulties (including difficulty in communicating distress) that appear to be a causative, contributory or triggering factor of their violence or aggression?

2. Are there particular communication skills or strategies that are, or could be, helpful?

Individuals with a first language other than English

First language

Lack of information from professionals is sometimes associated with frustration, and, in a small proportion of clients, possible violence or aggression (Richter 2006). Research has found that many individuals who speak little or no English have found it particularly difficult to engage in communication with health professionals or access information about services (Tribe and Raval 2003). This has included people who are deaf (Byrt *et al.* 2007), recipients of district nursing (Peckover and Chidlaw 2007) and services for individuals with learning disability (Addo and Smith 2008), mental health problems (Tribe and Raval 2003) and who are recovering from stroke (Kelson *et al.*1998). Several authors have described widespread discriminatory attitudes in wider society and within health services towards people with disabilities (Barnes and Mercer 2003; Byrt *et al.* 2007). Research has shown that many people recovering from strokes encounter considerable frustration because of a lack of staff efforts to understand their communications and a tendency of professionals to assume that patients cannot understand, or are confused, when this is not the case (Royal College of Physicians and College of Health 1998). Peckover and Chidlaw (2007, p. 377) comment that, amongst their research findings:

> Key issues were a lack of provision of District Nursing services to some clients, and failures to meet clients' language and communication needs, and although reflecting organizational constraints, such continuing inequities were largely unquestioned.

The NICE (2005) *Guideline on Violence states* (pp. 28f):

> ...Each service should have a policy that outlines the procedures for dealing with service users who have disabilities, including those with physical or sensory impairment and/or other communication difficulties.

Relevant interventions with individuals whose first language is not English are considered later in this chapter.

Questions for reflection/discussion

1. To what extent are the observations of Peckover and Chidlaw (2007) applicable to your own area of work/practice placement?

2. To what extent is it possible to assess, prevent and reduce violence and aggression of clients who: a) do not use words to communicate; b) use words, but who do not speak English?

Individuals who are refugees or seeking asylum

Refugees and asylum seekers

Recently, there has been an increasing number of individuals who are refugees or seeking asylum in the UK, some of whom are clients of health, social and other services (Maddern 2004; Maffia 2008; Marrington-Mir and Rimmer 2007) or in prisons and detention centres (HM Inspector of Prisons 2009a). Many of these individuals have suffered the traumas of war, terrorism and torture, as well as adverse events, including racism, since coming to the UK. Unfortunately, admission to services may compound the individual's suffering. 'For someone previously detained and tortured, it is likely to be an intensely negative experience to be detained in hospital' (Sewell 2009, p. 106). The authors' experience and the literature suggests that understanding, and endeavouring to empathise with the experiences of people who are refugees or seeking asylum, is crucial in attempts to relieve their distress, and for a small minority of individuals, in preventing and reducing violence and aggression (Heptinstall *et al.* 2004; Maddern 2004; Maffia 2008; World Health Organisation 2004). Interpreting and translating services that can accurately convey individuals' experiences are crucial in understanding and relieving individuals' distress, and any accompanying violence and aggression (Papadopoulos 2003).

'Zak', a young man admitted to a mental health unit, constantly shouted at other clients and staff, and occasionally physically assaulted them. When he felt able to trust his Named Nurse, he told her that, in his country of origin, he had witnessed, at the age of 10, his brother being shot by the militia of another neighbouring nation with whom his country was at war. He had also witnessed other people being shot and tortured. Zak sought asylum in England, and was admitted to the mental health unit when he had been in the country for only a few weeks. Professionals' ideas concerning 'mental health' were alien to his culture.

It was clearly necessary to understand this young man's experiences and meanings in interventions both to relieve the distress and other features of what professionals perceived to be 'post-traumatic stress disorder' and to prevent and reduce resultant violence and aggression.

Maffia (2008) points out that mental health [and it could be added, other] services may be culturally alien to many people who are refugees or asylum seekers, particularly if professionals fail to understand how each individual understands her or his problems. The latter would include any violence and aggression and underlying causative factors, including post-traumatic stress disorder, which involves a range of distressing psychological and physical symptoms arising from the serious effects of war, terrorism, separation from, or loss of family members/partners, sudden changes of culture and for some individuals, experience of stigmatisation and discrimination in the UK (Maddern 2004). However, some authors have questioned the appropriateness of this diagnosis, which may not accord with individuals' cultural understandings of their difficulties (Tribe and Morrisey 2003) or may detract from problems of greater importance to them, including their strengths and present sources of stress (Papadopoulos 2003). It has been argued that, in work with refugees and people seeking asylum, there is a need for staff self-awareness, cultural awareness, effective non-verbal communication, appreciation of the individual's perspective and appropriate use of interpreters (Heptinstall *et al.* 2004, Maddern 2004; Maffia 2008; Papadopolous 2006; Tribe and Morrisey 2003).

Some individuals with post-traumatic stress disorder express their considerable distress through violence or aggression, sometimes a manifestation of understandable anger about their experiences (Grieger *et al.* 2008), as was the case with 'Zak' (described earlier in this chapter). In addition, servicemen and women who have been involved in wars sometimes develop post-traumatic stress disorder, with, for example, flashbacks of violent scenes in which they or their comrades were shot. Some of these individuals have high levels of arousal (see Chapter 5) and marked violence and aggression on their return to civilian life, although other factors such as substance use and a long history of (non-war) violence may be contributory factors in some individuals (Grieger *et al.* 2008). Clearly, the deeply traumatic events experienced by many servicemen and women need to be approached with empathy in all interventions, including those to prevent and reduce violence and aggression (Combat Stress 2009).

The cultural and diversity needs of individuals who are prisoners

Individual needs of prisoners

Bartlett (2004) refers to the 'dual discrimination' that sadly, occurs when people both have mental health problems or learning disability and a history of offending. Harris *et al.* (2008) comment on the increased risk of both social exclusion and physical and mental health problems and substance use amongst prison inmates in comparison with the general population. Substance use particularly increases the risk of violence and aggression (Dugmore 2009). Within penal institutions, 'women, young offenders, older prisoners and those from minority ethnic groups have distinct health needs' (Harris *et al.* 2008, p. 56), which are not always met (HM Inspector of Prisons 2009a).

Relevant factors related to violence and aggression in prisons include the following:

- 'Black and minority ethnic prisoners...in all male prisons... reported more victimization by staff than by other prisoners' (HM Inspector of Prisons 2009a, p. 26). (As discussed in Chapters 8 and 10 authoritarianism and other negative staff attitudes are sometimes a factor contributing to violence and aggression, Meehan, *et al.* 2006; Morrison 1992.)

- Although there are examples of good practice, individuals who are 'foreign nationals' have often spent long periods 'in prisons, uncertain about their status and future' (HM Inspector of Prisons 2009a, p. 52), with increased occurrences of self-harm, and sometimes, inadequate assessment and care related to this. Many of these prisoners have received insufficient information with a lack of interpreters (Harris *et al.* 2008; HM Inspector of Prisons 2009a).

- Although some prisons encourage contact with children and adult relatives (HM Inspector of Prisons 2009a), women prisoners are often in establishments long distances from their families. This was also reported by Harner (2004), who found that many women were separated from their children, with few opportunities to see them.

- The above factors would be likely to engender frustration, and associated violence and aggression in some individuals (Linsley 2006).

Individuals in immigration detention centres

Immigration detention centres

HM Inspector of Prisons (2009a) identified deficits in some immigration detention centres. These related to several factors identified in the literature as crucial in preventing and reducing violence and aggression, and considered elsewhere in this book. They include a lack of staff respect; inadequate assessment and interventions for individuals who had experienced 'torture or ill-treatment' and 'women ... held in largely male centres' in deprived environments (HM Inspector of Prisons 2009a, p. 55). In addition, some people have been detained for long periods whilst awaiting decisions about their situation. This, with other factors, would be likely to engender frustration, and possible aggression in some individuals. Many children suffer detrimental effects from detention (Stern 2006), aggravated by delayed social work assessment (HM Inspector of Prisons 2009a) and previous traumatic experiences.

HM Inspector of Prisons (2009a) and Stern (2006) indicate several points about communication in prisons, which are relevant to staff in other services. Findings include the following:

- Examples of good inter-staff communication, but also lack of communication between staff in relation to both self-harm and violence and aggression, including bullying by other prisoners.

- The very obvious need for many prisoners, especially people with mental health problems and/or learning disabilities, to communicate their distress and their difficulties, but with a lack of opportunities to do so. Research findings suggest that non-verbal and verbal communication is crucial to preventing and reducing violence and aggression (Linsley 2006; Richter 2006).

- Limited opportunities for people to express distress or frustration may contribute to, or trigger some prisoners' violent and aggressive behaviours. Frustration can contribute to some individuals' aggression, as considered earlier in this book.

- Long periods isolated in cells (caused partly by shortage of staff) and limited time to associate with other prisoners or engage in meaningful activity increases isolation and boredom; and reduces opportunities for support from peers or staff. Chapter 4 has considered the role of boredom and lack of meaningful activities in contributing to violence and aggression.

- Nursing and medical assessment at reception to prison varies, with some individuals' mental health problems being unrecognised.

- There is sometimes a lack of communication, including relevant information, between professionals in mainstream health services and their colleagues providing health care and treatment in prisons.

- Some prisoners have not been offered treatment and care to enable them to safely withdraw from alcohol or other drugs.

(Durcan 2008a, 2008b; HM Inspector of Prisons 2009a; Stern 2006)

Prisoners' expressed needs for communication

Prisoners' need to communicate

Durcan (2008b) stated that, in surveys of 'prison mental health care', individuals reported, amongst other needs, the importance of 'someone to talk to' about their feelings and problems, 'help in a crisis', and 'access to psychological therapy and advice and medication' (Durcan 2008b, p. 300). In both Durcan and Knowles (2006) and Durcan (2008a), many individuals reported that other prisoners' bullying was a problem. Other difficulties found in the Durcan and Knowles (2006) study were 'concerns about family and significant others and difficulty in communicating with these (including limited visits)', 'having no one they can trust to talk to' and 'unresolved life traumas' (Durcan and Knowles 2006, quoted in Durcan 2008a, pp. 292f). All of these factors are relevant to preventing violence and aggression, as indicated elsewhere in this book. Durcan (2008b) indicates the need for mental health and learning disability nurses to work with prisoners who have experienced abuse and other trauma in childhood and later in life. This author also comments on the importance for individuals of working with a staff member they trust over an extended period, without being moved to another prison before therapeutic work has been completed.

Communicating with young people in 'a prison therapeutic community'

However, there are several prison therapeutic communities, with a considerable emphasis on communication and opportunities for prisoners to examine problems in depth (Parker 2007). Wood (2007) comments on the importance of developing caring, communication and the setting of clear limits in a respectful way, within a therapeutic relationship with young people in 'a prison therapeutic community' (Wood 2007, p. 149). Her comments apply to working with clients with violent and aggressive behaviours in other settings:

> ...It is important to focus on the component of 'care' that tends to be marginalized, if not held as taboo, within a prison

environment. A genuine capacity to care on the part of staff members working in a therapeutic environment for young offenders is the most powerful treatment tool available to staff.

The therapeutic relationship is the template on which all therapeutic interventions take place … If young people feel valued and validated for their positive potential, they will use this as a foundation on which to control and contain their own and others' behaviour...

Empathy is a two-way emotional exchange. Young people who have given no thought to their victims, through the capacity to care modelled by staff, begin to consider what they have done to others. The notion of staff caring leads to young offenders starting to care about themselves, and this can be the precursor to caring about others in a more global sense.
(Wood 2007, p. 156)

Although the authors agree with these values, Wood (2007) does not refer to evidence, other than her own experience, to support the above statements.

Grief and loss

Grief and loss

Violence and aggression, and other expressions of anger can sometimes be a way of expressing grief and loss, for example, in relation to the death of a loved one, or in response to bad news, such as being given a diagnosis of a terminal illness (Lugton 2002; Manos and Braun 2006). Thus, Wright (2002) gives a moving account of a father who thumped a wall, following the death of his two-year-old son. Sweet (1998, p. 27) points out that, in relation to bereavement, 'it is essential for [staff] to acknowledge and accept whichever reaction manifests itself'.

Some people tend to externalise grief and other feelings through aggressive or violent behaviours, as this is easier to express than depression or fear (Barker 2005). Individuals with learning disabilities may find it particularly difficult to comprehend death, or to express feelings about a loved one who has died. Some authors have outlined ways to help these people grieve (Dodd *et al.* 2008; MacHale and Carey 2002).

An example of loss expressed as aggression is a young woman ('Jan'), who is very concerned about her new diagnosis of multiple sclerosis. Presenting as tough and unafraid, and 'not to be messed with' is crucial for 'Jan' to have self-respect and gain the respect of her peers. Consequently (and perhaps, unintentionally), 'Jan' is rude and hostile to staff working with her.

In the authors' experience it is essential to try to understand the reason for an individual's aggressive behaviour, rather than adopting an authoritarian stance or ignoring him or her. Such approaches may increase Jan's aggression (Morrison 1992), and mean that her underlying fears and concerns are unrecognised. It would be more helpful for the worker to:

- indicate concern and caring non-verbally (e.g., by anticipating and meeting her needs)

- take what Jan says seriously: 'I hate you, you're not helping.' 'I'm sorry about that. What can I do to help?'

- enable Jan to safely express feelings in a way that she feels is safe, and in her own time and pace.

The rights of individuals with learning disabilities

Learning difficulties

HM Government (2009) indicates the discrimination and social exclusion that individuals with learning disabilities have experienced; and outlines ways to enable these people to be socially included:

> This strategy is written from a human rights approach on the fundamental principle that people with learning disabilities have the same human rights as everyone else, and sets out further steps for this to happen. It responds to the Joint Committee on Human Rights report 'A Life Like Any Other?' (House of Lords and House of Commons, 2008) that adults with learning disabilities are particularly vulnerable to breaches of their human rights.
> (HM Government 2009, pp. 4f)

This document particularly refers to the importance of considering 'people with more complex needs ... people from black and minority ethnic groups and newly arrived communities ... people with autistic spectrum conditions', as well as 'offenders in custody and in the community' (HM Government 2009, p. 5), often with histories of violent offending.

Communicating with individuals with learning disabilities

The 'complex needs' referred to in HM Government (2009, p. 5) include those related to communication. Several authors describe, in relation to children, young people and adults with learning disabilities, violence and aggression and other forms of so-called 'challenging behaviours' as ways that clients communicate distress, anxiety, pain, frustration and other feelings and experiences. These behaviours may also be in response to stress, e.g., a changed situation which the individual finds hard to understand. Most individuals with learning disabilities and 'challenging behaviours' have difficulty communicating their needs or their distress or stress in other ways. There is emphasis in the literature on the importance of using a variety of methods of non-verbal and other forms of communication, adapted to the specific needs and cognitive and other abilities of the client to reduce both her or his distressing or stressful feelings and experiences, as well as violence and aggression (Addo and Smith 2008; Challenging Behaviour Foundation 2009; Kevan 2003; Royal College of Psychiatrists *et al.* 2007).

Violence and aggression as communication in individuals with learning disabilities

Several authors outline ways that some aggressive behaviours in individuals with learning disabilities can be reduced by providing other means for them to communicate or express feelings (Addo and Smith 2008; Emerson 2001; Kevan 2003; Royal College of Psychiatrists *et al.* 2007). Kevan (2003) comments that if the individual does not understand the worker's communication, this can result in violence or aggression because 'the communicative environment is experienced as confusing, anxiety arousing, overwhelming and/or threatening ... As such, this environment becomes aversive to the individual, who then does all she can to escape or avoid it, including exhibiting challenging behaviour ...' (Kevan 2003, p. 79).

The frustration-aggression hypothesis (Dollard *et al.* 1939, cited in Turnbull and Paterson 1999) may partly explain violence and aggression in response to the experiences described, above, by Kevan (2003). The individual in these circumstances may feel understandably frustrated and/or distressed because she or he is overwhelmed by the experience of threat or anxiety, and has few means to express or otherwise communicate distress, other than through violence or aggression. It can be argued that adapting communication to the needs of the individual with learning disability (as well as people with mental health problems, including dementias) is likely to reduce distress, frustration and 'challenging behaviours'. Royal College of Psychiatrists *et al.* (2007, p. 35) outline the need for careful assessment of the strengths and problems in communication of people with learning disabilities, for example, through 'signs or symbols' and for workers to be trained in the use of particular communication skills, adapted to the individual's needs, including the need to ensure an environment which reduces extraneous noises. For example, it might be easier to communicate with a client in the absence of a vacuum cleaner or a loud television music channel nearby.

However, Addo and Smith (2008) comment that inequalities between the client with a learning disability and workers are compounded because of the latter's failure to use communication which is understood by the client. 'Staff frequently overestimate the comprehension of service users' (Addo and Smith 2008, p. 66, citing Bartlett and Bunning 1997). This can engender frustration and stress, expressed through aggressive behaviours in some clients. This may be prevented if active listening is used, with clients being given time to use their own preferred means of communication. It is also important to convey information in ways that the client understands (Addo and Smith 2008).

Moss's (1998) comments (below) apply, also, to some individuals with mental health problems (Gamble and Brennan 2006a):

> Working with people who do not use complex speech requires the use of other sources of information for communication
>
> Watching and listening to movement, facial expressions and sound accesses a rich source of communication, often overlooked in the more verbally-based therapies. Becoming aware of, and using, non-verbal communication helps overcome the anxiety that can be aroused by working with someone who does not speak, or whose speech is limited or perseverative [i.e., repeating the same word or phrase many times over].
>
> (Moss 2002, p. 187)

Conclusion

This chapter has considered the need to assess and respond to individuals' specific needs related to communication and aspects of diversity. The next chapter considers this further, in relation to workers' attitudes and the needs of individuals with dementia and other conditions resulting in changes to brain structure.

Chapter 10
More on individuals with specific communication needs

Research findings suggest that positive staff attitudes (see Box 10.1) are of key importance in all aspects of client care, including the prevention and reduction of violence and aggression (Jahoda and Wanless 2005; Meehan *et al.* 2006; Morrison 1992). Attitudes include beliefs that certain values and skills are important in preventing and reducing violence and aggression, particularly in relation to respect for the individual and valuing his or her integrity (Paterson and Leadbetter 1999, p. 97). (See, also, the core principles listed in Chapter 3.)

Box 10.1   **Attitudes**

Attitudes have been defined as '…Favourable or unfavourable evaluations of, and reaction to, objects, people, situations or other aspects of the world…' (Smith *et al.* 2003). Attitudes, including those that may reduce or worsen violence and aggression, have the following components:

- Cognitive, involving thoughts, beliefs and opinions. (E.g., stereotypes involve beliefs that certain types of patients will all have similar characteristics: 'He's a young man wearing a hood, so he's bound to be aggressive.')

- Affective, involving emotions and feelings. (E.g., prejudices are strong negative or positive feelings about an individual or a group: 'Not another client with personality disorder. I can't stand them. They always cause trouble.')

- Behavioural, involving the behaviour or action taken by the individual. (This can include discrimination, i.e. strongly negative or positive action taken towards a particular group of people. E.g., a worker always refusing to communicate with clients if they are aggressive.)

(Smith *et al.* 2003)

The link between staff attitudes, feelings and reactions to adults and children with learning disabilities and violence and aggression

Staff attitudes

Several studies have found a link between staff attitudes, feelings and reactions to children and adults with learning disabilities and the extent of violent and aggressive behaviours in these individuals (Emerson 2001; Hastings and Brown 2002; Jahoda and Wanless 2005; Tynan and Allen 2002). These findings are likely to be relevant, also, to clients in mental health and other settings. Researchers have found 'a general relationship between challenging behaviour', including violence and aggression, and 'levels of stress or strain experienced by carers' (Emerson 2001, p. 151, citing several studies). Research findings suggest that clients' violent and aggressive behaviours have sometimes been linked to strong negative attitudes from workers (Hastings and Brown 2002; Jahoda and Wanless 2005; Tynan and Allen 2002), which, in some instances, subsequently resulted in their withdrawal from engagement or communication with clients (Emerson 2001). These findings are similar to that of a pioneering study of nurses' attitudes in general hospitals (Stockwell 1972). This found that general nurses tended to withdraw from engagement or interaction with patients they disliked, including those who were seen as 'unpopular' or 'difficult' (Duxbury 2000).

Workers with negative attitudes may use personal attitudes and beliefs as a basis for their responses to clients' violence or aggression. In some cases, this may reinforce the violence or aggression (Emerson 2001; Jahoda and Wanless 2005; Turnbull and Paterson 1999). There may be moral judgements of the client's behaviours, rather than using the client's perspectives and valid and reliable assessments to inform interventions (Crichton 1997; Jahoda and Wanless 2005). In some cases, staff may have negative attitudes or unhelpful responses reinforced by their peers (Emerson 2001, p. 151):

> A range of 'informal' rules ... is likely to exert a powerful influence on carers and care staff. Peer groups within the workplace and other relatives within family settings shape each other's behaviour by defining the nature of the 'problem' and what should be done about it, monitoring each other's performance against these (often implicit or unstated)

aims, and providing effective (if not always constructive) feedback. In service settings, it is often possible to identify processes of socialization by which new staff are taught the 'tricks of the trade' by the existing staff group ... Informal rules ... may support practices which are either irrelevant to, or at odds with, the explicit aims of the service or the advice of ... professional staff

Unless staff receive adequate support and clinical supervision to enable them to be aware of negative attitudes, and the need to work professionally with clients, this may result in staff behaving abusively towards clients (White *et al.* 2003). The above findings have clear implications (as do many other research findings cited in this book) for the provision of good quality staff support, clinical supervision and relevant education.

A critique of some of the above findings

A critique

However, based on their research findings, Jahoda and Wanless (2005) argue that staff attitudes towards clients with 'challenging behaviours' are more complex than earlier studies suggest. They state that research interviews do not always reflect the complexity and changing nature of staff relationships with clients with learning disabilities.

Lucas *et al.* (2009) comment that research examining staff attitudes to individuals with learning disability and 'challenging behaviours' (including violence and aggression) often uses vignettes of hypothetical clients to assess workers' attitudes, rather than considering their attitudes to real-life clients. From their own research, Lucas *et al.* (2009) conclude that staff's stated attitudes to vignettes are nothing like the attitudes demonstrated in their responses to clients' challenging behaviours in the settings where they work.

Jahoda and Wanless (2005) conclude that staff often have complex attitudes towards individuals with 'challenging behaviours'. These attitudes may vary over time:

The responses [in a research interview on violence and aggression] given by staff highlighted the emotional arousal experienced [at the time of the incident], yet they tempered these responses in line with their professional responsibilities...

The meaning of the workers' appraisals can only be understood in the context of the wider relationships which they have with clients ... In [some] instances, the strength of the workers' negative emotional reactions may not stem from a dislike of the clients.

An interesting observation from the interview process was that some staff who appeared warm and empathic about the client's needs gave what seemed to be, on paper, the most hostile answers. One might speculate that emotive answers suggest an emotional link with the client, and that staff who give more 'professional' answers are in some cases, more disconnected, or even 'burned out'...

(Jahoda and Wanless 2005, p. 549)

Practical application of research findings on workers' attitudes

Application of research findings

Research findings on staff attitudes can help workers in a variety of settings to consider:

- the need for staff self-awareness and honesty about attitudes towards clients, including feelings, during and after incidents of violence and aggression

- the need to recognise that initial feelings and attitudes (e.g. anxiety, annoyance) are natural and human, in the face of a difficult, and sometimes, frightening situation.

- the need to ensure that:

  - any negative feelings and attitudes do not adversely affect the care of the client (the study of Jahoda and Wanless (2005) suggests that staff were able to work effectively with clients if they successfully resolved any negative attitudes)

  - there are opportunities for all staff involved to share with colleagues how they felt at the time of the incident, and subsequently. Such opportunities should include informal support, regular clinical supervision, and debriefing if the incident is serious.

Attitudes in mental health services

Attitudes

As mentioned earlier, Meehan *et al.* (2006) report research studies which have found that negative staff attitudes and 'controlling behaviour' (Meehan *et al.* 2006, p. 19) escalate aggression. In Meehan *et al.*'s (2006) study of a secure hospital, clients perceived provocative staff comments (including being 'put down') and custodial, rather than caring attitudes, as creating 'much more tension in the unit and this gave rise to aggression' (Meehan *et al.* 2006, p. 23). Several studies have found that positive staff attitudes are crucial to clients with a diagnosis of personality disorder feeling understood and respected (Ashman 2001; Byrt *et al.* 2006; Castillo 2003; Horn *et al.* 2007). The influence of both positive and negative attitudes on work with individuals with aggressive behaviours and personality disorder was referred to in Chapter 6. Service users with this diagnostic category have reported both helpful staff attitudes, and being dismissed and labelled in a judgemental way, e.g., as 'manipulative' or 'attention seeking' (Castillo 2003, Castillo *et al.* 2001, Fallon 2003). Although *Personality Disorder: No Longer a Diagnosis of Exclusion* (National Institute for Mental Health in England and Department of Health 2003) has required all NHS mental health trusts to set up specialist services for this client group, many individuals with personality disorder have experienced negative attitudes and rejection in the past. This needs to be borne in mind when these individuals are hostile towards workers (Byrt *et al.* 2006).

> It was decided that both my partner and myself had borderline personality disorder at a meeting to which we were not invited. As a result of this diagnosis, of which we were not initially informed, we were both refused all services and support ... Now [professionals] are tainting my life with the vindictive use of stigma.
> (John 2000, p. 2)

Other individuals have reported negative changes in staff attitudes towards them once a personality disorder diagnosis has been established (Castillo 2003; Fallon 2003). In one study, nurses in secure hospitals expressed more judgemental attitudes towards clients with personality disorders; and said they would use restrictive measures such as seclusion and restraint with these people, compared with clients with a diagnosis of mental illness (Crichton 1997). This has clear implications for these nurses' responses to clients' violence and aggression. However, positive attitudes from staff have been described by some individuals who have received treatment in specialist units, some of which have admitted individuals with aggressive behaviours (Bree *et al.* 2003; Castillo 2003; Fallon 2003; Perseius *et al.* 2003).

Respecting and validating individuals with dementias

Respecting those with dementias

Research findings suggest that older people with dementias are also often subject to negative attitudes and that violence and aggression of these individuals cannot be understood or responded to without considering the wider social context and services providing care (Baldwin and Capstick 2007). Research has indicated considerable ageism (discrimination towards older people), both within health services and in wider society (Rudge 2002), which can result in older people's understandable anger. In some health services, people with Alzheimer's Disease and other dementias have received a lack of validation, that is, staff acknowledgement of, and respect for, their individuality, present and past identities as people, and strengths and abilities (Baldwin and Capstick 2007; Kitwood 1997). These individual characteristics have often been ignored, with a 'failure to understand the value and meaning of their communications' (Byrt 2001, p. 76).

This lack of validation of the individual indicates denial of her or his personhood, defined by Kitwood (1997, p. 13) as 'a standing or status, bestowed by one individual on others'. This denial of personhood includes 'invalidation: the ignoring or discounting of a dementia sufferer's subjective states', including assertive or aggressive anger and the individual's underlying 'feelings of distress or bewilderment', as well as objectification: 'treating a person like a lump of dead matter; to be measured, pushed around, drained, filled, polished, dumped' (Kitwood 1993, p. 104).

In invalidation, a situation can arise where the individual's anger is ignored and written off as a manifestation of confusion. This reaction may result in further distress and anger and an unrelieved 'vicious circle'. Invalidation can also be reflected in failure to address the client by her/his preferred name and the use of patronising speech (Box 10.2).

Box 10.2   **Staff's indiscriminate use of clients' first names and other familiar forms of address**

One aspect of disrespect relates to calling a client by a name other than the one she or he wishes the worker to use, and using 'baby talk' (Brown and Draper 2003, pp. 15f) or patronising speech in conversation with them. This could result in clients' understandable frustration and possible aggression and other forms of anger. Brown and Draper (2003) reviewed the research on ways in which older clients are addressed by staff. In some instances:

...Older people are addressed in a simplified vocabulary with a high-pitched tone of voice and slow speech...

...The assumed use of older adults' first names ... as well as terms of endearment (such as 'honey' or 'sweetheart') may ... be used. In many respects ... [workers'] speech resembles that which an adult would use when speaking with a language-learning child ... terms used to describe this pattern of speech include 'baby talk'...

...Overall, the findings of ... studies suggest that older people tend to dislike [this type of] speech ...

(Brown and Draper 2003, pp. 15f)

Brown and Draper (2003) conclude that the way in which nurses address, and communicate with older people reflects ageism.

Lovegrove (2002) gives an example of nurses failing to address her 92-year-old neighbour with her preferred name:

... So here we are again in another nursing home ... From habit, I've told [the staff] that she's known by her second name, Enid, but they insist on calling her Leonora, her first name ...
(Lovegrove 2002, p. 12)

The message from Lovegrove (2002) is that clients should always be asked what name they prefer the worker to address them by, including the use of titles, such as 'Ms' and 'Mr'.

Validation refers to attempts to value the individual, and take seriously her or his communication. 'Validation ... involves accepting and acknowledging the reality and power of another's experience, emotions and feelings ...' (Davies *et al.* 2006, p. 520). This includes validating, rather than dismissing, anger. People with dementias and allied conditions can be validated through effective verbal and non-verbal communication, with attempts to understand their experiences and behaviours, including violence and aggression and the underlying reasons for them (Goldsmith 1996; Davies *et al.* 2006; Stokes 2002).

An important part of validation is awareness of the individual's previous and present life experiences (Kindell and Griffiths 2006), as described by the client and her or his carers at home. This helps to ensure good quality care, including the maintenance of the individual's personhood and the continuation of her or his valued identities, roles and activities (Baldwin and Capstick 2007; Neno *et al.* 2007). It also helps workers to understand the reasons for aggression and prevent and reduce this. For example, Goldsmith (1996) described an older woman with Alzheimer's disease ('Mrs Jones') who assaulted staff who attempted to help her to wash or bathe. It was discovered, through a detailed history, that she had been raped when young. When workers attempted to help Mrs Jones with her personal needs, she feared that she was being raped. Once staff realised this, they understood the reasons for Mrs Jones's violent behaviour, and were especially sensitive in their efforts to help her attend to her physical hygiene. Goldsmith (1996) also describes an older man who became agitated and potentially aggressive when workers tried to dissuade him from getting up at 4.00 am. It was then discovered that he had been a farmer, and had risen at this time throughout his life. This gentleman became happier and less agitated when enabled to get up whenever he wished.

Communicating with individuals with learning disability, dementias, acquired brain injury and stroke

Other conditions

The following suggestions, based on the authors' experience and the literature, may help to reduce the isolation and distress, sometimes manifested in violent and aggressive behaviours, of many individuals with learning disability who understand some verbal conversation, and individuals with dementias, acquired brain injury, strokes and other conditions resulting in structural changes to the brain (Richards *et al.* 2007). These conditions may result in misinterpretation or misunderstanding of other people's communication: a factor contributing to violence and aggression (Stokes 2002). Chawner (2003) gives a detailed account of ways that staff developed communication with an older person with dementia, in order to improve her quality of life, decrease her distress, and reduce aggressive behaviours.

Besides the aspects of communication outlined in earlier chapters, the following are proposed:

- Because some of these individuals have 'difficulty in locating sounds', where possible, 'speak to [the individual] face to face' (Oddy 2003, p. 18), with your head level to her or his head. Facing the individual also facilitates lip reading in some individuals who are deaf.
- For this and other reasons, 'address the person frequently by name' (Oddy 2003, p. 18).
- Ensure that the individual is addressed by her or his preferred name and title, with avoidance of indiscriminate use of endearments (such as 'Gran') unless the individual expresses a preference for these (see Box 10.2).

Aids to hearing, vision and speech

Hearing, vision and speech aids

Individuals' sense of isolation, frustration and any aggressive behaviours are likely to be compounded by difficulties in hearing, seeing or speaking. Therefore the following points should be borne in mind:

- With the individual's agreement, testing of hearing, sight and dental health needs to be carried out early during assessment.
- Ensure that individuals have the following, if they need them:
- hearing aids – check that these are working
- spectacles – check that these are appropriate for near sight or distance
- contact lenses – check that these are correctly and comfortably inserted
- dentures – check these are comfortable and fitted correctly.

Hearing, visual and dental aids are essential for effective communication, and individuals' self-esteem and ability to carry out everyday tasks (Arnold and Ryan 2007).

Communicating with individuals with short-term memory loss

Short-term memory loss

If the individual has short-term memory loss (i.e., difficulty in remembering things soon after they have happened), it may be necessary to patiently and clearly repeat what has been said. Many people with dementia, acquired brain injury or recovering from stroke, find it easier to understand statements one at a time (Bryan and Maxim 2006; Oddy 2003). For example, 'Tea is on the table', 'Can I help you to your chair' and 'Your daughter rang to say she's visiting you' are more likely to be understood if said separately. The following sentence is less likely to be understood: 'Tea is on the table, so shall I help you to your chair, and your daughter rang to say she's visiting you'. Giving information clearly, in a form that can be easily remembered, may help to reduce the individual's isolation and vulnerability and hence, reduce the likelihood of frustration and associated aggression (Bryan and Maxim 2006; Oddy 2003).

Difficulty in 'finding the right words'

'Finding the right words'

Some individuals have difficulty finding the right words. This is known as 'nominal dysphasia' (Oddy 2003, p. 19) and may occur in individuals with damage to parts of their brain concerned with speech. It can occur as a result of dementia, strokes, acquired brain injury and other conditions (Richards *et al.* 2007). Oddy (2003) suggests that these individuals are enabled 'to express themselves as well as they can, without stepping in too quickly to help them. Watch their facial expression and body language; their face and body posture give valuable clues to what they are trying to say. If necessary, help them to find the right word: Do you mean toilet or tablet?' (Oddy 2003, p. 19).

Alternative methods of communication

Attention to these aspects of communication may help to reduce the client's understandable frustration, and possible aggression, as may alternative methods of communication, such as, the use of writing clearly on a whiteboard or pictures representing essential items. The latter are often used for individuals recovering from strokes. (See Box 10.3 for examples.) The arts have also been used to enable older people to communicate effectively and creatively, through, for example, creative writing, dance and acting (Greenwood 2009; Kulik and Schweitzer 2002).

Box 10.3

The use of alternative means of communication

'Staff made efforts to understand Dad's communication problems and the consequences for him. Both family and staff continued to communicate through touch, gestures and writing clearly on his whiteboard ...

'Nursing staff enabled us to communicate with our father through the things which he had always liked or enjoyed ... We looked with Dad at his photograph albums, which included his most treasured snaps and a record of his past and his achievements ...

'Our father was always a very keen and highly skilled gardener ... This was reflected in the many pot plants ... in his room [in an orthopaedic ward], including ones which he could smell, as well as see ...

'As our father became progressively more ill, verbal communication, using the whiteboard, became increasingly difficult. It was possible to communicate through touch. Dad often squeezed our hands ... At times, he also appeared to enjoy the smell of citrus pot pourri.'
(Byrt, C. *et al.* 2003, pp. 175f).

Other interventions with individuals with dementias and allied conditions

Other interventions

Finally, this chapter will briefly consider other interventions with individuals with dementias and other conditions resulting in damage to the structure of the brain. Many of these interventions could also apply to individuals with other mental health problems and/or learning disability. These interventions include the anticipation of a wide range of the client's needs, and the reduction of frustration and consequent aggression in a minority of clients.

- Ensuring safety (see Chapter 4), for example, through keeping 'dangerous objects out of reach' (Bonner 2005, p. 41).

- Use of the communication skills outlined earlier in this chapter: in particular, speaking clearly, ensuring the individual can hear, or see to lip read, and using brief phrases/sentences which she or he can process easily (Stokes 2002).

- Endeavouring to understand the reasons for the individual's behaviour through listening to her or him and to her or his carers at home (Bryan and Maxim 2006).

- Careful assessment of all the stressors that are associated with the individual's violence or aggression (Goldsmith 1996; Royal College of Psychiatrists *et al.* 2007).

- Reducing all possible sources of stress and distress, e.g., pain or other symptoms, excessive noise which is unwelcome to the individual, not having enough personal space: e.g., when eating, missing opportunities for exercise. (Several authors have described the role of stress in causing, or contributing to violence and aggression in younger and older individuals with dementias and learning disabilities (Bonner 2005; Emerson 2001; Stokes 2000; Stokes 2002).)

- Awareness of the individual's need for personal space, privacy and dignity. Stokes (2002) indicates that violence and aggression in individuals with dementias are sometimes related to:

  > Entering [her/his] personal space without invitation or explanation (or if one is provided, it is inadequate, for it is ambiguous; fails to appreciate that the person may be hard of hearing; does not take into account their receptive [or cognitive] difficulties, or is not repeated).
  > (Stokes 2002, p. 142)

- Sensitivity to the individual's previous, as well as present, life experience. Within the parameters of safety, enable previous life styles to continue, for example, enabling an individual who always rose and went to bed early, because of her or his work, to continue to do so if she or he wishes (Goldsmith 1996).

- Particular respect for the individual's privacy and dignity in relation to her or his toilet and bathing/showering needs, with recognition and meeting of personal preferences and views: e.g., about a worker of the same gender providing assistance (Neno et al. 2007).

- Respect for the individual's culture, diversity and religion, in relation, for example, to toilet and bathing needs, dress, food, space for prayer (Neno et al. 2007).

- Enabling these and other choices to contribute to the individual's quality of life and essential physical, psychological, cultural, spiritual and other needs, as well as preventing agitation and possible aggression (Goldsmith, 1996).

- Careful consideration of the use of bed rails and related items, following a risk assessment, since some individuals may feel confined by them, and respond with frustration, and possible aggression (Darcy 2007).

- A physical environment to reduce disorientation and associated frustration: e.g., toilet, bedroom and other doors clearly labelled, with toilet doors, for example, all in the same distinctive bright colours (Redfern and Ross 2006). This may help the individual to maintain dignity and privacy, with consequent reduced agitation and/or aggression.

- Some individuals may benefit from distraction or diversion from triggers of their aggression (Stokes 2002).

- Avoidance of both institutionalisation and sudden changes of routine which result in stress, and consequent aggression in a minority of clients (Stokes 2002).

- Establishing whether or not reality orientation is helpful or not. For some individuals, reality orientation: e.g., in relation to where the person is, or a reminder that a partner or relative is visiting, may be helpful and reassuring. For other people 'Exposing a confused person to the painfulness of a present characterized by a loss of persons, places and things can result in anger and abuse, as they live and know a reality of years ago ...' (Stokes 2002, p. 143).

Conclusion

This chapter has considered the relevance to preventing and reducing violence and aggression of workers' attitudes, and the communication and other needs of clients with learning disabilities and with dementias and other conditions resulting in changes in brain structure. The next chapter considers the relevance of individuals' physical health needs to their well-being and the prevention and reduction of violence and aggression.

Chapter 11
Clients' physical health needs

This chapter is concerned with the assessment and provision of care related to clients' physical health needs in relation to the prevention and reduction of violence and aggression. Topics covered include the role of exercise, diet and nutrition, the needs of people with both learning disabilities and physical illness, and the care of individuals with delirium.

The National Institute for Clinical Excellence (NICE) (2005) *Guideline on Violence* states:

> The physical health needs of the service user should be assessed on admission or as soon as possible thereafter and then regularly reassessed. The care plan should reflect the service user's physical needs.
> (NICE 2005, p. 28)

These points are also considered, in relation to individuals with learning disabilities, in Royal College of Psychiatrists, *et al.* (2007).

Questions for reflection/discussion

1. Can you think of an instance where interventions to meet a client's physical health needs or deficits contributed to the prevention or reduction of violence or aggression?

2. Is this an area that could receive greater emphasis in your own area of work/practice placement?

The relevance of nutrition

Relevance of nutrition

Several authors have considered nutritional deficiencies, including lack of essential minerals, vitamins and other nutrients in childhood (Liu and Wuerker 2005). Liu *et al.* (2004) found that:

> Malnutrition at age three years ... predisposes to neuro-

cognitive deficits, which, in turn, predispose to persistent, externalising behaviour problems throughout childhood and adolescence. The findings … suggest that reducing early malnutrition may help reduce later antisocial and aggressive behaviors.

(Scarpa and Raine 2008, pp. 161f, citing Liu *et al.* 2004)

Research suggests that violence and aggression can be prevented if individuals drink sufficient fluids and have balanced diets which include all essential nutrients (NPI Center 2008; University of Oxford 2008). These findings, in wider populations and amongst prisoners, are likely to have relevance to clients of social care and health services. For example, some people become increasingly irritable or aggressive if they have hypoglycaemia (low blood sugar) from diabetes. Giving sugar, followed by a snack rich in complex carbohydrates, such as a sandwich, would improve the individual's physical well-being, and also reduce aggression (Mistry 2009; Morrison and Bennett 2009). It may be appropriate to offer a drink or food to other clients with aggressive behaviours, if, for example, they are hungry or thirsty, with subsequent physical discomfort. Research findings suggest that high caffeine intakes (e.g., from coffee and some fizzy soft drinks) can increase aggression in some individuals (Martin *et al.* 2008). This could have implications for interventions to help some individuals to replace fluid high in caffeine with other drinks that they enjoy.

Byrt and Doyle (2007) outline the care of an individual ('Mr Clive Crimson'), who was experiencing the hypomanic phase of a bipolar mental illness. This resulted in physical over-activity, and distractibility, with difficulty in concentrating on most activities for a sustained period. This included eating a large meal. Clive found it easier to consume nutritious snacks and drinks, and so these were provided, with a fluid and food intake and output chart to ensure that he was drinking sufficient fluids, eating a sufficient amount of nutritious foods, and passing adequate amounts of urine (Archibald 2008). These measures not only contributed to Clive's physical health, but may have prevented violence or aggression, given his recent history of these behaviours, and the links between poor nutritional status and violent behaviours (NPI Center 2008; University of Oxford 2008). Dehydration, with inadequate intake of fluids and reduction in urine production could result in delirium (acute confusional state), which can also contribute to aggression. (This is considered later in this chapter.)

Improving nutrition in prisons and the effects on violence and aggression

Studies have found that improving individuals' diet, including the use of dietary supplements, can result in 'significant reduction in antisocial and violent behaviour' (NPI Center 2008). University of Oxford (2008) reports on a study of the effects of improving prisoners' nutrition in three penal establishments:

> The new trials build on previous research carried out at ... HM Young Offenders' Institution, Aylesbury ... In that study, nutritional supplements were given to ensure that inmates' diets reached recommended UK dietary standards. The researchers found that prisoners who consumed the active nutrient capsule committed ... 37% fewer violent offences.
>
> Professor Stein and colleagues believe that the reason why supplements can have such a large effect is because the proper function of nerve cell membranes and signalling molecules [in the brain] depend upon adequate amounts of minerals, vitamins and essential fatty acids in the diet.
> (University of Oxford 2008)

Laurance (2008) comments:

> The theory behind the trial is that when the brain is starved of essential nutrients, especially omega-3-fatty acids, which are a central building block of brain neurons [nerve cells], it loses 'flexibility'. This shortens attention span and undermines self-control.

Lawrence (2008) states that prisoners often 'make unhealthy choices', but Condon et al. (2007) comment that many prisoners are not able to choose healthy diets or have access to exercise or programmes to help them give up smoking.

The value of exercise in reducing and channelling violence and aggression

The value of exercise

Research findings indicate the role of exercise in reducing aggressive anger, sometimes as a means to channel it through physical activity (Adams 2002; Biddle and Mutrie 2008; Faulkner and Taylor 2005). In addition, research suggests that, following exercise, many people also experience reductions in depression and anxiety and various symptoms of mental illness (Adams 2002; Biddle and Mutrie 2008; Morrison and Bennett 2009), which may underlie violence and aggression. Many individuals experience increases in self-esteem (Biddle and Mutrie 2008). There is 'a more positive mood through the increased output of endorphins and active seeking of physical and cognitive diversions to cope with thoughts' (Adams 2002, p. 124). The successful relief of stress, from exercise, is also important, given the role of stress in contributing to some individuals' violence and aggression (Hodgins *et al.* 2009). In an exercise programme for women with a diagnosis of personality disorder who were clients in a medium security ward, there was a 'statistically significant improvement in service users' self-reported feelings of relaxation, happiness and calmness following engagement in personal training sessions' (Savage *et al.* 2009, p. 32).

Tetlie *et al.* (2009) report that patients particularly valued sharing sporting activities with a staff member, and that this contributed to the development of therapeutic relationships. In this study of an exercise programme in a secure hospital:

> One of the patients [who had participated in the exercise programme] talked about avoiding fights because he was not bored, which is an example of the importance of having a meaningful schedule in an inpatient setting: 'When I work out, I relax more easily, and I don't get into fights then, partly because I'm not bored'.
> (Tetlie *et al.* 2009, p. 37, quoting the views of an individual who is a secure hospital patient).

Exercise also contributes to social inclusion and recovery (Carless and Sparkes 2008; Perkins and Repper 2009) and results in physical health gains (Hensley, 2008), including reductions in obesity and blood pressure, improved sleep, and if sustained, decreased risk of heart disease, diabetes and some forms of cancer (Biddle and Mutrie 2008; Morrison and Bennett 2009).

Safety related to clients' risk of harm to self or others

Access to exercise equipment, and to facilities outside the ward environment needs to be informed by risk assessments related to violence and aggression, as well as self-harm, in case clients are likely to harm themselves or others (Tetlie *et al.* 2009). However, exercise may be a means to divert clients from thoughts of violence to self or others and of channelling aggression in a creative way (Adams 2002; Cashin *et al.* 2008). In line with Health and Safety regulations, the safety of any equipment used must be evaluated (Fuller 2004).

Clients' physical health also needs to be assessed before exercise programmes are implemented. For example, individuals with obesity and/or certain physical health conditions, such as heart disease, would be at risk if they exercised strenuously because of the strain exerted on the heart and other organs (Biddle and Mutrie 2008; Lloyd-Williams and Mair 2005; Piperidou and Bliss 2008). Any risks related to clients' mental health problems also need to be considered: for example, certain types of exercise might over-stimulate an individual experiencing the hypomanic or manic phase of a bipolar mental illness (Beech 2009), and, in some circumstances, possibly potentiate aggression. An important aspect of assessment, in relation to exercise programmes, is to evaluate clients' motivation. This may be affected, for example, by distressing symptoms of mental illness, including depression. The effects of antipsychotic medication may affect the extent to which people are alert or drowsy during the day, with consequent effects on motivation (Healy 2005). Motivation may also be affected by living in an institutionalised, understimulating environment (Keen and Barker 2009) and by the extent to which clients perceive exercise to be an enjoyable activity (Biddle and Mutrie 2008). Individuals' perceptions of exercise, and their motivation to engage in it, are also likely to be affected by previous experiences e.g., at school (Biddle and Mutrie 2008).

An important aspect of assessment is to ask the client what sort of exercise she or he would enjoy. This should involve offering a range of activities, and asking clients what they would like to choose. For example, at one point, women patients at a medium security unit said they would like exercises with an aerobics instructor, and so these were provided (Byrt *et al.* 2001).

The individual's culture, age, gender and spirituality might influence attitudes to exercise and activities chosen by the client, but assumptions should not be made (Griggs *et al.* 2009). In relation to gender, for example, the film 'Billy Elliott' is a moving story about a boy's wish to become a ballet dancer, and how this was gradually accepted by his father and older brother and their workmates. Billy Elliott's dance on dustbins after a family row is a vivid example of how exercise can be used to positively channel aggression and frustration (Hall 2000).

Some clients' spiritual needs might make it difficult for them to exercise at particular times of day. For example, an individual might need specific times to pray. It might be difficult for a Muslim client to exercise if they have not eaten for several hours during Ramadan.

Self-efficacy, locus of control, self-esteem and body image

Clients' perceptions, and motivation to exercise, relate to their self-efficacy (belief that they can achieve goals, e.g., when exercising) and locus of control (how far they feel they are responsible for, and able to influence, their exercise programmes and the achievement of positive results) (Biddle and Mutrie 2008; Morrison and Bennett 2009). Self efficacy and locus of control also have implications for clients' beliefs that they are able to control their aggression and express it assertively. Workers need to take this into account in interventions to prevent and reduce violence and aggression.

Research suggests that some people benefit from the sense of control that exercise gives them (Morrison and Bennett 2009), which may be particularly beneficial for individuals who find it difficult to control aggression. A vivid example of an individual gaining control through physical activity is given in Alan Sillitoe's (1959) short novel *The Loneliness of the Long Distance Runner*, later made into a film. The hero, at an institution for offenders, finds that he can gain control over his life by running – eventually faster than his competitors.

Opportunities for exercise in prisons and the relevance to other services

Prisoners' lack of opportunities for sufficient exercise is outlined in HM Inspector of Prisons (2009a) and in research by Durcan (2008a) and Durcan and Knowles (2006). Condon *et al.* (2008) indicate the links between lack of exercise in prisons and links with increased risks of heart disease, diabetes and other physical ill health. Cashin *et al.* (2008, p. 66) examine 'the relationship between exercise and hopelessness in prison'. This paper makes links between the physical and spiritual needs of individuals in prison. The authors review the connection between lack of exercise and physical, psychological and spiritual ill health.

Box 11.1

Aspects of health promotion and related work at 'Cedarview'

'Cedarview' (a pseudonym) is an NHS medium security unit with a primary healthcare nursing team, whose work is concerned with links between patients' physical and mental health, with consequences for reducing violence and aggression and for health promotion:

- The primary healthcare nursing team work with colleagues in the care and treatment of individuals with diabetes, which sometimes develops as a side effect of antipsychotic medication, such as Clozapine and Olanzapine (British National Formulary 2009). In some individuals, the diabetes can worsen symptoms of mental illness, and potentiate violence and aggression, e.g., because of hypoglycaemia (low blood sugar).

- Weight gain can also occur as a side effect of some antipsychotics (British National Formulary 2009) and as a result of lack of motivation and a sedentary life style (Archibald 2008). Patients at Cedarview have individualised fitness programmes, with access to a wide range of physical activities, including a well equipped gym and multi-gym. Bearing in mind research findings in this area, it is likely that access to exercise will decrease violence and aggression and increase individuals' self-esteem, as well as leading to weight loss and improved physical health and well-being (Biddle and Mutrie 2008).

- Many clients, like people elsewhere, have used nicotine as a protective factor against hallucinations, delusions and other distressing symptoms of mental illness (McChargue et al. 2002), some of which are associated with violence and aggression. The primary healthcare nurses, in liaison with patients and with other staff, have enabled patients to cease smoking, in line with the local NHS Trust policy. Care plans and their implementation have assessed, amongst other factors, specific stressors that contribute both to patients' smoking and to violence and aggression. Patients have been enabled to find other means to manage stress and resultant anger, e.g., through exercise and the use of psychosocial interventions (described in Chapter 12).

The physical health of individuals with learning disabilities

Physical health

This is considered by Royal College of Psychiatrists et al. (2007) in relation to individuals with learning disabilities and 'challenging behaviours'. This document, like the NICE (2005) *Guideline on Violence*, advises the assessment of underlying 'medical problems' and 'referral for further assessment and investigations ... where necessary' (Royal College of Psychiatrists *et al.* 2007, p. 27). Conditions causing pain are considered, including 'headaches and migraine ... earache and toothache ... urinary tract infections', abdominal pain and cancers. Some individuals with learning disabilities, dementia and acquired brain injury have difficulty communicating that they have pain, which has sometimes been unrecognised, with consequent worsening of physical health, frustration, and possible aggression (Kunz *et al.* 2009; McAuliffe *et al.* 2009; Michael 2008; Royal College of Psychiatrists *et al.* 2007).

Lack of access to physical health care for individuals with learning disabilities is reported in both Mencap's (2007) report *Death by Indifference* and in Michael (2008, p. 7):

> People with learning disabilities find it much harder than other people to access assessment and treatment for general health problems ... Parents and carers of adults and children with learning disabilities often find their opinions ignored by healthcare professionals.

The rights of individuals with learning disabilities to physical health assessment and treatment have been emphasised (HM Government 2009; World Health Organisation and Montreal PAHO/WHO Collaborating Centre for Training in Mental Health 2007). This is necessary, not only for individuals' health and well-being, but to prevent and reduce violence and aggression when these are used as ways to communicate pain and physical symptoms. Careful observation and anticipation of individuals' needs are crucial. One of the authors worked with a young man with learning disability with limited verbal communication. Careful observation for signs that he was in pain (e.g., from toothache) not only ensured adequate pain relief and the meeting of other physical health needs, but also reduced violent behaviours.

Adverse experiences in a General Hospital as contributive to violence and aggression in individuals with learning disability

Adverse experiences

This is outlined by Jones (2004) who refers to the sources of stress to individuals with learning disabilities who are admitted to general hospitals. To overcome this problem, learning disability liaison nurses have recently been appointed to work with staff in general hospitals (Garvey 2008; Pointu *et al.* 2009). Some individuals with learning disability and dementia may be violent or aggressive because of the stress and distress they experience in unfamiliar surroundings and with strange and frightening procedures and interventions (Jones 2004; Pointu *et al.* 2009).

Jones (2004) highlights some of the problems experienced by 'Julie', an individual with learning disabilities who was admitted to a surgical ward:

- Lack of information for surgical ward staff about Julie's learning disability before her admission made it difficult to plan her nursing care at this time.

- Julie was distressed at not being able to eat or drink before her general anaesthetic and surgery – and there was difficulty in explaining this to her in a way that she could understand. (This has implications for the production of materials, such as pictures, to explain to individuals with learning disabilities, as well as some other clients, their admission, care and treatment in general hospitals.)

- 'The situation was made worse by [Julie's] being in a strange environment and being approached by people whom she did not know' (Jones 2004, p. 149).

- Because of Julie's high anxiety, and difficulty in trusting nurses, she could not be persuaded to have her pulse, temperature and blood pressure taken.

- Jones (2004) considers ethical concerns about giving Julie's medication covertly (that is, in a drink without her knowledge) because Julie would not take it in any other way.

- Jones (2004) also considers some health professionals' prejudiced attitudes towards clients with learning disabilities.

The last part of this chapter will consider the care of individuals experiencing delirium.

The individual with delirium

Delirium

Delirium (also called acute confusional state and toxic confusional state) is a condition which usually lasts for a few hours to a few days, and has an underlying physical cause. It can occur at any age, but is commonest in young children and older people and is more frequent in men. The individual has alterations or changes in alertness and consciousness (Macleod 2007; Royal College of Physicians and British Geriatric Society 2006). She or he has difficulty in sustaining or focusing attention, and has impairment of 'short term memory' (O'Keeffee 1999, p. 5), that is, finding it hard to remember things which have happened recently. The person also has a lack of 'orientation for time' (O'Keeffee 1999, p. 5), and has little idea of the approximate time of day, week or year. She or he may be lethargic and depressed or agitated and aggressive (Macleod 2007; Royal College of Physicians and British Geriatric Society 2006).

Delirium tremens is a condition occurring in individuals who are dependent on alcohol, but who suddenly withdraw from it, e.g., because they cannot access supplies because of acute illness or other reasons. Besides the other features of delirium, the individual experiences often terrifying visual hallucinations of many small insects or animals, and experiences severe shaking and anxiety. She or he may be violent or aggressive, e.g., attempting to fight the hallucinatory creatures (Kipping 2009; Rassool and Winnington 2006) or because of 'paranoid delusions' (Kipping 2009, p. 495) that other people wish to harm her or him. Delirium tremens is now uncommon, although some individuals experience milder forms of alcohol withdrawal (Healy 2005).

In delirium, the client's speech is difficult to follow, and hard to understand, with statements that do not appear logically connected. However, the connections may be more obvious if time is spent communicating with the client, and this may reduce anxiety and aggression. Delusions and hallucinations (defined on p 108) are common, particularly when it is dark. Visual hallucinations can involve seeing things which may be frightening. The individual may be uncertain what is 'real' and 'unreal' (Macleod 2007; O'Keeffee 1999; Royal College of Physicians and British Geriatric Society 2006), as was found by Andersson et al. (2002) in interviews with people who had experienced delirium.

... the patients experienced themselves as being in a vacuum, or a torpor and/or slumbering ... the surroundings were experienced through a mist.

... Both the confusion in itself and the content that was revealed in their thoughts and 'dreams' during the confusion were experienced as real and at the same time unreal, which

gave rise to uncertainty about whether the scene really happened, which was frightening for some …
(Andersson *et al.* 2002, p. 656)

Risk factors for developing delirium are indicated in Box 11.2. Many of the conditions listed affect the functioning of the brain because of, for example, lack of oxygen as a result of heart failure, toxins from infections and lack of nutrients from lack of adequate nutrition which may accompany, or be caused by, problematic and heavy drinking (Macleod 2007; Royal College of Physicians and British Geriatric Society 2006).

Box 11.2

Risk factors for developing delirium

- Commoner in young children, older people and men
- Infections and high temperature, especially in older people and young children
- Dementia
- Severe and multiple physical illness
- Visual difficulties
- Effects of medication
- Problematic alcohol use, resulting in delirium tremens and milder forms of alcohol withdrawal
- Dehydration
- Poor nutrition
- Heart failure
- Both hypertension (high blood pressure) and hypotension (low blood pressure)
- Fractures (especially of the femur in older people)
- Depression
- Low social interaction

(Macleod 2007; Rahkonen *et al.* 2001; Royal College of Physicians and British Geriatric Society 2006)

Interventions in caring for individuals with delirium

In caring for individuals with delirium, there is an overlap between meeting clients' physical and psychological needs and preventing and reducing aggression. Nursing, medical and other professional care, to meet the individual's physical needs and treat the underlying cause, will help to reduce both the delirium, and concomitant agitation and aggression (Macleod 2007; Royal College of Physicians and British Geriatric Society 2006). For example, antibiotics would reduce the number of toxins affecting the brain and producing delirium in a child or older person with a high temperature. Sponging with tepid water would not only help to reduce the client's heat and discomfort, but possibly be experienced as soothing and reassuring. A client with severe heart and/or lung failure might become aggressive because insufficient oxygen is reaching her or his brain. The giving of oxygen, and measures such as sitting the client upright in bed with plenty of pillows (unless this is contraindicated) could reduce both the delirium and any accompanying aggression, as well as improve the client's physical health (Macleod 2007; Naldrett 2007; Royal College of Physicians and British Geriatric Society 2006).

Anticipating, and meeting the client's needs, especially when she or he may not be able to express them, may also reduce agitation and aggression in delirium and delirium tremens. This can include realising that the individual is in pain and providing medication to relieve it; or that she or he needs a drink, a bedpan or access to spectacles or hearing aid. Symptoms of delirium, including aggression, were considerably reduced in one client once her serious constipation was treated (Byrne, 1997; Macleod, 2007; Royal College of Physicians and British Geriatric Society, 2006)

Interventions in caring for individuals with delirium tremens

For a client with delirium tremens undergoing detoxification (withdrawal from alcohol), plenty of fluids and adequate nutrition are essential and make the process as safe and comfortable for the client as possible (Rassool and Winnington 2006). Both excessive alcohol and an accompanying lack of Vitamin B2 (thiamine, British National Formulary 2009), minerals and other nutrients can affect the functioning of the brain and produce delirium, so a nourishing diet and extra Vitamin B2 is given. In addition, adequate (non-alcoholic) fluids and nutritious food could relieve a dry mouth and other distressing symptoms and this could contribute to the prevention or lessening of aggression. Agitation and aggression, and the other very distressing effects of alcohol withdrawal could also be reduced by enabling detoxification through prescribing a reducing regimen of a long-acting benzodiazepine (diazepam or chlordiazepoxide) over a period of about a week. 'Close monitoring of the client is required because of the risks if he or she drinks alcohol while taking benzodiazepines, and because of the severe complications that can be associated with withdrawal (for example, seizures)' (Kipping 2004, p. 507). Detoxification for new prisoners is described as unsatisfactory in some prisons, but others provide continuous input by nurses (HM Inspector of Prisons 2009a).

Communication skills with individuals with delirium and delirium tremens

Many of the communication skills with individuals with dementia and acquired brain injury, outlined in Chapter 10, are relevant to the care of individuals experiencing delirium and delirium tremens. They include the worker's introduction of her or himself by name, active listening, speaking clearly, but quietly, and in short sentences and giving information briefly, avoiding overloading the client. It is also important to be prepared to repeat information, without impatience, and to recognise that the client has difficulty remembering. Impatience is likely to increase agitation and may precipitate or increase aggression (Byrne 1997; Macleod 2007; Royal College of Physicians 2006). 'Reassurance and explanation' (Byrne 1997, p. 180) may be helpful, especially if the client is very anxious, with the sensitive use of touch if the individual finds this comforting. It may, however, be seen as threatening, especially in individuals with delirium tremens and paranoid delusions (Kipping 2009).

Empathy is needed to attempt to understand the client's experiences, as indicated by Andersson *et al.* (2002) in the following extract:

> ... The findings ... indicate that what takes place during the acute confusional state [i.e., delirium] is not nonsense, but probably a mix of the patient's life history, their present situation, and above all, a form of communication concerning their emotional state and inner experience in this new situation...
>
> (Andersson *et al.* 2002, p. 662)

Practical experience and the literature suggest that causes of anxiety, such as visual hallucinations, should be acknowledged, not dismissed. It may be helpful to assure individuals that they are safe, and to provide orientation to remind the client where she or he is, the name of the staff member working with her or him, or the time of day. One of the authors found that one man with delirium tremens was able to accept assurances that the small insects he was perceiving were the result of alcohol withdrawal. However, some clients may not be able to accept or believe explanations or orientation. Contradicting or arguing with the client is likely to cause distress, and precipitate or escalate aggression, and should be avoided. Interpreters should be provided for clients who do not understand or speak English or who are communicating in another first language. Not being able to understand other people could add to the isolation and agitation experienced by individuals with delirium (Tribe and Raval 2003).

From their research, Fagerberg and Jonhagen (2002) provide findings which may aid understanding of the reasons for some clients' aggression as a result of delirium:

> Aggressiveness was a way of handling the threat the informants felt ...Irritation and aggression were directed towards staff who did not show consideration and understanding for the feelings of threat the informants were trying to express ...

> [Clients'] experience of threat is something nurses and [other] health care professionals must take into account when caring for temporarily confused patients).

> An awareness of the reasoning that lies behind the patients' behaviour could contribute to an understanding of why patients can become aggressive ...
> (Fagerberg and Jonhagen 2002, pp. 342 and 344).

Byrne (1997) comments that most requisite communication skills '...require time, which may be in short supply ... The lack of such an investment in time will, however, not only worsen the patient's mental state, but inevitably require more staff time later ...' (Byrne 1997, p. 180).

The use of bed rails and alternatives with older people

In some services, bed rails (sometimes called 'cot sides' or 'bed sides') and other restraints are used to prevent older people with delirium or dementia from being aggressive or violent towards others, and/or from harming themselves. The use of bed rails should be based on a risk assessment of whether or not they reduce agitation or aggression. In some instances, this may be increased, with the individual feeling trapped, imprisoned or disempowered (Darcy 2007; Naldrett 2007; Royal College of Nursing 2008). Darcy (2007) reports that the use of bed rails in one facility for older people was reduced following staff training on assessment and alternative interventions. Bed rails may provide comfort and safety for some individuals with delirium, as well as safety for others, but the literature suggests their use should be based on individualised assessments, rather than being used for all people with delirium (Darcy 2007; Naldrett 2007; Royal College of Nursing 2008). Other interventions, including care that meets individuals' physical needs, effective communication skills and the provision of a safe, beneficial environment may be more likely to ensure safety. The Royal College of Physicians (2006, p. 9) guidelines state that physical restraint must never be used with older people with delirium and propose 'keeping the use of sedatives and major tranquillisers to a minimum', as these drugs can precipitate or worsen delirium in these individuals. However, the guidelines recommend gradually increasing doses of Haloperidol (an antipsychotic: major tranquilliser for people with mental illness) for older people with delirium and aggressive or violent behaviours.

Providing a safe, beneficial environment for individuals with delirium and delirium tremens

If individuals with delirium and delirium tremens are cared for in single rooms, other staff should be readily available and contactable if there is violence or aggression. Delirium may be reduced if clients have access to spectacles/contact lenses and hearing aids, and it is ensured that these are working. Avoidance of an over-stimulating environment, with excessive noise and light, has been recommended. The Royal College of Physicians (2006) recommend the following:

- 'Appropriate lighting levels for time of day.'
- 'Use of clocks and calendars.'
- 'Continuity of care from nursing staff.'
- 'Encourage ... mobility and engagement in activities and with other people.'
- The client should 'be approached and handled gently.'

- 'Encouragement of visits from family and friends' may reduce anxiety and disorientation.
- Give the client's family information and 'encourage [them] to bring in familiar objects and pictures from home'.
- Enable sleep at night ('use milky drinks at bedtime, exercise during the day').

(Royal College of Physicians 2006, p. 9)

Conclusion

This chapter has considered various aspects of clients' physical health needs, and their relevance in preventing and reducing violence and aggression. The next chapter reviews various psychotherapeutic approaches.

Chapter 12
Psychosocial interventions, including cognitive behavioural therapy

The next two chapters will consider selected psychotherapies and related approaches and their role in preventing and reducing violence and aggression. Psychosocial interventions, including cognitive behavioural therapy are described in Chapter 12. In Chapter 13, we will consider behavioural therapy, mentalisation-based therapy, empathic anger management, psychodynamic psychotherapy and therapeutic community principles.

Psychotherapy has been described (Moyo 2008, p. 89, citing Barker 1999) as including:

> ... a number of interventions, all of which use talking and listening to bring about relief from distress. Barker (1999) defines psychotherapy as psychological treatment of problems of living, by a trained person, within the context of a professional relationship, involving removing, reducing or modifying specific emotional, cognitive or behavioural problems, and/or by promoting social adaptation, personality development and/or personal growth. Psychotherapy may be conducted with individuals, groups or families.

Types of psychotherapy for individuals with violent and aggressive behaviours have any or all of the following aims, depending on the type of psychotherapy (Aiyegbusi and Clarke-Moore 2009; Dryden 2007; Gabbard *et al.* 2007; Jones 2004; O'Donahue and Graybar 2008):

- Providing support, empathy, unconditional positive regard.
- Helping the individual to more effectively understand her or himself and the reasons for their violence and aggression.
- Ascertain the causative and contributory factors and triggers of violence and aggression.

- Enable the individual to safely express anger, and underlying feelings, such as depression, anxiety and bereavement.
- Help the client to recognise and develop positive coping strategies and strengths.
- Aid her or him in identifying specific problems related to the expression of anger and related areas.
- Enable the individual to find practical ways of managing anger, recognise positive and creative aspects of this emotion and aid her or him to express this assertively, rather than aggressively or passively (avoid 'bottling it up', see Chapter 1).
- Apply the insights gained in psychotherapy to practical situations in everyday life, what Maxwell Jones called 'living-learning situations' (Jones 1968).

Some types of psychotherapy have other aims, and these will be considered during this chapter and Chapter 13. All psychotherapy requires the informed consent of the client, except that some forms of behavioural therapy may be used with the agreement of a carer at home or an advocate, if a client does not have the capacity to consent (Mandelstam 2009; Richards and Mughal 2009), e.g., because of severe learning disability or the later stages of dementia.

Psychosocial interventions for individuals with mental illness

Individuals with mental illness

In the broadest sense, the term 'psychosocial' can refer to any interventions which take account of psychological and social aspects of the individual's life and health (Barker 2009). Within mental health services, psychosocial interventions usually refer to a group of approaches aimed to prevent or reduce 'stress' and 'distress' experienced by individuals with mental illness, and/or particular 'problems and symptoms' (Byrt 2007, p. 57), including violence and aggression (Rogers and Vidgen 2006). Psychosocial interventions are also used to prevent 'relapse or an exacerbation of symptoms' (Byrt 2007, p. 57). A wide range of therapies is included within psychosocial interventions, the most frequent involving cognitive behavioural therapy, including approaches to anger management (Rogers and Vidgen 2006) and psychoeducation (sometimes called illness education).

The following account illustrates the use of psychosocial

interventions with 'Ms Amrit Kaur', a young woman of 27 who generally enjoys spending time with her family, listening to music and cooking. Amrit has occasionally worked in catering, although none of her jobs have lasted more than a few months. Amrit sometimes enjoys going to the gym. She is very fond of animals and has a pet cat at home. Since the age of 17, Amrit has had three brief admissions to hospital, followed by community interventions. Over the last 18 months, Amrit has been an inpatient in an acute mental health unit, and subsequently, in a treatment and recovery service for people with mental illness and has now chosen to live at home with her parents. Amrit sometimes has command hallucinations (auditory hallucinations which tell her to attack people to prevent them from harming her (Maden 2007)). On two occasions four years ago, she attacked her sister (who does not live at home) because she believed she was influencing her thoughts, although there was no evidence that this was the case. Amrit's belief that her sister and other women wish to harm her (when there is no evidence that this is the case) is known as a paranoid delusion (Ryan 2009).

Note the description, above, of Amrit as an individual, not just a 'client with schizophrenia'. Some writers on psychosocial interventions emphasise an approach which is concerned with the whole person, including her or his significant relationships and their strengths, aptitudes and goals, which can positively influence psychosocial interventions (Gamble and Brennan 2006a; Gamble and Ryrie with Curthoys 2009). These are also the concern of recovery approaches which emphasise that individuals should not be seen solely in terms of risk, signs and symptoms and 'problems', but as individuals with various aspirations, talents, and roles: e.g., 'daughter', 'girlfriend', 'skilled cook' and 'Kings of Leon fan' (Perkins and Repper 2009; Tew 2005; Watkins 2007). At the same time, the present authors suggest that workers' commitment to recovery principles can coexist with approaches that endeavour to relieve individuals' distress, enable them to find solutions to problems, and assess and manage risk effectively.

Assessment

When Amrit left the Treatment and Recovery Service to live with her parents, Priti, the professional working with Amrit, undertook a thorough assessment, with her participation, to identify her

Assessment

specific strengths, needs and problems and how these related to her management of anger. Risk assessments and other assessments (see Box 12.1) were conducted during Amrit's stay at the treatment and recovery service, before she left, and whilst she was living at home. From these risk and other assessments, the following conclusions were arrived at:

- During the first few months of Amrit's stay in the Treatment and Recovery Service, she had difficulty in expressing anger verbally because of thought block: 'a sudden stoppage of all thoughts' (Craig 2006, p. 92), and a feature of her schizo-phrenia. The thought block resulted in Amrit's initial difficulty in articulating anger verbally, which appeared partly to explain a few violent episodes which occurred soon after her admission to the Treatment and Recovery Service. However, Amrit no longer experienced thought block (probably because this had responded to her Olanzapine, a type of atypical antipsychotic medication (Healy 2005)). She said she found it helpful to talk about her voices, associated anxiety and aggression, and related experiences.

- Amrit's risk to her sister was reduced, as she had not experienced command hallucinations telling her to attack her during the last four years and did not have paranoid delusions about her. Her sister lived over 100 miles from Amrit and her parents.

- She still had command hallucinations telling her to attack others, but the voices were not specific about particular people (targets) she should attack. She also had some paranoid delusions about young women in general, but these were not focused on anyone in particular. (Care was taken to establish that Amrit had not been abused or otherwise harmed by women, either in the past or present.)

- Amrit had never experienced command hallucinations telling her to attack her parents, or any thoughts of doing so.

- Over the last 18 months, Amrit had not acted on the command hallucinations by assaulting anyone.

- However, she was distressed by the command hallucinations, and sometimes anxious that she might act on them, but did not have thoughts of harming or killing herself.

- Amrit and her parents were keen to live together as a family, although they recognised that sometimes there were arguments and disagreements about how Amrit should be spending her time. All three agreed that they were concerned at the extent to which they shouted at each other, and Amrit said that this made her voices worse and made it more difficult to concentrate or 'think straight', an example of sensory overload. In the Treatment and Recovery Service, Amrit's anxiety and occasional violence appeared to be triggered by a combination of distressing and intrusive voices and thoughts and times when other residents were aggressive and the ward was noisy (Byrt 2007).

- Amrit was not at risk of neglecting herself, was motivated to achieve her goals and aspirations, and had the love and support of her family.

- Previous adverse experiences with professionals or services may make it difficult for some clients to trust staff enough to feel able to talk about distressing symptoms and other problems (Gamble and Brennan 2006a; Gamble et al. 2009). In addition, many clients from minority ethnic groups have found that mental health services are insensitive, and fail to take account of their cultural or spiritual needs and the ways they perceive their distress (Marrington-Mir and Rimmer 2007; Sewell 2009). Consequently, these individuals may not have the outlet of safe, verbal expression of their anger and other feelings. The extent to which Amrit and her parents found the service culturally sensitive was assessed, and they indicated their satisfaction with this area.

Box 12.1

Assessments of Amrit's strengths, needs, problems and symptoms

The following assessments were made of Amrit's strengths, needs, problems and symptoms:

- 'Health of the Nation' (HoNOS) Scale. Includes a 'social functioning' scale.
- 'Social Functioning Scale' (SFS). 'It covers seven main areas of social functioning, [including] social engagement [and] interpersonal behaviour … It can provide a guide to goals and interventions'
- 'Manchester Symptom Severity Scale' (KGV). 'It identifies the type and

severity of psychiatric symptoms ... A KGV assessment provides a global measure of common psychiatric symptoms (feelings/thoughts) experienced with a psychosis'

- 'Positive and Negative Syndrome Scale' (PANSS). This assesses positive symptoms (which include hallucinations and delusions, and negative symptoms, including the extent, for example, to which people feel motivated, have difficulty in thinking, or have flatness in mood, with difficulty experiencing enjoyment or interest.
- 'Schedule for the Assessment of Negative Symptoms'
- 'Delusions Rating Scale ... Consists of six items which range from the amount of preoccupation to the intensity of distress and disruption'
- 'Beliefs About Voices Questionnaire'.
- 'Auditory Hallucinations Rating Scale ... Addresses distress control and belief re origin of voices, in addition to how client experiences voices'

(Quotations above are from Gamble and Brennan 2006b, p. 121)

After four weeks at home with her parents, Amrit's assessment revealed various effective coping strategies and problems. These will be considered in relation to particular interventions:

Family interventions

Priti asked Amrit and her parents, Mrs Kaur and Mr Singh, if they would like to reduce the amount of apparent tension and anger within the family, and the resulting distress that all three said that this caused them. Professionals must obtain clients' informed consent to all psychosocial interventions, and this was the case with Amrit and her parents. Family interventions, a type of psychosocial intervention, were started, with weekly sessions in the home. Amrit and her parents were asked to record both happy and enjoyable events in the family, and events resulting in tension and anger (Gamble *et al.* 2009; Gillam 2001).

The diary and subsequent discussions revealed that all three family members, especially Amrit, felt happier when she was left to her own devices and choices about how to spend her time. Mrs Kaur and Mr Singh led very busy lives at both work and home, but both parents and Amrit particularly enjoyed the rare times when they went out together and shared a relaxing activity such as a film. In contrast, Mrs Kaur and Mr Singh felt very anxious if Amrit stayed in bed until mid-morning and refused breakfast (a problem explored by Gamble *et al.* 2009) or did not participate in household tasks. This sometimes resulted in violent shouting between Amrit and her parents, and in addition, there were sometimes loud disagreements between Mrs Kaur and Mr Singh about how to tackle what they saw as Amrit's 'problems'. Similar family dynamics have been described in the literature (Gamble *et al.* 2009; Gillam 2001; Kuipers *et al.* 2002).

In her interventions with the family, Priti needed to be very sensitive to their culture, including what they felt to be familial norms and expectations and how they perceived anger and other emotions, and their expression (Sewell 2009). This is part of psychoeducation (sometimes called illness education), which arguably, should include the professional learning from the family, including the identified client, as well as giving information to the family to consider (Gamble *et al.* 2009; Keen and Barker 2009). Priti explained about the role of high expressed emotion in contributing to a worsening or a recurrence of symptoms of schizophrenia. She outlined how high expressed emotion consists of over-involvement and considerable aggressive anger and hostility from either family members or professionals towards the individual, who then experiences greater levels of stress (Byrt 2007; Gamble *et al.* 2009; Keen and Barker 2009). Priti mentioned a study which found that individuals with schizophrenia in India had lower relapse rates than those in London and that this related to the amount of expressed emotion in the home (Leff 2001). In explaining this, Priti endeavoured to be non-judgemental, and indicated, through her non-verbal and verbal communication, that she was not blaming Amrit or her parents and that she recognised the stress that they could experience. (Sadly, blame has been experienced by some carers of individuals with schizophrenia (Fisher 2003).) Amrit said that she wasn't surprised that her parents were stressed when she spent long periods in bed, but sometimes she didn't feel motivated. 'And what is there to get up for?' she said.

Finding solutions as a family

Priti asked Amrit, Mrs Kaur and Mr Singh whether they thought high expressed emotion was relevant to their situation. They said that it made a lot of sense, although, as Mr Singh rightly said to Priti: 'If you lived here, your expressed emotion would probably be high as well.' Priti acknowledged that that was possible.

The family discussed with Priti how expressed emotion could be reduced. The following action was agreed:

- As the family enjoyed going out together, it was agreed that Amrit, Ms Kaur and Mr Singh would watch a film and go out for a meal once a week.

- It was agreed, in line with Amrit's request, that if she was not up, Ms Kaur would call her only twice, at 9.00 am and 9.30 am before setting out for work. (This example is based on Gamble *et al.* 2009). She would not insist that Amrit had breakfast.

- Amrit would explore, initially with Priti, reasons to get up in the morning. Amrit said she would like to do a catering course and eventually, return to her work as a cook. Vocational rehabilitation, including supported employment, is an aspect of psychosocial interventions (Droughton and Williams 2002) and has been an important part of treatment in the Van der Hoeven Clinic, Utrecht, a secure hospital for people with histories of violent offending (Wiertsema and Derks 1997). Amrit stated, and her parents and Priti agreed, that attending a catering course and working in the café in a local community centre might provide distraction from her command hallucinations and thoughts of harming other people.

- Not all people with schizophrenia find medication helpful (Healy 2005). However, Amrit felt that her antipsychotic medication had helped her symptoms to some extent, and was keen to continue taking it. She mentioned that she tended to forget to take it, so a medication concordance progamme was introduced. This psychosocial intervention is usually called a medication compliance programme (McCann 2001; Zygmunt 2002). Priti and Amrit preferred the term concordance, as this represented a shared decision by Amrit, her consultant psychiatrist and Priti, about the type and doses of medication that would be most helpful (Keen and Barker 2009). The medication concordance programme included replacing bottles of tablets with a dosset box, with clearly marked compartments for different times and days of the month (Butt *et al.* 2008). Various aids to memory were also devised. For example, one dose was due immediately after Amrit's daily favourite television programme, so a large coloured note was placed on top of the television in her bedroom.

Outcome of these psychosocial interventions

Priti continued to work with Amrit and her family over several months. Despite some setbacks over this time, the following positive outcomes occurred:

- The family felt that it had not been possible to go out for a film and meal every week, but they had been able to achieve this more frequently than in the past. They agreed that these had been relaxing events which had strengthened their relationship and reduced tension.

- Mrs Kaur sometimes found it hard to resist calling Amrit more than twice in the morning, but Amrit was getting up more frequently to attend her catering course and her voluntary work in the community centre. She was also thinking of applying for a part-time catering job in a local sandwich bar.

Cognitive behavioural therapy

CBT

Cognitive behavioural therapy (CBT) was another psychosocial intervention used with Amrit. Box 12.2 summarises some of the main features of CBT. (See, also, Clarke and Wilson 2009; Simmons and Griffiths 2009.)

Box 12.2

Cognitive Behavioural Therapy

'Cognitive behavioural therapy (CBT) aims to:

- Assess and measure precisely:
  - The nature and frequency of a particular problem [e.g., aggression] or symptom.
  - The distress associated with this problem or symptom.
  - Any stressors (i.e., things that cause stress) and other triggers that seem to precipitate the problem [e.g., aggression] or symptom.
- Use specific, clearly stated interventions to reduce or relieve symptoms, problems and associated distress and stress.
- Focus, not only on individuals' problems and symptoms, but on their strengths and positive coping strategies. In CBT, ideally, individuals should be enabled to recognize and develop these, and to use them to resolve or reduce symptoms and problems.
- Use precise measures to assess the extent that the interventions have been successful in reducing or alleviating symptoms or problems and/or associated stress and distress.'

(From: Bowness et al. 2008, p. 224, citing Doyle et al. 2006; Rogers and Vidgen 2006)

Amrit remained distressed by her command hallucinations (voices telling her to attack other people (Maden 2007)) and paranoid delusions (suspicious beliefs that other young women would harm her, when there was no evidence that this had ever happened in the past or present). By the time she was referred for CBT, Amrit had managed to stop herself from responding to the command hallucinations over the previous two years, and had not thought of harming her sister.

During the first stage of Amrit's CBT, there was a two week assessment of the following:

- The frequency and intensity of her command hallucinations (voices). Frequency here refers to how often the voices occurred. Amrit was asked to record the time of day and the date that she experienced the voices.

- The intensity of her voices. Amrit was asked to rate the intensity on a scale of 1 (very low) to 10 (very high). Intensity here refers to how prominent the voices were: from very intrusive to being in the distant background or not present, and from very loud to very soft.

- The amount of anxiety and anger she felt in response to them. Anxiety and anger were each measured on a scale of 1 to 10.

- Whether Amrit's anger was assertive (a creative response to the voices, e.g., channelling anger through a workout in the gym) or involved aggressive thoughts (e.g., of harming others) or violent response (e.g., shouting at someone or hitting them. Chapter 1 considers differences between assertion and aggression.

- Triggers: things which appeared to precipitate or worsen the voices.

- Positive coping strategies used by Amrit, which reduced the intensity of the voices, and/or the accompanying anxiety and anger.

Once the initial assessment of the above was completed, Anna, the cognitive behavioural therapist, and Priti discussed with Amrit possible strategies that she could use to reduce the intensity of the voices and her anxiety and anger. These included the following, which were included in a multidisciplinary care plan:

- Distraction, with Amrit spending time with her cat, listening to Kings of Leon music, and cooking. Amrit found these activities soothing and relaxing (Byrt 2007). The initial assessment showed that intensity of voices, anxiety and anger was worse when Amrit was lying on her bed in the daytime and better when she was engaged in activities that she found enjoyable. (However, it was acknowledged that, at times, lying on her bed for short periods could be an effective way for Amrit to relax and recover (Byrt, 2007).)

- Channelling anger and anxiety and reducing stress. In line with research findings, going to the gym helped Amrit to reduce the stress caused by her voices, and effectively channelled her anger in a positive and enjoyable way, which lifted Amrit's mood (Biddle and Mutrie 2008; Faulkner and Taylor 2005).

- Listening to a relaxation tape helped Amrit to reduce psycho-logical and physical arousal through guided imagery (enabling relaxing thoughts) and reducing tension in various muscles (Muir-Cochrane 2009).

- When required ('pro re nata', PRN) medication could also have been used, but Amrit, Priti, Anna and her consultant psychiatrist all agreed that this was unnecessary

Evaluation and outcome

The success of these measures was assessed by asking Amrit to rate the intensity of the voices, her anxiety and anger on a scale of 1 to 10 before and after each intervention. Six months after her sessions with Anna, the cognitive behavioural therapist, had ended, and with the continued use of the strategies, Amrit reported marked decreases in the intensity of voices, and far less concomitant anxiety and anger. It was found that listening to Kings of Leon music and going to the gym were the most helpful strategies, overall. One of the changes that most pleased Amrit was her part-time job cooking in a supermarket café. 'I've now got more reasons to get up', she commented.

Amrit also reported less frequent and less intrusive command hallucinations, and her paranoid delusions about other young women harming her largely disappeared. Amrit, her parents and the professional team agreed that improvements were probably as a result of the combination of psychosocial interventions and antipsychotic medication. This was in line with NICE (2009) guidelines on the treatment of individuals with schizophrenia, which argues that research findings suggest that this combination produces the best outcomes. However, Raguram *et al.* (2002) found that many individuals with schizophrenia made good recoveries, without medication, in a low expressed emotion environment in a Hindu temple.

CBT to explore clients' experiences of hallucinations and delusions

Another use of CBT, not used with Amrit, 'is exclusively focused on beliefs and ongoing patterns of thinking' (Birchwood and Jackson 2001, p. 121):

> ... Therapist and client collaborate to explore the meanings that [clients] attribute to events. They examine the evidence for and against specific beliefs, meanings or attributions; devise challenges to habitual patterns of thinking and reacting; and employ logical reasoning, and other neglected, personal experiences to develop more rational and effective alternative responses...
>
> (Keen and Barker 2009, p. 221)

For example, one individual, known to one of the authors, had considerable anxiety and thoughts of assaulting people wearing combat clothes, as he had the delusional belief that these people had been sent by the Ministry of Defence to attack him. CBT was used to help him question the nature of these beliefs. Over time, he was able to realise that people wearing combat clothing were not 'out to get him'. His anxiety and his thoughts of attacking such people gradually diminished, and eventually disappeared.

CBT would be used in this way only if:

- such approaches did not increase the individual's distress
- the individual felt ready to explore delusions, hallucinations and other symptoms (this was usually the case with the individual concerned, but the professional working with him did not insist that he think in certain ways)
- the individual would be likely to be at a recovery stage, rather than experiencing the effects of acute schizophrenia (this was true of the individual described above; when he had, on one occasion, a relapse of psychotic symptoms, the CBT was temporarily discontinued).

A critique of CBT

There are many programmes referred to as 'anger management', most of which include components of CBT (Bede *et al.* 2008; Bowness *et al.* 2008). Anger management programmes have, for example, been widely used in prisons (HM Prison Service 2009). Reviews of CBT anger management are reported to have high levels of success (Bowness *et al.* 2008; Rogers and Vidgen 2006, citing Beck and Fernandez 1998) and, it has been argued, should be far more available to the general public (Mental Health Foundation 2008). 'Anger management' recently appears to be commonly used in everyday speech; and has even been the topic of a 2009 television advertisement for a well known chain of fast food outlets (Alarcon 2009).

However, critics have argued that CBT proponents perceive 'anger' and 'anger management' in simplistic ways, without appreciating the complexity of aggression and causative and contributory factors (Joseph 2001; Parker-Hall 2009):

> Although the research evidence is generally taken to support the effectiveness of cognitive-behavioural approaches ... there have been critics. Some question the extent to which the research findings can be generalised to routine clinical settings and say that the approach has been overhyped ...Others are more critical. Smail (1996), for example, writes:
>
> > 'Cognitive behaviourism' embod[ies] an ... extraordinarily simplistic collection of ideas about how people come to be the way they are, and what they can be expected to do about it ... Such ideas ... ring particularly hollow when they come to be applied in the clinical setting, where people's difficulties are often complex and intractable ...' (Smail, 1996)
>
> ... Behaviour therapies have traditionally been neglectful of the social setting in which therapy takes place and of the relationship which develops between the therapist and the client, although more recent writers in the behavioural tradition have begun to recognise the importance of the therapeutic relationship...
>
> (Joseph 2001, p. 112, quoting Smail 1996)

CBT has been criticised for imposing views and values, rather than enabling individuals to arrive at their own solutions to problems, including managing anger. This has been seen as related to imbalances in power between client and therapist, with an emphasis on the latter's 'expertise' and on clients' 'maladaptive' methods of coping, rather than on their positive attributes (Fox 1999; Parker-Hall 2009). The emphasis on negative behaviours has been seen by Parker-Hall (2009) as being judgemental, and failing to value and validate the individual's potential to develop positive coping strategies and solutions. However, some cognitive behavioural therapists emphasise the latter (Bowness *et al.* 2008). Fox (1999) outlines her research findings that prisoners were 'forced' to accept psychologists' cognitive-behavioural explanations of their (the prisoners') aggressive and other behaviours, in order to get parole. Failure to accept these explanations could be interpreted as negative, and lacking commitment to therapy. In contrast, six clients in a medium security ward using CBT describe mainly positive effects. These authors emphasise the importance of clients finding their own solutions to managing anger, rather than have these imposed on them, but also describe power imbalances between clients and professionals (Bede *et al.* 2008).

Conclusion

This chapter has considered psychosocial interventions, including cognitive behavioural therapy, particularly related to the care, treatment and recovery of one individual. The next chapter will consider other types of psychotherapy and therapeutic communities as a setting in which psychotherapy is practised.

Chapter 13
Other types of psychotherapy and therapeutic communities

This chapter reviews a few of the many psychotherapies used in the prevention and reduction of violence and aggression. Behavioural therapy, mentalisation-based therapy, empathic anger management are outlined. The chapter concludes with a consideration of psychodynamic psychotherapy and therapeutic community principles, with reference to the care and treatment of one individual.

Behavioural therapy

Behavioural therapy

Behavioural therapy focuses mostly on the individual's behaviours, rather than on the accompanying thoughts and feelings (McKenzie 2008; Royal College of Psychiatrists *et al.* 2007), as is the case with cognitive behavioural therapy (Clarke and Wilson 2009; Simmons and Griffiths 2009), which was considered in the last chapter. Slevin (2007) provides an overview of the application of behavioural therapy, using functional analysis (outlined later in this chapter), in the care of individuals with learning disabilities and 'challenging behaviours', including violence and aggression. Shlosberg (2003, p. 95, citing Teri and Gallagher-Thompson 1991) points out that, whilst cognitive behavioural therapy 'highlights the association between thoughts, feelings and behaviours ... those individuals with advanced young onset [or older onset] dementia may benefit from a more behavioural focus, whereas cognitive approaches are more appropriate from early stage dementia'.

Behavioural therapy, and later, cognitive behavioural therapy have been developed, as a set of treatment approaches, since the early twentieth century. To begin with, behavioural therapy was restricted to treatment based on classical and operant conditioning.

Behavioural therapy is an attempt to change behaviour which is perceived to be maladaptive, including violence and aggression. It does so by drawing on the methods used, and the findings made, by experimental psychologists in their study of both normal and abnormal behaviour (Curwen *et al.* 2000).

Operant conditioning, the development of behavioural therapy and its relevance to the present

Occasionally, the term 'behaviour modification' has been used interchangeably with behaviour therapy. Therapists using operant conditioning as a means of treatment have often preferred this term (Curwen *et al.* 2000). Others, at least in the past, have argued that the term 'behavioural therapy' should be used to distinguish this approach from others (Kring and Davison 2007). In the 1950s, several researchers suggested that therapists could change overt behaviour, such as aggression, though reward and punishment (Skinner 1953). In the belief that therapists could, through operant conditioning, exercise some control over the often complex and frenetic behaviour of some hospitalised patients, many experimentally minded psychologists determined to attempt to bring some order into the chaos of institutions for individuals with severely aggressive behaviours (Kring and Davison 2007). In addition to the familiar use of praise, tokens and food as positive reinforcers and of verbal or physical punishment as negative reinforcers, operant therapists developed other means to establish positive behaviours. The so called 'Premack Principle' held that in a given situation, a more probable behaviour could serve as a reinforcer for a less probable behaviour (Premack 1959). Nowadays, it would be seen as extremely unethical to consider any form of punishment as an appropriate professional response to violence and aggression (Department of Health 2008a) or to see approval, particular foods and other essentials as 'rewards', rather than as rights and essential needs. It is important that methods used in behavioural therapy are not perceived by clients and their families as punitive, do not lead to deprivations of essentials to which people are entitled and result in positive outcomes for clients (Royal College of Psychiatrists, *et al.*, 2007).

The client's perspective in assessments in behavioural therapies

The client's perspectives and experience of the problem should always be emphasised in behavioural, as well as cognitive behavioural therapies (Rogers and Vidgen 2006; Shlosberg 2003). For example, Naldrett (2007) outlines ways that understanding the life history of an individual with dementia helps with appreciation of her or his apparently problematic behaviours, including violence and aggression. Aggressive and apparently 'restless' behaviour may indicate that the individual is orientated to a time in the past when she or he was particularly busy, for example, preparing for a daughter's wedding. Attempts to make the individual 'sit down and rest' and fit into an institutionalised ward or nursing home routine could increase her or his frustration, and possibly potentiate aggression, particularly if it were insisted that the individual sit down (Naldrett 2007).

Appreciation of the individual's life history and perspectives is also emphasised in the literature on individuals with learning disabilities (Royal College of Psychiatrists, *et al.*, 2007; Slevin 2007) and younger people with mental illness (Gamble and Brennan 2006a). A 'life chart' is sometimes completed with clients, as a component of psychosocial interventions. This helps to identify factors in the individual's life which have both increased and reduced stress and thus, the precipitation or worsening of symptoms. Factors protecting against stress are also identified (Gamble and Brennan 2006a).

Functional assessment and functional analysis in behavioural therapy

According to Royal College of Psychiatrists *et al.* (2007, p. 28), in relation to individuals with learning disabilities, 'functional assessment' involves 'structured observation and other methods of behaviour to generate hypotheses [ideas stated in such a way that they can be tested (Gerrish and Lacey 2006)] about the challenging behaviour, antecedents which might be acting as stimuli for the behaviour and consequences which may be reinforcing it. These hypotheses are then tested out ...'.

For example, 'Mr Ezra East' is an individual with a severe learning disability and no communication through words. Through structured observation recording his behaviour, it is observed that his violent behaviours (hitting other people) occur at times when there is a lot of noise, e.g., from other residents at mealtimes or when there is a loud television programme or music. This noise distresses Ezra; he cannot understand the source of the noise or communicate his wish to avoid it. The noise is the antecedent and the consequence is Ezra's hitting people (his behaviour). Based on this functional assessment, it could be ensured that:

- Ezra has his meals on his own or with a few other residents who are generally quiet at mealtimes
- his areas for living, relaxation and activities are relatively quiet, and free from television, music and other noise that he finds distressing, and cannot cope with.

The assessment would establish whether or not these changes to Ezra's environment resulted in less distress, and fewer incidents of violent behaviour. The assessment, and consequent changes to Ezra's environment constitute behavioural therapy. If the underlying thoughts and feelings were to be considered in depth, it would constitute cognitive behavioural therapy (as with Amrit Kaur, see Chapter 12). At the start of his behavioural assessment, it is difficult to understand, in depth, Ezra's feelings and thoughts underlying his behaviour, as he finds it hard to articulate these. For this reason, the behavioural therapy assessment concentrates on Ezra's behaviour. However, the structured observation makes it possible to infer, and better understand, his thoughts and feelings (e.g., related to his dislike of noise) and to take appropriate action to modify his environment.

The difference between functional assessment and functional analysis is considered in Royal College of Psychiatrists *et al.* (2007):

> The terms functional assessment and functional analysis are used interchangeably by some clinicians. Generally, functional assessment is a more inclusive term that refers to a range of approaches to establish the function of the behaviour, while functional analysis refers to more structured techniques that require manipulating antecedents and consequences, in order to establish their functional relationships.
>
> (Royal College of Psychiatrists *et al.* 2007, p. 28)

For example, if functional analysis is used with Ezra, this could involve observing his behaviours and inferred feelings, and perhaps, thoughts, during time in his usual noisy environment, in a setting with minimal noise and in a sensory stimulation room (see Chapter 4) where there were quiet, but pleasant and soothing noises (International Snoezelen Association 2009). Ezra's violent and other behaviours could then be compared in the three environments (Royal College of Psychiatrists *et al.* 2007). Thought would need to be given to the ethics of this environmental manipulation, and whether it would be likely to increase his distress. Informed consent by a relative or advocate would be required (Mandelstam 2009).

Risk assessments and risk management in behavioural therapy, using 'antecedent–behaviour–consequence' (ABC) principles

ABC principles

These principles of assessment are often used in behavioural therapy, as part of a functional assessment or functional analysis, with individuals with learning disability (Kelly 2008; Royal College of Psychiatrists *et al.* 2007; Slevin 2007), dementia (McGeorge 2007; Shlosberg 2003; Stokes 2000) and other mental illnesses (Rogers and Vidgen 2006). Antecedent–Behaviour– Consequence (ABC) principles of assessment include evaluation of:

- Antecedents: factors which appear to precipitate or precede a particular behaviour.
- Behaviour(s): things that people do or say (including violence and aggression).
- Consequences: things that happened as a result of the behaviour, including responses that may have reinforced it (Shlosberg 2003; Slevin 2008).

The application of ABC principles: 'ABC analysis' (from Shlosberg 2003, p. 100)

ABC analysis, as explained by Shlosberg (2003) involves asking a series of questions as listed below. Shlosberg applies this method in relation to people with dementia, but it can also apply to many other clients.

Box 13.1

ABC analysis (from Shlosberg 2003, p. 100)

Date/Time

Antecedent

What were they doing immediately before the behaviour occurred?

Who was there/wasn't there?

Behaviour

Describe precisely what happened.

Where did it occur?

What did the person do?

Consequences

What happened immediately after the incident?

How did others respond?

Background

Has anything happened during the day to cause distress?

Has there been a change in routine?

ABC analysis is, in part, a type of risk assessment tool which measures the extent to which an individual is likely to harm self and/or others and the nature, frequency and intensity of this risk (Maden 2007; Morgan and Wetherell 2009; Woods and Kettles 2009). These sources give further details of risk assessment and prediction.

Assessment, implementation and evaluation of behavioural therapy, like other psychotherapies, require training, education and supervision (McKenzie *et al.* 2006). These authors describe their research on the extent to which staff implemented 'formal behavioural guidelines consistently or appropriately' (McKenzie *et al.* 2006, p. 28). They conclude:

> Even when staff report no difficulty in implementing guidelines, the ability to implement them in practice is low. This suggests a need for a new approach including organisational commitment, staff training and involving the whole team in a collaborative approach.
> (McKenzie *et al.* 2006, p. 32)

Mentalisation-based therapy

Mentalisation-based therapy

According to Bateman and Fonagy (2004), individuals with borderline personality disorder find it difficult to mentalise. Mentalisation has been defined as the interpretation of the individuals':

> own and others' actions ... Mentalisation is the sense we have of ourselves and others around us. Our actions are linked to our mental states: feelings, beliefs, desires and needs. Therefore, when we interact with our environment

and the people within it, we use our understanding of another person's behaviour.

(Gibson 2006, p. 54)

Difficulties with mentalisation in individuals with borderline personality disorder

Individuals with borderline personality disorder experience problems in mentalisation in the following areas, which are relevant to their sense of self and relationships with others:

- The individual has difficulty in recognising that she or he, and other people, are experiencing anger and other feelings.

- This may make it hard for the individual to empathise with others, or to appreciate 'the effects of their behaviour [including violence and aggression] ... on other people' (News-Medical Net 2006).

- It may also be very difficult for the individual to accept, or perhaps, understand other perspectives, including those of staff who work with them. This may make it difficult for the client to benefit from interventions, unless workers attempt to understand her or his difficulties, and adapt their interventions accordingly.

- She or he is likely to attribute her or his own feelings to others, which is known as psychic equivalence. For example:

  - If a client feels angry, they may wrongly assume that the worker is angry, and react to the worker, accordingly.
  - If the client thinks that she or he is a 'worthless person', this may be reflected in her or his assumption that the worker thinks so, too. This may result in the client's rejection of, and hostility towards, the worker.

- This psychic equivalence is related to the individual's difficulty in distinguishing what is his or her own fantasy or imagination and what is happening in external 'reality'.

(Bateman and Fonagy 2004; Gibson 2006; News-Medical.Net 2006).

Reasons for problems with mentalisation in individuals with borderline personality disorder

Reasons relate to childhood environmental factors and biological factors and their influence on self-concept and the development of 'personality disorder':

- The child does not have a satisfactory relationship, with close, attachment to parents (Bateman and Fonagy 2004). (Attachment is considered in Chapter 3 and the next section of this chapter.)

- This includes the way the parents respond (e.g., through violence and aggression) to the child and his or her feelings (Gibson 2006).

- This lack of attachment makes it difficult for the child to:

  - distinguish internal fantasy and imagination from external reality

  - successfully recognise his or her own feelings, including aggression and other forms of anger

  - correctly understand the feelings of others, including whether or not they are angry

  - empathise with others (Bateman and Fonagy 2004)

The role of attachment in developing mentalisation

It has been argued that the recognition of feelings in oneself and others, and the development of empathy, are affected by the extent to which an individual develops attachment to at least one parent figure. Attachment includes the bond between child and parents and the extent to which the latter 'provide safety and security' and 'respond to their children's interactions in a sensitive manner' (Gibson 2006, p. 54), demonstrating interest and engagement with them. Bateman and Fonagy (2004) state that the individual's ability to mentalise is also influenced by 'genetic factors' and 'the physical structure of the brain and processes within it' (Gibson 2006, p. 55, citing Bateman and Fonagy 2004; Gallagher and Frith 2003).

'Mentalisation-based treatment' (Bateman and Fonagy 2004)

Interventions based on mentalisation share the following characteristics. As with therapeutic community principles, there is concentration on considering problems in the 'here and now' (Gibson 2006, p. 55), that is, in the present, rather than the past (Bateman and Fonagy 2004). 'Focusing on the past encourages the patient to remain in the past. The primary aim of the therapist is to assist the patient to mentalise' (Gibson 2006, p. 55). Important goals include validating the client's experience, and taking this seriously, but also, within the context of valuing the individual, questioning her or his perceptions, including enabling her or him to distinguish between untrue fantasies/imaginations about other people and what they think (e.g., that they are thinking aggressive thoughts towards the client) and the 'reality' of who they are and what they actually think. The individual is enabled to monitor and reflect on anger and other feelings and accompanying thinking and other cognitive processes. This is partly achieved through the worker's efforts to 'offer an alternative explanation and develop different insights' (Gibson 2006, p. 55).

Example of the application of mentalisation-based therapy

The worker, who is trained in mentalisation-based therapy, explores with the client specific situations, and her or his perceptions of their own, and other people's interpretations. For example, 'Mr Fred Fonz' clenches his fist and ventilates verbal abuse towards the worker. Underlying this behaviour is Fred's belief that the worker must 'completely hate' him because she has politely apologised for not being able to meet his request immediately.

In mentalisation-based therapy, the worker acknowledges Fred's feelings, but feeds back that she does not hate Fred, feels positively towards him, and has only delayed meeting his request because of an urgent phone call (Bateson and Fonagy 2004; Gibson 2006). This feedback would be given at an appropriate time, and in a way that would not increase further violence

In a randomised controlled trial, patients receiving mentalisation-based therapy were compared with a group of patients receiving 'structured clinical management' (Bateman and Fonagy 2009, p. 1355). Compared with the latter group, people receiving mentalisation-based therapy 'showed a steeper decline of both self-reported and clinically significant problems' (Bateman and Fonagy 2009, p. 1355).

Empathic anger management

Empathic anger management

Client-centred principles of communication are considered in Chapter 6. Client-centred (also called person-centred or humanistic) approaches have informed interventions in services for individuals with learning disabilities (Brewster and Ramcharen 2005), mental health problems (Barker 2009) and older people (Naldrett 2007).

Parker-Hall (2009) describes empathic anger management, based, in part, on Carl Rogers' three core client-centred principles: 'congruence, unconditional positive regard and empathy' (Freeth 2007, p. 127). In empathic anger management, emphasis is placed on listening to the client, and understanding, in a non-judgemental way, the reasons why she or he has difficulties in managing her or his anger.

Parker-Hall (2009) distinguishes between positive aspects of anger (including 'adult rage') and 'hot' and 'cold' rage. 'Adult rage' includes positive anger against injustice and results in 'social activism' (Parker-Hall 2009, p. 182). 'Hot rage', in Parker-Hall's (2009) classification, appears to have similar characteristics to aggression (outlined in Chapter 1). Parker-Hall (2009, p. 90) likens hot rage to a cooking 'pot' whose lid 'flies off', with an expression of anger which others see as aggressive, and which disregards their needs and rights. In contrast, individuals with 'cold rage' (Parker-Hall 2009, p. 91), which appears similar to passive expressions of anger, internalise or 'bottle up' their anger, which is denied. These people may appear unresponsive to other individuals' anger or other feelings and find it difficult to appreciate that the expression of anger could be positive.

Over ten empathic anger management sessions, clients have opportunities to explore the ways they express (or do not express) anger in relation to childhood and later experiences. The client's anger is assessed in the first session, using the 'pot' model. Her or his expression of hot or cold rage is seen, in part, as a way of coping with past or present traumas. The therapist endeavours to be compassionate, take seriously the client's experiences, and help her or him to develop their own solutions and decisions, rather than have these imposed by the therapist. The client's ability to achieve this is stressed. The therapist enables people with hot rage to 'contain' their anger and express it assertively, rather than aggres-sively. Individuals with cold rage are helped to 'recognise and name' (Parker-Hall 2009, p. 113) various emotions, including anger and its physiological concomitants. Parker-Hall stresses the value of individuals and their experiences and emphasises that these should be positively affirmed. The client-centred principles accord with those of therapeutic communities (Byrt 2006; Winship 2009, described later in this chapter), aspects of psychosocial interven-tions described by Gamble et al. (2009), and the tidal model of nursing (Barker and Buchanan-Barker 2005). However, Parker-Hall (2009) could, perhaps, give more consideration to the limitations of empathic anger management. It is also worth considering whether it is possible to combine client-centred principles with other therapeutic interventions. For example, research suggests that individuals with personality disorders benefit from a combination of different therapeutic approaches, rather than a single intervention or type of psychotherapy (Livesley 2007).

Psychodynamic psychotherapy

Psycho-dynamic psychotherapy

Sigmund Freud (1856–1939) is often regarded as the first and perhaps most popular, if controversial, proponent of psychodynamic or psychoanalytic explanations of aggression. Freud (1967) considered aggression to be instinctual and inevitable. He described the energy of 'Thanatos' (the death instinct) as building up within the individual until it is ultimately discharged, either outwardly through overt aggression or inwardly in the form of self-harm. Freud added that society could never eliminate the exhibition of aggressive behaviour, which, he considered, accounted for so many wars throughout human history. However, society could channel and modify its intensity by promoting certain positive emotional attachments between people and through sublimation: a mental defence mechanism enabling individuals to channel and express aggressive, as well as sexual drives, e.g., through engaging in physical exercise and sporting activities or producing aggressive paintings or poems (Freud 1967).

Psychodynamic theory and psychotherapy are based on the work of Sigmund Freud and his followers (Dryden 2007; Gabbard *et al.* 2007). Freud, and some thinkers before him, postulated the existence of various levels of consciousness in the human mind:

- The conscious mind consists of memories and feelings of which we are immediately aware.

- The unconscious mind includes memories and feelings, including those that are distressing to the individual, and conflicts (i.e., problems that cannot be easily resolved, and which result in considerable distress).

- Sigmund Freud and subsequent psychoanalysts and other psychodynamic psychotherapists argued that the unconscious mind influences our behaviour, including the expression of anger, for reasons that are beyond our conscious awareness, that is, the motivations for our behaviour are unconscious. (Dryden 2007; Gabbard *et al.* 2007).

Box 13.2 considers Freud's concept of mental defence mechanisms; and considers their application to workers' responses to clients' violence and aggression:

Box 13.2

The use of mental defence mechanisms by workers and clinical supervision

'In response to stress, an individual may attempt to cope by adopting mental defence mechanisms ... unconscious processes used to cope with negative emotions as found in sustained aggression' (Linsley 2006, p. 88). Defence mechanisms are used by everyone in daily life. They usually enable people to cope effectively, but in certain instances, they may interfere with staff members' ability to communicate with, and respond to clients. Linsley (2006, p. 87) lists several examples. Examples of mental defence mechanisms include the following:

Displacement

A manager does not bother to check how 'Millie', a Care Assistant, is feeling after she has been racially abused by a client. Millie, understandably, feels hurt and angry. Instead of being angry with the manager, she displaces her anger onto another client (not the one who abused her) by telling him abruptly, and in an authoritarian way, that she cannot deal with his request. This is an example of the defence mechanism of displacement.

In this instance, Millie's displacement, although understandable, is not a professional or ethical way to respond and it might result in an aggressive response from the client on whom Millie is displacing her anger.

Projection

After an incident of violence, 'Fred', the professional in charge, blames his colleagues for not managing the situation effectively. In this instance, 'Fred' finds it so painful to acknowledge his own failings in responding to the situation, that he blames his colleagues, instead. Here, 'Fred' is using a mental defence mechanism known as projection.

Denial

An example of denial would be: 'Violent clients never make me feel anxious. I can tackle any incident of violence on my own, without any difficulty at all'. It is possible that a worker who said this would not consciously feel anxiety, but this would probably be at the expense of honest self-reflection. In addition, the worker's belief that she or he could 'tackle any incident of violence on my own' could result in putting her or himself, patients and colleagues at risk.

Support of staff and clinical supervision, with an experienced professional, can enable workers to reflect on their interventions to prevent and reduce violence and aggression, and become aware of unconscious and other factors that influence their care of clients (Linsley 2006).

Psychodynamic theory and therapy: An example

(References that are relevant to the following account include: Dryden 2007 and Gabbard *et al.* 2007).

'Libby' is a young woman who enjoys going to night clubs with her friends and is a talented artist. She has been assessed as having a mild learning disability and a 'personality disorder', a term avoided in some therapeutic communities (Campling and Birtle 2001). Libby feels, and expresses, aggressive anger towards her parents, and also to professionals and other people whom she sees as authority figures.

Psychodynamic psychotherapy, based on psychodynamic theory enables Libby to explore early memories, feelings and conflicts concerning her parents. As a toddler, Libby suffered considerable physical and sexual abuse from both parents, which, understandably, produced considerable feelings of rage and hatred towards her parents. According to psychodynamic theory, these feelings and the actual abuse were so painful that Libby repressed the associated memories, that is, she pushed them from her conscious mind into her unconscious. This means that she is unable to remember the abuse or the unbearable feelings associated with it.

In addition, according to the psychodynamic theorist/therapist, Libby is not consciously aware that her feelings towards her parents are transferred onto people who remind her of her parents – including staff members and other people that she sees as authority figures: a process known as transference (Byrt 2006; Jones 2005). This is sometimes expressed as violence and aggression towards these people.

In the past, Libby has been admitted to both learning disability and mental health services, and once, to prison. Although workers have tried to be empathetic and supportive, Libby has found it hard to trust them and (to the bewilderment of the workers), has often been violent or aggressive towards them and rejecting of offers of help. Libby has occasionally also expressed bewilderment about her behaviour, saying 'I don't know what makes me behave like this'.

Some workers have been able (e.g., through clinical supervision) to express and resolve their own hurt feelings with colleagues (Bateman and Fonagy 2004). These nurses are able to consistently support and value Libby as an individual (despite her hostility towards them) through the application of Rogerian core principles of congruence, empathy and unconditional positive regard (Freeth 2007).

Other workers feel unable to resolve their negative feelings and develop what, in psychodynamic theory is called counter-transference. This term refers to strong positive or negative feelings that a staff member develops towards a client, partly because of the client's behaviour, but also because unconsciously, and without her or his awareness, the client reminds the staff member of a parent or other significant person (Dryden 2007; Gabbard *et al.* 2007; Nelson-Jones 2006).

Resolution of Libby's distress and reduction of her aggression through psychodynamic principles

According to psychodynamic theory, applied to psychodynamic psychotherapy, Libby's distress and resultant problems, including aggressive anger, can be resolved by:

● giving Libby a chance to talk freely about anything that comes into her head (this is called free association)

● through the process of free association, enabling Libby to remember (bring from the unconscious to the conscious mind) the repressed memories, and associated feelings, of her early childhood physical and sexual abuse

● enabling her transference to the psychotherapist (a professional with training in psychodynamic psychotherapy) of her formerly repressed and understandable feelings of rage and hatred towards her parents.

● through expressing and exploring this rage and hatred:

  ● there may be a resolution of these feelings, not only towards the therapist, but towards other authority figures who remind Libby of her parents

  ● Libby may experience positive gains from understanding herself better, and from being able to express, and eventually resolve, painful feelings.

(Dryden 2007; Gabbard *et al.* 2007; Nelson-Jones 2006)

Some of the differences between psychodynamic and cognitive behavioural therapies are given in Box 13.3.

Initially, Libby met with the therapist on her own (individual psychodynamic psychotherapy), rather than with other clients (group psychodynamic psychotherapy). However, it became clear that Libby needed more support during the day, and her therapist recommended, with Libby's agreement, a referral to a day centre run as a therapeutic community.

Box 13.3

Some differences between psychodynamic and cognitive behavioural therapy

Differences between psychodynamic and cognitive behavioural therapy include the following:

- Cognitive behavioural therapy involves precise, quantitative measures of a problem or symptom (e.g., aggressive behaviours). In psychodynamic therapy, assessment is concerned with relatively unquantifiable feelings, memories and experiences of the individual.

- Cognitive behavioural therapy targets specific problems and symptoms, with precise goals, e.g., the individual will be able to cope with frustrations assertively, with a measurable decrease in threats to assault others. Psychodynamic psychotherapy is more concerned with the resolution of painful, repressed feelings, memories and conflicts through transference and with wider changes in the individual, rather than a diminution of specific problems and symptoms.

- Whilst many cognitive behavioural therapists are concerned with the individual's past and its link with present problems or symptoms, this is generally explored in greater depth in psychodynamic psychotherapy.

(Dryden 2007; Gabbard et al. 2007; Nelson-Jones 2006)

However, in practice, some therapists and services combine cognitive behavioural, psychodynamic and other approaches (Byrt et al. 2005; Campling et al. 2004).

Therapeutic community principles

Therapeutic community principles

Therapeutic community principles have been used in the treatment of people with a variety of problems, and who often receive a diagnosis of personality disorder (Campling 1999). However, Campling and Birtle (2001, p. 132) point out that many clients dislike this term, and suggest alternatives which are less likely to stigmatise clients.

In therapeutic communities, the whole social environment is intended to be therapeutic. There are many opportunities for residents to safely express and discuss feelings, thoughts, problems and views. Most therapeutic communities have structured programmes of psychotherapy groups and other group activities to facilitate this. In addition, there are often 'crisis meetings', which a resident can call at any time of the day and night to explore particular concerns. These opportunities, as well as the process of living and working together, enable residents to 'learn about themselves and their problems, including relation-ship difficulties' (Byrt 1999, p. 67). This can include situations involving violent or aggressive anger, as illustrated in the following example.

'Libby' and her psychodynamic psychotherapist agreed that she might benefit from attending a day centre with therapeutic community principles. For many years, Libby had felt unable to tell anyone about the rejection of her parents, or their sexual and physical abuse of her when she was a child. She had kept her feelings of despair and rage to herself, but sometimes felt better after physically attacking or shouting at other people or cutting herself. On an initial assessment visit at the therapeutic community, Libby said she had a 'short fuse', and wanted to be able to express her anger assertively, rather than aggressively.

For the first few weeks after starting at the therapeutic community, Libby found it hard to trust anyone, isolated herself from other people and was frequently verbally hostile, with occasional threats to hit people. Staff and other residents continued to be supportive to Libby, regardless of her behaviour. Occasionally, Libby was invited to discuss what was troubling her, and feedback was given to her, so that she was aware of how her behaviour affected others. However, the timing of feedback was carefully chosen, to avoid escalating Libby's verbal violence at times when she was particularly hostile.

After a few weeks, Libby commented on how surprised she was that her views were listened to and taken seriously; and said that, for the first time in her life, she felt valued. She apologised for her behaviour, and said that she felt that she behaved as she did to keep people at a distance, in case they could not be trusted. Gradually, Libby was able to use psychodynamic psychotherapy groups to gain an understanding of how this related to her early experiences of abuse and rejection, but also appreciate that her aggressive behaviours could lead to further rejection.

Libby also started to explore events in the day to day life of the therapeutic community, in order to understand herself better. For example, she was understandably angry when another resident criticised the standard of her washing up, and responded by shouting abuse, throwing a plate at him, and breaking several mugs. When Libby was calmer, a crisis meeting was called in order that she could learn from the incident. In this, and subsequent meetings, Libby gradually learnt that her anger, especially when criticised, was linked to her understandable feelings towards critical, hostile and rejecting parents. She also learnt that when people were critical, this did not necessarily mean that they were rejecting her; and was encouraged to practice ways of expressing her anger assertively, rather than aggressively. As she learnt to do this, she found that she could listen to a criticism, and either take it on board, or disagree, assertively and quietly.

The warmth, concern and interest which Libby experienced from staff, and at times, from other residents, provided her with a 'corrective emotional experience' (Ratigan and Aveline 1988): a realisation that at least some people did care about her, and could be trusted. As this occurred to Libby, she realised that she did not need to be hostile in order to keep people away from her.

Various group activities in the therapeutic community gave Libby a chance to develop or discover abilities and talents, which she could use to contribute to other members, e.g., her cooking skills, or to channel her anger creatively. The expressive use of the arts in the latter area has been described (McArdle and Byrt 2001) and Libby was able to express some of her anger through the paintings she produced in a creative art group, and eventually, in the frenetic work-outs with other residents which she started, and led each morning.

Communication in 'Libby's' therapeutic community

One of the main aims of a therapeutic community (and ideally, of any service providing care) is to ensure good communication. This involves staff being accessible and approachable and facilitating residents' discussion of issues of concern to them. There also needs to be good communication between staff, including those of different disciplines, partly so that there can be an understanding of events in the life of the therapeutic community, and of group dynamics (i.e., the communication, inter-relationships and roles of group members) (Rawlinson 1999; Winship 2009). For example, if Libby is aggressively hostile, and frequently the recipient of other residents' angry feelings, staff would need to be aware of this, and consider ways to enable both Libby and the other residents to understand their anger, e.g., in psychotherapy groups and other activities, and to consider assertive and creative ways of expressing it (Byrt 2006).

Staff communication is also facilitated through regular staff support groups. These provide opportunities for staff to consider their interventions and relationships with patients and can increase self awareness, in relation, for example, to countertransference: strong feelings, positive or negative, in response to residents (including their aggression), which are sometimes influenced by significant relationships, especially in the staff member's past (Bree *et al.* 2003, Kelly *et al.* 2004).

Research on therapeutic communities

Research at a high security hospital in Canada found that a therapeutic community worsened features of psychopathy (Harris *et al.* 1994, see Chapter 7). There have been 'mixed results for recidivism [reoffending] amongst individuals treated in prison and secure hospital' therapeutic communities (Byrt 2006, p. 203), but several studies of Grendon Prison therapeutic communities have found lowered rates of offending and aggressive behaviours (Parker 2007). Residents with histories of violence also often report relief of anxiety and other underlying painful feelings (Lees *et al.* 2004). The number of UK prison therapeutic communities has increased considerably recently, especially for individuals dependent on alcohol and other drugs (Phoenix Futures 2009), a factor which increases the risk of violence (Kipping 2009). Most NHS therapeutic communities now operate only during the day (Pierce and Haigh 2008), but residential therapeutic communities, for individuals with mental health problems and/or learning disabilities, are run by voluntary organisations, including the Arbours Association (2009), Camphill Village Trust (2009), L'Arche (2009) and Phoenix Futures.

Conclusion

Health and social care workers are required to deal with a variety of challenges during the course of their work. Occasionally, this includes dealing with and managing aggression and potentially aggressive and violent behaviour. Indeed, care workers are often in the frontline when such behaviour occurs and therefore need a range of skills and competencies in order to care for and manage aggressive behaviour appropriately and effectively.

As highlighted, the concepts of aggression and violence are wide ranging and consequently, the information provided in this book has focused on a selection of the most salient issues which are relevant to care workers working in close contact with clients and their relatives and friends.

This book has examined some of the concepts, theories and models, relating to aggressive and violent behaviour in care settings and has explored some of the management strategies to deal with, and respond to, such behaviour. Care workers deal with more aggressive incidents than most other occupational groups and staff who have been on the receiving end of an aggressive or violent attack need the opportunity to talk about their experience, and need assistance to develop strategies to avoid the recurrence of such incidents. Care managers must also be receptive to the therapeutic and interpersonal climate within their respective area of work. The health and social care environment must accommodate the inevitable stresses and strains that care workers will encounter. Moreover, adequate resources should be available for in-service training and education of care workers who need to maintain a high level of interpersonal and other clinical skills. However, the problem of aggression and violence cannot be addressed purely by investing in staff development and policy making. In addition, issues need to be explored in wider society and a selection of these issues have been addressed in this book. Attention also needs to be paid to the recruitment of staff, who need to be valued, respected and receive appropriate resources. Indeed, the issue of resources is an important one and situations where staff have to 'fight' for resources are not particularly conducive to creating a healthy work environment. Care workers, many of whom have been on the receiving end of violence and aggression in care facilities, could be part of the solution if their potential as role models and educators is exploited.

References

Abderhalden, C., Hahn, S., Bonner, Y.D.B., and Galeazzi, G.M. (2006). Users' perceptions and views on violence and coercion in mental health. In Richter, D., and Whittington, R. (eds) *Violence in Mental Health Settings. Causes, Consequences, Management*. New York: Springer.

About.Com: Biology (Undated). Website. The Limbic System. www.biology.about.com/od/anatomy/c/aa042205a.htm (accessed August 2009).

Adams, L. (2002). Nursing interventions and future directions with exercise therapy. In Kettles, A.M., Woods, P., and Collins, M. (eds) *Therapeutic Interventions for Forensic Mental Health Nurses*. London: Jessica Kingsley.

Addo, M.A. (2006). Culture, spirituality and ethical issues in caring for clients with personality disorder. In National Forensic Nurses' Research and Development Group (eds) *Aspects of Forensic Mental Health Nursing: Interventions with People with 'Personality Disorder'.* London: Quay Books, Mark Allen Health Care.

Addo, M., and Smith, I. (2008). Equality and diversity: Respecting the person with a learning disability. In National Forensic Nurses' Research and Development Group: Kettles, A.M., Woods, P., and Byrt, R. (eds) *Forensic Mental Health Nursing: Capabilities, Roles and Responsibilities*. London: Quay Books, MA Healthcare, Ltd.

Aiyegbusi, A., and Byrt, R. (2006). Gender and sexuality. In: National Forensic Nurses' Research and Development Group: Woods, P., Kettles, A.M., Byrt, R., Addo, M., Coffey, M., Collins, M., Doyle, M., Garman, G., and Watson, C. (eds) *Aspects of Forensic Mental Health Nursing: Interventions with People with 'Personality Disorder'.* London: Quay Books, MA Healthcare, Ltd.

Aiyegbusi, A., and Clarke-Moore, J. (eds) (2009). *Therapeutic Relationships with Offenders. An Introduction to the Psychodynamics of Forensic Mental Health Nursing*. London: Jessica Kingsley.

Alarcon, C. (2009). Burger King to promote Angry Whopper launch. *Marketing Week*. 14 September. www.marketingweek.co.uk (accessed 14 September 2009).

Alexander, J. (2004). Ward Rules for Patient Conduct. Unpublished PhD thesis. London: City University.

Allen, D. (2002). Behaviour change and behaviour management. In Allen, D. (ed.) *Ethical Approaches to Physical Interventions*. Kidderminster: British Institute of Learning Disabilities (BILD).

Andalo, D., and agencies (2004). NHS urged to combat institutional racism. *The Guardian*, 12 February 2004. www.guardian.co.uk/society/2004/Feb/12/mentalhealth.raceintheUK2. (accessed 14 August 2009).

Andersson, E.M., Halberg, I.R., Norberg, A., and Edberg, A.K. (2002). The meaning of acute confusional state from the perspective of elderly patients. *International Journal of Geriatric Psychiatry* 17: 652–63.

Andrews, M.M., and Boyle, J.S. (eds) (2008). *Transcultural Concepts in Nursing Care*. Philadelphia: Lippincott, Williams and Wilkins.

Appleby, L. (2007) Foreword. In Department of Health, *Best Practice in Managing Risk. Principles and Evidence for Best Practice in the Assessment and Management of Risk to Self and Others in Mental Health Services*. London: Department of Health.

Arbours Association. (2009). Website. www.arboursassociation.org (accessed 14 September 2009).

Archibald, G. (2008). Role of the forensic mental health nurse in nutrition: Towards recovery. In National Forensic Nurses' Research and Development Group: Kettles, A.M., Woods, P., and Byrt, R. (eds) *Forensic Mental Health Nursing: Competencies, Roles, Responsibilities*. London: Quay Books, MA Healthcare, Ltd.

Arnold, E. (2007a). Developing therapeutic communication skills in the nurse-client relationship. In Arnold, E., and Boggs, K. U. (eds). (5th edn). *Interpersonal Relationships. Personal Communication Skills for Nurses*. St. Louis, Missouri: Saunders Elsevier.

Arnold, E. (2007b). Intercultural communication. In Arnold, E., and Boggs, K.U. (eds) *Interpersonal Relationships. Professional Communication Skills for Nurses* (4th edn). St. Louis, Missouri: Saunders Elsevier.

Arnold, E., and Boggs, K.U. (2007). *Interpersonal Relationships. Personal Communication Skills for Nurses* (5th edn). St. Louis, Missouri: Saunders Elsevier.

Arnold, E., and Ryan, J.W. (2007). Communicating with older adults. In Arnold, E., and Boggs, K. (eds) *Interpersonal Relationships. Professional Communication Skills for Nurses* (5th edn). St. Louis, Missouri: Saunders Elsevier.

Ashman, D. (2001). Desperately seeking understanding. *Mental Health Today* October, 30–31.

Astrom, S., Karlsson, S., Sandvide, A., Bucht, G., Eisemann, M., Norberg, A., and Saveman, B.-I. (2004). Staff's experience of and the management of violent incidents in elderly care. *Scandinavian Journal of Caring Science* 18: 410–16.

Atakan, Z. (2008). Severe mental illness and substance abuse. In Beer, M.D., Pereira, S., and Paton, C. (eds) *Psychiatric Intensive Care* (2nd edn). London: Greenwich Medical Media.

Atkinson, D., Jackson, M., and Walmsley, J. (1997). *Forgotten Lives: Exploring the History of Learning Disability*. Kidderminster: BILD Publications Ltd.

Atkinson, R.L., Atkinson, R.C., Smith, E.E., Bem, D.J., and Nolen-Hoksema, S.(2000). *Hilgards's Introduction to Psychology* (13th edn). Fort Worth: Harcourt College Publishers.

Audit Commission (1999). *Safety in Numbers. Promoting Community Safety*. London: Audit Commission.

Bailey, R.H. (1977). *Violence and Aggression*. Amsterdam: Time-Life Books.

Baldwin, C., and Capstick, A. (eds) (2007). *Tom Kitwood on Dementia: A Reader and Critical Commentary*. Maidenhead: Open University Press.

Barker, G.T. (2005). Dying to be Men. Youth, Masculinity and Social Exclusion. London: Routledge/Taylor and Francis Group.

Barker, P. (1999). Talking Cures. A *Guide to the Psychotherapies for Health Care Professionals*. London: NT Books.

Barker, P.(ed.) (2009). *Psychiatric and Mental Health Nursing: The Craft of Caring* (2nd edn). Arnold: London.

Barker, P., and Buchanan-Barker, P. (2005). *The Tidal Model. A Guide for Mental Health Professionals.* Hove: Brunner-Routledge, Taylor and Francis Group.

Barlow, T. (2003). What colour is aggression? *Mental Health Practice* 7(4): 32–3.

Barnes, C., and Mercer, G. (2003). *Disability.* Cambridge: Polity Press.

Bartlett, A. (2004). Fashions in psychiatric care: Implications for sense of self. In Crisp, A.H. (ed.) *Every Family in the Land: Understanding Prejudice and Discrimination Against People with Mental Illness.* London: Royal Society of Medicine Press.

Bartlett, C., and Bunning, K. (1997). The importance of communication partnerships: A study to investigate the communicative exchanges between staff and adults with learning disabilities. *British Journal of Learning Disabilities* 26: 148–53.

Barnes, C., and Mercer, G. (2003). *Disability.* Cambridge: Polity Press.

Barton, R. (1966). *Institutional Neurosis* (2nd edn). Bristol: John Wright.

Bateman, A., and Fonagy, P. (2004). *Psychotherapy for Borderline Personality Disorder.* Oxford: Oxford University Press.

Bateman, A., and Fonagy, P. (2009). Randomized controlled trial of outpatient mentalization based therapy versus structured clinical management in borderline personality disorder. *American Journal of Psychiatry* 166(12): 1355–64.

Beale, D. (1999). Managing violence and aggression towards NHS staff working in the community. *NT Research* 4(2): 87–98.

Beck, R., and Fernandez, E. (1998). Cognitive behavioral therapy in the treatment of anger: a meta-analysis. *Cognitive Therapy and Research* 22, 63–74.

'Bede', 'Colm', 'Algy', 'Dirk', 'Ezra', 'Ferg' and Byrt, R. (2008). Managing anger creatively: Patients' views and experiences. In National Forensic Nurses' Research and Development Group: Kettles, A.M., Woods, P., and Byrt, R. (eds) *Forensic Mental Health Nursing: Competencies, Roles, Responsibilities.* London: Quay Books, MA Healthcare Ltd.

Beech, I. (2009). The person with a diagnosis of bipolar disorder. In Barker, P. (ed.) *Psychiatric and Mental Health Nursing. The Craft of Caring* (2nd edn). London: Hodder Arnold.

Beer, M.D. (2008). Psychiatric intensive care units and low secure units: Where are we now? *Psychiatric Bulletin* 32: 441–3.

Beer, M.D., Pereira, S., and Paton, C. (eds) (2008). *Psychiatric Intensive Care* (2nd edn). London: Greenwich Medical Media.

Biddle, S.J.H., and Mutrie, N. (2008). *Psychology of Physical Activity. Determinants, Well-Being and Interventions* (2nd edn). London: Routledge, Taylor and Francis Group.

Birchwood, M., and Jackson, C. (2001). *Schizophrenia.* Hove: Taylor and Francis.

Bjorkly, S. (2006). Psychological theories of aggression: Principles and application to practice. In Richter, D., and Whittington, R. (eds) *Violence in Mental Health Settings. Causes, Consequences, Management.* New York: Springer.

Blair, R.J.R. (2009). The amygdala and ventromedial prefrontal cortex: Functional contributions and dysfunction in psychopathy. In Hodgins, S., Viding, E., and Plodowski, A. (eds) *The Neurological Basis of Violence: Science and Rehabilitation.* Oxford: Oxford University Press.

Blair, R.J., Perschardt, K.S., Budhani, S., Mitchell, D.G., and Pine, D.S. (2006). The development of psychopathy. *Journal of Child Psychology and Psychiatry* 47: 262–76.

Blofeld, Sir J. (2003). *Independent Inquiry into the Death of David Bennett. An Independent Inquiry Set Up by Norfolk, Suffolk and Cambridgeshire Strategic Health Authority Under HSG(94)27.* London: HM Government. Available at www.doh.gov.uk (accesses 9 February 2010).

Blom-Cooper, L. (1992). *Report of the Committee of Inquiry into Complaints at Ashworth Hospital.* London: HMSO.

Blom-Cooper, L. (2008). *The Penalty of Imprisonment. Why 60% of the Prison Population Shouldn't Be There.* London: Continuum.

Blunden, R., and Allen, D. (1987). *Facing the Challenge: An Ordinary Life for People with Learning Disabilities.* London: King's Fund.

Boggs, K.U. (2007). Communication styles. In: Arnold, E., and Boggs, K. U. (2007). *Interpersonal Relationships. Personal Communication Skills for Nurses* (5th edn). St. Louis, Missouri: Saunders Elsevier.

Bonner, C. (2005). *Reducing Stress-Related Behaviours in People with Dementia. Care-Based Therapy.* London: Jessica Kingsley.

Bose, S. (2009). Containment and the structured day. In Aiyegbusi, A., and Clarke-Moore, J. (eds) *Therapeutic Relationships with Offenders. An Introduction to the Psychodynamics of Forensic Mental Health Nursing.* London: Jessica Kingsley.

Bowers, L. (2002). *Dangerous and Severe Personality Disorder: Response and Role of the Psychiatric Team.* London: Routledge.

Bowers, L., Crowhurst, N., Alexander, J., Callaghan, P., Eales, S., Guy, S., McCann, E., and Ryan, C. (2002). Safety and security policies on psychiatric acute admission wards: Results from a London-wide survey'. *Journal of Psychiatric and Mental Health Nursing* 9: 427–33.

Bowers, L., Jarrett, M., and Clark, N. (1999). Absconding. Part 1. Why patients leave. *Journal of Psychiatric and Mental Health Nursing* 6(3): 199–205.

Bowness, S., 'Algy', Byrt, R., Ngeh, R., Mason, L., and Wray, C. (2008). Managing anger creatively: An overview'. In National Forensic Nurses' Research and Development Group: Kettles, A.M., Woods, P., and Byrt, R. (eds) *Forensic Mental Health Nursing: Competencies, Roles, Responsibilities.* London: Quay Books, MA Healthcare, Ltd.

Braithwaite, R. (2001). *Managing Aggression.* London: Routledge/Community Care.

Brechin, A., and Walmsley, J. (eds) (1989). *Making Connections. Reflecting on the Lives and Experiences of People with Learning Difficulties.* London: Hodder and Stoughton/Open University.

Bree, A., Campling, P., and Liderth, S. (2003). Empowerment in mental health: the therapeutic community model. In Dooher, J., and Byrt, R. (eds) *Empowerment and the Health Service User.* Dinton, Salisbury: Quay Books, Mark Allen Publishing.

Brewster, J., and Ramcharan, P. (2005). Enabling and supporting person-centred approaches. In Grant, G., Goward, P., Richardson, M., and

Ramcharan, P. (eds) *Learning Disability. A Life Cycle Approach to Valuing People.* Maidenhead: Open University Press.

British Association of Social Workers (1988). *Violence to Social Workers.* London: BASW.

British Medical Association (2007). Bullying and Harassment in the Workplace. Web page: www.bma.org.uk/wa/employmentandcontracts/morale/motivation/ bullyingWales.jsp (last accessed 18 January 2010).

British National Formulary (2009). Website. www.bnf.org/bnf/ (accessed 14 September 2009).

British Society of Rehabilitation Medicine and Royal College of Physicians (2003). *Rehabilitation Following Acquired Brain Injury.* London: British Society of Rehabilitation Medicine and Royal College of Physicians.

Britten, N., and Shaw, A. (1994). Patients' experiences of emergency admission: How relevant is the British Government's Patients' Charter? *Journal of Advanced Nursing* 19(6): 1212–20.

Brown, A., and Draper, P. (2003). Accommodative speech and terms of endearment: Elements of a language mode often experienced by older adults. *Journal of Advanced Nursing* 41(1): 15–21.

Bryan, K., and Maxim, J. (eds) (2006). *Communication Disability in the Dementias.* London: Whurr Publishers.

Buckholtz, J.W., and Meyer-Lindenberg, A. (2009). Gene-brain associations: The example of MAOA. In Hodgins, S., Viding, E., and Plodowski, A. (eds) *The Neurological Basis of Violence: Science and Rehabilitation.* Oxford: Oxford University Press.

Buckingham, A. (2003). Bottling up problems. *Emergency Nurse* 11(2): 14–15.

Buckley, E.R. (2000). Abusive clients. *RCM Midwives Journal* 3(1): 10.

Buckley, M.J. (2003). *World of the Body: Limbic System.* Oxford: Oxford University Press. Accessed via: Answers.com (undated). Limbic System. www.answers.com (last accessed 12 January 2010).

Bullock, J., and MacKenzie, S. (2003). The menopause. In Jukes, M., and Bollard, M. (eds) *Contemporary Learning Disability Practice.* Dinton, Salisbury: Quay Books/Mark Allen Publishing.

Burbach, R. (2008). Substance abuse disorders. In Simon, R.I., and Tardiff, K. (eds) *Textbook of Violence Assessment and Management.* Washington, D.C.: American Publishing, Inc.

Burnard, P. (1999). *Counselling Skills for Health Professionals* (3rd edn). Cheltenham: Stanley Thornes.

Buss, A. (1961). *The Psychology of Aggression.* New York: Wiley.

Butt, M.A., Mallick, S., Syed, Y., and O'Neal, H. (2008). Adherence and the dosset box. Letter, 19 March in *British Medical Journal.* Rapid Responses to Clinical Review: Milton, J.C., Hill-Smith, I., and Jackson, S.H.D. (2008). Prescribing for older people. *British Medical Journal* 336: 606–9.

Byrne, E.J. (1997). Acute and sub-acute confusional states (delirium) in later life. In Norman, I.J., and Redfern, S.J. (eds) *Mental Health Care for Elderly People.* New York: Churchill Livingstone.

Byrt, C., Weeks, M., and Byrt, R. (2003). Making empowerment a reality: a personal account. In Dooher, J., and Byrt, R. (eds) *Empowerment and the Recipients of Health Care.* Dinton, Salisbury: Quay Books, Mark Allen Publishing.

Byrt, C. (2009). *Personal communication.* Abertillery. CEB Consultancy, PLC.

Byrt, R. (1999). Nursing the psychosocial environment. In Campling, P., and Haigh, R. (eds) *Therapeutic Communities. Past Present and Future.* London: Jessica Kingsley.

Byrt, R. (2001). Power, influence and control in practice development. In Clark, A., Dooher, J., and Fowler, J. (eds) *The Handbook of Practice Development.* Dinton, Salisbury: Quay Books.

Byrt, R. (2006). Nursing interventions in therapeutic communities. In National Forensic Nurses' Research and Development Group: Woods, P., Kettles, A.M., Byrt, R., Addo, M., Coffey, M., Collins, M., Doyle, M., Garman, G., and Watson, C. (eds) *Aspects of Forensic Mental Health Nursing: Interventions with People with 'Personality Disorder'.* London: Quay Books, MA Healthcare, Ltd.

Byrt, R. (2007). Towards therapeutic environments: Alternatives and solutions. In National Forensic Nurses' Research and Development Group: Kettles, A.M., Woods, P., Byrt, R., Addo, M.A, Coffey, M., and Doyle, M. (eds) *Forensic Mental Health Nursing: Forensic Aspects of Acute Care.* London: Quay Books, MA Healthcare.

Byrt, R. (2008a). Power and participation in forensic services: An introduction. In National Forensic Nurses' Research and Development Group: Kettles, A.M. Woods, P., and Byrt, R. (eds) *Forensic Mental Health Nursing: Competencies, Roles, Responsibilities.* London: Quay Books, MA Healthcare, Ltd.

Byrt, R. (2008b). Negative control or life saving? Perspectives on power. In National Forensic Nurses' Research and Development Group: Kettles, A.M., Woods, P., and Byrt, R. (eds) *Forensic Mental Health Nursing: Competencies, Roles, Responsibilities.* London: Quay Books, MA Healthcare, Ltd.

Byrt, R., and Doyle, M. (2007). Prevention and reduction of violence and aggression. In National Forensic Nurses' Research and Development Group: Kettles, A.M., Woods, P., Byrt, R.., Addo, M.A, Coffey, M., and Doyle, M (eds) *Forensic Mental Health Nursing: Forensic Aspects of Acute Care.* London: Quay Books, MA Healthcare, Ltd.

Byrt, R., and Hardie, T. (2007). Cultural sensitivity and cultural competence. In National Forensic Nurses' Research and Development Group: Kettles, A.M., Woods, P., Byrt, R., Addo, M.A, Coffey, M., and Doyle, M (eds) *Forensic Mental Health Nursing: Forensic Aspects of Acute Care. London.* Quay Books, MA Healthcare, Ltd.

Byrt, R. with James, L. (2007). Towards therapeutic environments: Challenges and problems. In National Forensic Nurses' Research and Development Group: Kettles, A.M., Woods, P., Byrt, R., Addo, M.A, Coffey, M., and Doyle, M (eds) *Aspects of Forensic Mental Health Nursing in Acute Mental Health Settings.* London: Quay Books, MA Healthcare.

Byrt, R., and Woods, P. (2006). Introduction. In National Forensic Nurses' Research and Development Group: Woods, P., Kettles, A.M., Byrt,

R., Addo, M., Coffey, M., Collins, M., Doyle, M., Garman, G., and Watson, C. (eds) *Aspects of Forensic Mental Health Nursing: Interventions with People with 'Personality Disorder'.* London: Quay Books, MA Healthcare, Ltd.

Byrt, R., Lomas, C., Gardiner, J., and Lewis, D. (2001). Working with women in secure environments. *Journal of Psychosocial Nursing and Mental Health Services* 39(9): 42–50.

Byrt, R., Wray, C., and 'Tom' (2005). Towards hope and inclusion: Nursing interventions in a medium secure service for men with 'personality disorders'. *Mental Health Practice* 8(8): 38–43

Byrt, R., Wetherell-Graley, R., 'R', Studley, R., James, L., Pocock, T., and D'Silva, K. (2006). Service user experiences and professional attitudes. In National Forensic Nurses' Research and Development Group: Woods, P., Kettles, A.M., Byrt, R., Addo, M., Coffey, M., Collins, M., Doyle, M., Garman, G., and Watson, C. (eds) *Aspects of Forensic Mental Health Nursing: Interventions with People with 'Personality Disorder'.* London: Quay Books, MA Healthcare, Ltd.

Byrt, R., Aiyegbusi, A., Hardie, T., and Addo, A. (2007). Cultural and diversity issues. In National Forensic Nurses' Research and Development Group: Kettles, A.M., Woods, P., Byrt, R., Addo, M.A, Coffey, M., and Doyle, M. (eds) *Forensic Mental Health Nursing: Forensic Aspects of Acute Care.* London: Quay Books, MA Healthcare.

Byrt, R., Hart, L., and James-Sow, L. (2008). Patient empowerment and participation: Barriers and the way forward. In National Forensic Nurses' Research and Development Group: Kettles, A.M., Woods, P., and Byrt, R. (eds) *Forensic Mental Health Nursing: Competencies, Roles, Responsibilities.* London: Quay Books, MA Healthcare, Ltd.

CALM Training Services, Ltd. (2008). CALM – Crisis, Aggression, Limitation and Management. Website. www.calmtraining.co.uk/ (last accessed 18 January 2010).

Camphill Village Trust (2009). Website. www.cvt.org.uk/ (accessed 9 February 2010).

Campling, P. (1999). Chaotic personalities: Maintaining the therapeutic alliance. In Campling, P., and Haigh, R. (eds) *Therapeutic Communities. Past, Present and Future.* London: Jessica Kingsley.

Campling, P., and Birtle, J. (2001). The need for an NHS policy on developing the role of therapeutic communities in the treatment of personality disorder. *Therapeutic Communities* 22(2): 131–42.

Campling, P., Davies, S., and Farquharson, G. (eds) (2004). *From Toxic Institutions to Therapeutic Environments: Residential Settings in Mental Health Services.* London: Gaskell.

Cannon, W. (1932). *The Wisdom of the Body.* New York: W.W. Norton.

Carless, D., and Sparkes, A.C. (2008). The physical activity experiences of men with serious mental illness: Three short stories. *Psychology of Sport and Exercise* 9: 191– 210.

Carr-Walker, P., Bowers, L., Callaghan, P., Nijman, H., and Paton, J. (2004). Attitudes towards personality disorders: Comparison between prison officers and psychiatric nurses. *Legal and Criminological Psychology* 9: 265–77.

Carson, E. (2007). Hidden Torment of Battered Men. BBC News, 13 February 2007. www.news.bbc.co.uk (accessed 9 February 2010).

Cashin, A., Potter, E., and Butler, T. (2008). The relationship between exercise and hopelessness in prison. *Journal of Psychiatric and Mental Health Nursing* 15: 66–71.

Cassidy, S.B., and Driscoll, D.J. (2009). Prader-Willi Syndrome. European *Journal of Human Genetics* 17(1): 3–13.

Castillo, H. (2003). *Personality Disorder: Temperament or Trauma?* London: Jessica Kingsley.

Castillo, H., Allen, L., and Coxhead, N. (2001). The hurtfulness of a diagnosis: User research about personality disorder. *Mental Health Practice* 4(9): 16–19.

Cawson, P., Wattam, C., Brooker, S., and Kelly, G. (2000). *Child Maltreatment in the United Kingdom: A Study of the Prevalence of Child Abuse and Neglect.* London: NSPCC.

Cembrowicz, S., Ritter, S., and Wright, S. (2001). Attacks on doctors and nurses. In Shepherd, J. (ed.) *Violence in Healthcare. Understanding, Preventing and Surviving Violence. A Practical Guide for Professionals* (2nd edn). Oxford: Oxford University Press.

Challenging Behaviour Foundation (2009). Website. www.thecbf.org.uk (accessed 15 September 2009).

Chaloner, C. (2000). Ethics and morality. In Chaloner, C., and Coffey, M. (eds) *Forensic Mental Health Nursing. Current Approaches.* Oxford: Blackwell Science, Ltd.

Chandler-Oatts, J., and Nelstrop, L. (2008). Listening to the voices of African-Caribbean mental health service users to develop guideline recommendations on managing violent behaviour. *Diversity in Health and Social Care* 5: 31–41.

Chartered Institute of Personnel and Development (CIPD) (2004). *Managing Conflict at Work: A Strategy of the UK and Ireland.* London. CIPD.

Chawner, L. (2003). Keeping a diary helped staff find their own solutions. *Journal of Dementia Care* Sept/Oct: 30–1.

ChildLine (1998). *Children and Racism.* London: ChildLine.

ChildLine (2005). *Every School Should Have One. How Peer Support Schemes Make Schools Better.* London: ChildLine.

ChildLine (2009). Website. www.childline.org.uk (last accessed 12 January 2010).

Citrome, L. (2008). Psychopharmacology and electroconvulsive therapy. In Simon, R.I., and Tardiff, K. (2008). *Textbook of Violence Assessment and Management.* Washington, DC: American Publishing, Inc.

Clarke, H., and Wilson, H. (eds) (2009). *Cognitive Behavioural Therapy for Acute Mental Health Units. Working with Clients, Staff and the Milieu.* Abingdon: Routledge, Taylor and Francis Group.

Collins, M., and Walford, M. (2008). Helping vulnerable adults to feel safe. *Journal of Adult Protection* 10(1): 7–12.

Collins, R. (2009). *Violence: A Microsociological Theory.* Princeton, NJ: Princeton University Press.

Combat Stress (2009). Website. www.combatstress.org.uk/ (accessed 14 September 2009).

Condon, L., Hek, G., and Harris, F. (2007). A review of prison health and its implications for primary care nursing in England and Wales: the research evidence. *Journal of Clinical Nursing* 16: 1201–9.

Condon, L., Hek, G., and Harris, F. (2008). Choosing health in prison: Prisoners' views on making healthy choices in English prisons. *Health Education Journal* 67(3): 155–66.

Cooke, D.J. (2008). Casting light on prison violence in Scotland: Evaluating the impact of situational risk factors. *Criminal Justice and Behavior* 35(8): 1065–78.

Corbett, K., and Westwood, T. (2005). 'Dangerous and severe personality disorder': A psychiatric manifestation of the risk society. *Critical Public Health* 15(2): 121–33.

Cowman, S. (2006). Safety and security in psychiatric clinical environments. In Richter, D., and Whittington, R. (eds) *Violence in Mental Health Settings. Causes, Consequences, Management.* New York: Springer.

Craig, T.K.J. (2006). Severe mental illness: Symptoms, signs and diagnosis. In Gamble, C., and Brennan, G. (eds) *Working with Serious Mental Illness. A Manual for Clinical Practice.* Edinburgh: Elsevier.

Crichton, J. (ed.) (1995). *Psychiatric Patient Violence: Risk and Response.* London: Duckworth.

Crichton, J. (1997). The response of nursing staff to psychiatric inpatient misdeameanour. *The Journal of Forensic Psychiatry* 8(1): 36–41.

Crowner, M.L. (2008). Schizophrenia and delusional disorder. In Simon, R.I., and Tardiff, K. (eds) *Textbook of Violence Assessment and Management.* Washington, DC: American Publishing, Inc.

Curwen, B., Palmer, S., and Ruddell, P. (2000). *Brief Cognitive Therapy.* London: Sage.

Cutcliffe, J. (2009). Engagement and observation of people at risk. In: Barker, P.(ed.) *Psychiatric and Mental Health Nursing: The Craft of Caring* (2nd edn). London: Arnold.

Dahlberg, L.L. (2008). Public health and violence: Moving forward in a global context. In Flannery, D.T., Vazsonyi, A.T., and Waldman, I.D. (eds) *The Cambridge Handbook of Violent Behavior and Aggression.* New York: Cambridge University Press.

Dale, C., and Gardner, J. (2001). Security in forensic environments: Strategic and operational issues. In Dale, C., Thompson, T., and Woods, P. (eds) *Forensic Mental Health: Issues in Practice.* Edinburgh: Bailliere Tindall/Royal College of Nursing.

Darcy, L. (2007). Reducing and/or minimising physical restraint in a high care, rural aged care facility. *International Journal of Evidence Based Healthcare* 5: 458–67.

Davenport, S. (2004). A gender-sensitive therapeutic environment for women. In Campling, P., Davies, S., and Farquharson, G. (eds) *From Toxic Institutions to Therapeutic Environments: Residential Settings in Mental Health Services.* London: Gaskell.

Davies, D., and Neal, C. (1996). Homophobia and heterosexism. In Davies, D., and Neal, C. (eds) *Pink Therapy: A Guide for Counsellors and Therapists Working with Lesbian, Gay and Bisexual Clients.* Buckingham: Open University Press.

Davies, S., Aveyard, B., and Norman, I.J. (2006). Person-centred dementia care. In Redfern, S.J., and Ross, F.M. (eds) *Nursing Older People.* Edinburgh: Churchill Livingstone Elsevier.

Davis, C. (2006). School's out for bullying. *Nursing Standard* 20(21): 24–5.

de Brito, S.A., and Hodgins, S. (2009). Executive functions of persistent violent offenders: A critical review of the literature. In Hodgins, S., Viding, E., and Plodowski, A. (eds) *The Neurological Basis of Violence: Science and Rehabilitation.* Oxford: Oxford University Press.

Department of Health (2002). *Mental Health Implementation Guide. National Minimum Standards for General Adult Services in Psychiatric Intensive Care Units (PICUs) and Low Secure Environments.* (Pereira, S., and Clinton, C. eds). London: Department of Health.

Department of Health (2003). *Secretary of State Directions on Work to Tackle Violence Against Staff or Professionals Who Work in, or Provide Services to, the NHS.* London: Department of Health.

Department of Health (2005). *Delivering Race Equality in Mental Health Care. An Action Plan for Reform. Inside and Outside Services and the Government's Response to the Independent Inquiry into the Death of David Bennett.* London: Department of Health.

Department of Health (2007). *Working with Lesbian, Gay, Bisexual and Trans (LGBT) People.* Author: Fish, J. London: Department of Health. August, 2007.

Department of Health (2008a). *Code of Practice, Mental Health Act 1983.* London: The Stationery Office.

Department of Health (2008b). *Healthier, Fairer and Safer Communities – Connecting People to Prevent Violence. Towards a Framework for Violence and Abuse Prevention.* Draft. 20 November. Available via: www.dh.gov.uk/en/publicationsandstatistics/Publications/PublicationsPolicyandGuidance/DH091772 (accessed 9 February 2010).

Department of Health (2009). *Single Equality Scheme, 2009-2012.* London: Department of Health. Available via: www.dh.gov Accessed 14 September 2009.

Dickenson, D., and Fulford, B. with Birley, J.L.T. (eds) (2000). *In Two Minds: A Casebook of Psychiatric Ethics.* Oxford: Oxford University Press.

Dimond, B. (2003). *Legal Aspects of Consent.* Dinton, Salisbury: Quay Books, Mark Allen Publishing, Ltd.

Dimond, B. (2008a). *Legal Aspects of Mental Capacity.* Oxford: Blackwell. Publishing.

Dimond, B. (2008b). *Legal Aspects of Nursing* (5th edn). Harlow: Pearson Education.

Dix, R., and Page, M.J. (2008). Physical environment. In Beer, M.D., Pereira, S., and Paton, C. (eds) *Psychiatric Intensive Care* (2nd edn). London: Greenwich Medical Media.

Dixon, J. (2006). Special considerations: Gender, violence, health and healthcare. In Linsley, P. (ed.) *Violence and Aggression in the Workplace. A Practical Guide for All Healthcare Staff.* Oxford: Radcliffe Publishing.

Dodd, P., Guerin, S., McEvoy, J., Buckley, S., Tyrrell, J., and Hillery, J. (2008). A study of complicated grief symptoms in people with intellectual disabilities. *Journal of Intellectual Disability Research* 52(5): 415–25.

Dollard, J., Doob, L.W., Miller, N.E., Mowrer, O.H., and Sears, R.R. (1939). *Frustration and Aggression*. New Haven: Yale University Press.

Dooher, J. (2006). *New Ways of Working in Mental Health Nursing*. London: Quay Books.

Dooher, J., and Byrt, R. (2003). *Empowerment and the Health Service User* Volume 2. Wiltshire: Quay Books.

Dooher, J., and Byrt, R. (2005). A critical examination of the concept of empowerment. In Cutcliffe, J.R., and McKenna, H. (eds) *The Essential Concepts of Nursing. Building Blocks for Practice*. Edinburgh: Elsevier. Churchill Livingstone.

Dowd, N.E. (2006). Introduction. In Dowd, N.E., Singer, D.G., and Wilson, R.F. (eds) *Handbook of Children, Culture and Violence*. London: Sage.

Doyle, M., Aiyegbusi, A. and Burbery, P. (2006). Personality disorder: Specialist psychological approaches. In National Forensic Nurses' Research and Development Group: Woods, P., Kettles, A.M. Byrt, R., Addo, M., Coffey, M., Collins, M., Doyle, M., Garman, G., and Watson, C. (eds) *Aspects of Forensic Mental Health Nursing: Interventions with People with 'Personality Disorder'*. London: Quay Books, MA Healthcare, Ltd.

Droughton, J., and Williams, S. (2002). Working and schizophrenia. In Harris, N., Williams, S., and Bradshaw, T. (eds) *Psychosocial Interventions for People with Schizophrenia. A Practical Guide for Mental Health Workers*. Basingstoke: Palgrave Macmillan.

Dryden, W. (ed.) (2007). *Dryden's Handbook of Individual Therapy* (5th edn). London: Sage Publications.

Dugmore, L. (2009). Risk of substance misuse. In Woods, P., and Kettles, A. (eds) *Risk Assessment and Risk Management in Mental Health Nursing*. Chichester: Wiley-Blackwell.

Durcan, G. (2008a). *From the Inside. Experiences of Prison Mental Health Care*. London: Sainsbury Centre for Mental Health.

Durcan, G. (2008b). Prison mental health nursing. In *National Forensic Nurses' Research and Development Group*: Kettles, A.M., Woods, P., and Byrt, R. (eds) Forensic Mental Health Nursing: Capabilities, Roles and Responsibilities. London: Quay Books, MA Healthcare, Ltd.

Durcan, G., and Knowles, K. (2006). *Policy Paper 5. London's Prison Mental Health Services: A Review*. London: Sainsbury Centre for Mental Health.

Duxbury, J. (2000). *Difficult Patients*. Oxford: Butterworth Heinemann.

Duxbury, J.A. (2002). An evaluation of staff and patients' views of strategies employed to manage patient aggression in both mental health and general nursing settings. *Journal of Psychiatric and Mental Health Nursing* 9: 325–37.

Duxbury, J.A., and Whittington, R. (2005). 'Causes and Management of Patient Aggression and Violence: Staff and Patient Perspectives'. *Journal of Psychiatric and Mental Health Nursing*. 50, (5), 469-478.

Duxbury, J.A., Bjorkdahl, A., and Johnson, S. (2006). Ward culture and atmosphere. In Richter, D., and Whittington, R. (eds) *Violence in Mental Health Settings. Causes, Consequences, Management*. New York: Springer.

Emerson, E. (2001). *Challenging Behaviour: Analysis and Intervention in People with Severe Intellectual Disabilities* (2nd edn). Cambridge: Cambridge University Press.

European Commission (2009). *Daphne Toolkit. A Campaign by People with Learning Disabilities Against Violence and Bullying of Young People with Learning Disabilities in Europe*. Available at: http://ec.europa.eu/justice_home/daphnetoolkit (accessed 9 February 2010).

Evans, S., and Byrt, R. (2002). The right to complain? In Dooher, J., and Byrt, R. (eds) *Empowerment and Participation: Power, Influence and Control in Contemporary Health Care*. Dinton, Salisbury: Quay Books/Mark Allen Publishing.

Fagerberg, I., and Jonhagen, M.E. (2002). Temporary confusion: A fearful *experience. Journal of Psychiatric and Mental Health Nursing* 9(3): 339–46.

Fairclough, P.L. (2002). *Living with Brain Injury*. London: Jessica Kingsley.

Fallon, P. (2003). Travelling through the system: the lived experience of people with borderline personality disorder in contact with the system. *Journal of Psychiatric and Mental Health Nursing* 10: 393–400.

Farrell, A.D., and Vulin-Reynolds, M. (2008). Violent behaviour and the science of prevention. In Flannery, D.J., Vazsonyi, A.T., and Waldman, I.D.,(eds). *The Cambridge Handbook of Violent Behavior and Aggression*. New York: Cambridge University Press.

Farrell, G.A., and Gray, C. (1992). *Aggression: A Nurses Guide to Therapeutic Management*. London: Scutari Press.

Faulkner, G.E.J., and Taylor, A.H. (eds) (2005). *Exercise, Health and Mental Health. Emerging Relationships*. London: Routledge/Taylor and Francis Group.

Fava, L. and Strauss, K. (2010). Multi-sensory rooms: Comparing effects of the Snoezelen and the stimulus proof environment on the behavior of adults with profound mental retardation. *Research in Developmental Disabilities* 31(1): 160–71.

Fawcett, B., and Waugh, F. (eds) (2008). *Addressing Violence, Abuse and Oppression. Debates and Challenges*. London: Routledge, Taylor and Francis Group.

Feeley, K., and Jones, E. (2008). Strategies to address challenging behaviour in young children with Down Syndrome. *Down Syndrome Research and Practice* 12(2): 153–63.

Ferns, T., and Chojnacka, I. (2005). Reporting incidents of violence and aggression towards NHS staff. *Nursing Standard* 19(38): 51–6.

Ferns, T., Cork, A., and Rew, M. (2005). Personal safety in the Accident and Emergency Department. *British Journal of Nursing* 14(13): 725–30.

Finnegan, R. (2004). Communicating humans ... but what does that mean? In Robb, M., Barrett, S., Komaromy, C., and Rogers, A. (eds) *Communication, Relationships and Care. A Reader*. London: Routledge, Taylor and Francis Group/The Open University.

Finnema, E.J., Dassen, T., and Halfens, R. (1994). Aggression in psychiatry: A qualitative study focusing on the characterisation and perception of patient agency by nurses working on psychiatric wards. *Journal of Advanced Nursing* 19(6): 1088–95.

Firth, W. (2004). Acute psychiatric wards: an overview. In Campling, P., Davies, S., and Farquharson, G. (eds.) *From Toxic Institutions to Therapeutic Environments: Residential Settings in Mental Health Services*. London: Gaskell.

Fish, J. (2006). *Heterosexism in Health and Social Care*. Basingstoke: Palgrave Macmillan.

Fisher, J. (2003). Participation and empowerment of users and carers in mental health services. In Dooher, J., and Byrt, R. (eds) *Empowerment and the Health Service User*. Dinton, Salisbury: Quay Books, Mark Allen Publishing.

Fitzgerald, K. (Undated). Neurological Disorders: Diencephalon. In Answers.com. www.answers.com/topic/diencephalon (accessed 9 February 2010).

Fitzgerald, P. (2003). A question of 'choices and space': Gay, lesbian and transgendered services in North Warwickshire. In Dooher, J., and Byrt, R. *Empowerment: and the Health Service User*. Dinton, Salisbury: Quay Books/Mark Allen Publishing.

Flannery, D.T., Vazsonyi, A.T., and Waldman, I.D. (eds) (2008). *The Cambridge Handbook of Violent Behavior and Aggression*. New York: Cambridge University Press.

Foakes, R.A. (2003). *Shakespeare and Violence*. Cambridge: Cambridge University Press.

Fontaine, K.L. (2009). *Mental Health Nursing* (6th edn). Upper Saddle River, NJ: Prentice Hall.

Ford, K.G., and Rigby, P. (2000). Managing and preventing aggressive behaviour. *Practice Nursing* 11(13): 9–11.

Ford, K; Middleton, J and Palmer, R. (1997). The Mental Health Training Needs of Primary Health Care Workers. *British Journal of Nursing*; 6 (21) 1244–1250.

re workers' training needs in mental health. *British Journal of Nursing* 6(2): 1244–50.

Foster, C., Bowers, L., and Nijman, H. (2007). Aggressive behaviour on acute psychiatric wards: Prevalence, severity and management. *Journal of Advanced Nursing* 58(2): 140–9.

Fox, J., and Gamble, C. (2006). Consolidating the assessment process: the semi-structured interview. In: Gamble, C., and Brennan, G. (eds). *Working with Serious Mental Illness. A Manual for Clinical Practice*. Edinburgh: Elsevier.

Fox, K.J. (1999). Changing violent minds: discursive correction and resistance in the cognitive treatment of violent offenders in prison. *Social Problems* 46(1): 88–103.

Freeth, R. (2007). *Humanising Psychiatry and Mental Health Care. The Challenge of the Person-Centred Approach*. Oxford: Radcliffe Publishing.

Freire, P. (1996). *The Pedagogy of the Oppressed*. Translated by Ramos, M.B. Harmondsworth: Penguin Books.

Freud, S. (1967). *The Ego and the Mechanism of Defence*. London: Hogarth Press.

Friis, S., and Helldin, L. (1994). The contribution made by the clinical setting to violence amongst psychiatric patients. *Criminal Behaviour and Mental Health* 4: 341–52.

Fuller, C. (2004). *Health and Safety Management: Principles and Best Practice*. Harlow: Financial Times, Prentice Hall.

Gabbard, G.O., Beck, J.S., and Holmes, J. (2007). *Oxford Textbook of Psychotherapy*. Oxford: Oxford University Press.

Gale, J., and Sanchez, B. (2005). Reflections on the treatment of psychosis in therapeutic communities. *Therapeutic Communities* 26(4): 485–94.

Gallagher, H.L., and Frith, C.D. (2003). Functional imaging of 'theory of mind'. *Trends in Cognitive Sciences* 7(2): 77–83.

Gallop, R., McCay, E., Guha, M., and Khan, P. (1999). The experience of hospitalisation and restraint of women who have a history of childhood sexual abuse. *Health Care for Women International* 20: 401–16.

Gamble, C., and Brennan, G. (eds) (2006a). *Working with Serious Mental Illness. A Manual for Clinical Practice*. Edinburgh: Elsevier.

Gamble, C., and Brennan, G. (2006b). Assessments: A rationale for choosing and using. In Gamble, C., and Brennan, G. (eds) *Working with Serious Mental Illness. A Manual for Clinical Practice*. Edinburgh: Elsevier.

Gamble, C., and Ryrie, I. with Curthoys, J. (2009). Psychosocial interventions. In Norman, I., and Ryrie, I. (eds) *The Art and Science of Mental Health Nursing* (2nd edn). Maidenhead: McGraw Hill Open University Press.

Garvey, F. (2008). Setting up a learning disability liaison team in acute care. *Nursing Times* 104(28): 30–31.

Gates, B. (ed.) (2007). *Learning Disabilities. Towards Inclusion* (5th edn). Edinburgh: Churchill Livingstone, Elsevier.

Gates, B., Gear, J., and Wray, J. (2000). *Behavioural Distress. Concepts and Strategies*. Edinburgh: Bailliere Tindall/Royal College of Nursing.

Gavlak, D., and Jamjoum, L. (2009). Rebuilding lives, healing minds. *Bulletin of the World Health Organisation* 87: 408–9. Available via: www.who.int/entitiy/bulletin/volumes/87/6/09 (accessed 9 February 2010).

Gelder, M., Mayou, R., and Cowen, P. (eds) (2001). *Shorter Oxford Textbook of Psychiatry* (4th edn). Oxford: Oxford University Press.

Gerrish, K., and Lacey, A. (2006). *The Research Process in Nursing* (5th edn). Oxford: Blackwell Publishing.

Gibson, B. (2006). Using mentalisation to treat patients with borderline personality disorder. *Nursing Standard* 20(51): 52–7.

Gillam, T. (2001). Listening to what Simon says. *Mental Health and Learning Disability Care* 4(7): 237–9.

Gilligan, J. (2001). *Preventing Violence*. London: Thames and Hudson.

Godfrey, J. (2003). The lesbian, gay man and transgendered experience as users of healthcare services. In Dooher, J., and Byrt, R. *Empowerment: and the Health Service User*. Dinton, Salisbury: Quay Books/Mark Allen Publishing.

Godin, P. (2006). *Risk and Nursing Practice*. Basingstoke: Palgrave Macmillan.

Goffman, E. (1968). *Asylums. Essays on the Social Situation of Mental Patients and Other Inmates*. Harmondsworth: Pelican.

Golding, J. (1997). *Without Prejudice: MIND Lesbian, Gay and Bisexual Mental Health Awareness Research*. London: MIND Publications.

Goldsmith, M. (1996). *Hearing the Voice of People with Dementia*. London: Jessica Kingsley.

Gournay, K., Benson, R., and Rogers, P. (2008). Inpatient care and management. In Soothill, K., Rogers, P., and Dolan, M. (eds) *Handbook of Forensic Mental Health*. Uffculme, Cullompton: Willam Publishing.

Government Office of the East Midlands (2009). Website. www.goem.gov.uk (accessed 9 February 2010).

Government Office of the East of England (2009). Website. www.go-east.gov.uk

Greenwood, P. (2009). Dance: Five-minute love affairs. *Journal of Dementia Care* 17(1): 30-1.

Grieger, T.A., Benedek, D.M., and Ursano, R.J. (2008). Posttraumatic stress disorder. In Simon, R.I., and Tardiff, K. (2eds) *Textbook of Violence Assessment and Management*. Washington, DC: American Publishing, Inc.

Griggs, I., Osley, R., and Bignell, P. (2009). Sexism in sport: It sidelines Britain's world-beaters. *The Independent on Sunday*. 22 March. Available via http://www.independent.co.uk/sport/general/others/sexism-in-sport-it-sidelines-britains-worldbeaters-1651319.html (last accessed 18 January 2010).

Gurney, S. (2009). The person with an affective/mood disorder. In Norman, I., and Ryrie, I. (eds) *The Art and Science of Mental Health Nursing* (2nd edn). Maidenhead: McGraw Hill Open University Press.

Hall, L. (2000). *Billy Elliot*. London: New Windmill Plays, Heinemann.

Hanlon, M. (2008). Men and violence. In Fawcett, B., and Waugh, F. (eds) *Addressing Violence, Abuse and Oppression. Debates and Challenges*. London: Routledge, Taylor and Francis Group.

Hare, R.D., and Neumann, C.S. (2008). Psychopathy as a clinical and empirical construct. *Annual Review of Clinical Psychology* 4: 217-46.

Harner, H.M. (2004). Relationships between incarcerated women: moving beyond stereotypes. *Journal of Psychosocial Nursing and Mental Health Services* 42(1): 38-46.

Harper-Jaques, S., and Reimer, M. (1998). Biopsychosocial management of aggression and violence. In Boyd, M.A., and Nihart, M.A. (eds) *Psychiatric Nursing*. New York: Lippincott-Raven.

Harris, D., and Morrison, E.F. (1995). Managing violence without coercion. *Archives of Psychiatric Nursing* 9(4): 203-10.

Harris, F., Hek, G., and Condon, L. (2008). Health needs of prisoners in England and Wales: The implications for prison healthcare of gender, age and ethnicity. *Health and Social Care in the Community* 15(1): 56-66.

Harris, G.T., Rice, M.E., and Cormier, C. A. (1994). Psychopaths: Is a therapeutic community therapeutic? *Therapeutic Communities* 15(4): 283-99.

Hart, D. (2008). Trapped within poverty and violence. In Fawcett, B., and Waugh, F. (eds) *Addressing Violence, Abuse and Oppression. Debates and Challenges*. London: Routledge, Taylor and Francis Group.

Hastings, R.P., and Brown, T. (2002). Behavioural knowledge, causal beliefs and self-efficacy as predictors of special educators' emotional reactions to challenging behaviours. *Journal of Intellectual Disability Research* 46(2): 144-50.

Healthcare Commission (2006). Fewer NHS workers report violence and abuse from patients and relatives – NHS Survey. From Healthcare Commission website (accessed January 2007): www.healthcarecommission.org.uk/

Healthcare Commission (2008). Audit throws spotlight on violence in mental health units and highlights areas for action. www.healthcarecommission.org.uk/ (accessed May 2008).

Healthcare Commission (2009a). *National Survey of NHS Staff, 2008*. Summary of key findings. Available via: www.cqc.org.uk/ (last accessed 12 January 2010).

Healthcare Commission (2009b). Report. Cited in Parish, C. (2009). Mental health services are failing people from ethnic minorities. *Mental Health Practice* 12(5): 3.

Health Services Advisory Committee (1997). Violence and Aggression to Staff in Health Services. Guidance on Assessment and Management. Sudbury: HSE Books.

Healy, D. (2005). *Psychiatric Drugs Explained* (4th edn). Edinburgh: Elsevier Churchill Livingstone.

Henley, A., and Schott, J. (1999). *Culture, Religion and Patient Care in a Multi-Ethnic Society*. London: Age Concern.

Hensley, M.A. (2008). Being bipolar and dealing with obesity: Personal lessons. *Psychiatric Rehabilitation Journal* 3: 247-8.

Heptinstall, T., Kralj, L., and Lee, G. (2004). Asylum seekers: A health professional perspective. *Nursing Standard* 18(25): 44-53.

Hill, J., Murray, L., Leidecker, V., and Sharp, H. (2009). The dynamics of threat, fear and intentionality in the conduct disorders. In Hodgins, S., Viding, E., and Plodowski, A. (eds) *The Neurological Basis of Violence: Science and Rehabilitation*. Oxford: Oxford University Press.

HM Government (1989). *The Children Act*. London: HMSO.

HM Government (1998). *Human Rights Act*. Chapter 42. London: HMSO.

HM Government (2004). *The Children Act*. London: HMSO.

HM Government (2006). *Equality Act*. London: The Stationery Office.

HM Government (2009). Valuing People Now: A Three-Year Strategy for People with Learning Disabilities. London: The Stationery Office.

HM Inspector of Prisons (2009a). *HM Inspector of Prisons for England and Wales. Annual Report*. London: The Stationery Office.

HM Inspector of Prisons (2009b). Publication of HM Inspectorate of Prisons Annual Report. January, 2009. Available at: www.inspectorates.homeoffice.gov.uk/hmprisons/ (accessed 9 February 2010).

HM Prison Service (2007). Offender behaviour programmes (OBPs). Online. Available from: www.hmprisonservice.govuk/adviceandsupport. (accessed 15 March 2009).

HM Prison Service (2009). Violence and Bullying. Available at: www.hmprisonservice.gov/uk/ (accessed 14 September 2009).

Hodgins, S., Viding, E., and Plodowski, A. (eds) (2009). *The Neurological Basis of Violence: Science and Rehabilitation.* Oxford: Oxford University Press.

Holmqvist, R., and Fogelstam, H. (1996). Psychological climate and countertransference in psychiatric treatment homes. *Acta Psychiatrica Scandinavica* 93(4): 288–95.

Home Office, National Institute for Mental Health in England and Department of Health (2006). *Tackling the Health and Mental Health Effects of Domestic and Sexual Violence and Abuse.* Report by Catherine Itzen. London: Home Office, National Institute for Mental Health in England and Department of Health.

Hopton, J. (1995). The application of the ideas of Frantz Fanon to the practice of mental health nursing. *Journal of Advanced Nursing* 21: 723–8.

Horn, N., Johnstone, L., and Brooke, S. (2007). Some service user perspectives on the diagnosis of borderline personality disorder. *Journal of Mental Health* 16(2): 255–69.

House of Lords and House of Commons Joint Commission on Human Rights (2008). *Seventh Report of Session, 2007–2008.* Volume 1. HL Paper 40-1. HC 73-1. 6 March 2008. London: The Stationery Office.

Howells, K., Daffern, M., and Day, A.. (2008). Aggression and violence. In Soothill, K., Rogers, P., and Dolan, M. (eds) *Handbook of Forensic Mental Health.* Uffculme, Cullompton: Willan Publishing.

Howitt, D. (2009). *Introduction to Forensic and Criminal Psychology* (3rd edn). Harlow: Pearson Education.

Hughes, L., and Owen, H. (eds) (2009). *Good Practice in Safeguarding Children: Working Effectively in Child Protection.* London: Jessica Kingsley.

Hunter, M.E., and Love, C.C. (1996). Total quality management and the reduction of inpatient violence and costs in a forensic psychiatric hospital. *Psychiatric Services* 47(7): 751–4.

Institute of Psychiatry Health Services Research Department (2002). *The Recognition, Prevention and Therapeutic Management of Violence in Mental Health Care.* London: United Kingdom Central Council for Nursing, Midwifery and Health Visiting. Available from: www.nmc-uk.org (accessed 9 February 2010).

International Snoezelen Association (2009). Website. www.isna.de/index2e.html (accessed 9 February 2010).

Ireland, J. (2002). *Bullying Among Prisoners: Evidence, Research and Intervention Strategies.* London: Brunner-Routledge.

Irwin, J. (2008). Challenging the second closet: Intimate partner violence between lesbians. In Fawcett, B., and Waugh, F. (eds) *Addressing Violence, Abuse and Oppression. Debates and Challenges.* London: Routledge.

Jackson, D., Clare, J., and Mannix, J. (2002). Who would want to be a nurse? Violence in the workplace – a factor in recruitment and retention. *Journal of Nursing Management* 10(1): 13–20.

Jahoda, A., and Wanless, L.K. (2005). Knowing you: the interpersonal perceptions of staff towards aggressive individuals with mild to moderate intellectual disabilities in situations of conflict. *Journal of Intellectual Disability Research* 49(7): 544–51.

Jansen, G.J., Dassen, T.W., and Groot Jabbink, G. (2005). Staff attitudes towards aggression in health care. *Journal of Psychiatric and Mental Health Nursing* 11: 172–8.

Jeffcote, N., and Travers, R. (2004). Thinking about the needs of women in secure settings. In Jeffcote, N., and Watson, T. (eds) *Working Therapeutically with Women in Secure Settings.* London: Jessica Kingsley.

Jeffcote, N., and Watson, T. (eds) (2004). *Working Therapeutically with Women in Secure Settings.* London: Jessica Kingsley.

John (2000). *The stigma of diagnosis. Dialogue 5,* Autumn/Winter. Sutton, Surrey. Henderson Hospital publication.

Jones, A. (2004). A shock to the system: Improving encounters with acute care. In Turnbull, J. (ed.) *Learning Disability Nursing.* Oxford: Blackwell Science.

Jones, A. (2005). Transference, countertransference and repetition compulsion. Some implications for practice' *Journal of Clinical Nursing* 14(10): 1177–84.

Jones, M. (1968). *Social Therapy in Psychiatry.* Harmondsworth: Penguin Books.

Jorgensen, K.N., Romma, V., and Rundmo, T. (2009). Associations between ward atmosphere, patient satisfaction and outcome. *Journal of Psychiatric and Mental Health Nursing* 16(2): 113–20.

Joseph, S. (2001). *Psychopathology and Therapeutic Approaches. An Introduction.* Basingstoke: Palgrave.

Kant, I. (1969). *The Moral Law: Kant's Groundwork of the Metaphysics of Morals* (Translated by Paton, H.J.). London: Hutchinson.

Kaplan, S.G., and Wheeler, E.G. (1983). Survival skills for working with potentially violent clients. *Social Casework* 64: 339–43.

Keen, T., and Barker, P. (2009). The person with schizophrenia. In Barker, P. (ed.) *Psychiatric and Mental Health Nursing: The Craft of Caring* (2nd edn). London: Arnold.

Keen, T., and Lakeman, R. (2009). Collaboration with patients and families. In Barker, P. (ed.) *Psychiatric and Mental Health Nursing: The Craft of Caring* (2nd edn). London: Arnold.

Kelly, M. (2008). Challenging behaviour. In Clark, L.L., and Griffiths, P. (eds) *Learning Disability and Impairments. Meeting Needs Throughout Health Services.* Chichester: John Wiley and Sons, Ltd.

Kelly, S., Hill, J., Boardman, H., and Overton, I. (2004). Therapeutic communities. In Campling, P., Davies, S., and Farquharson, G. (eds) *From Toxic Institutions to Therapeutic Environments: Residential Settings in Mental Health Services.* London: Gaskell.

Kelson, M., Ford, C., and Riggs, M. (1998). *Stroke Rehabilitation: Patient and Carer Views. A Report from the Intercollegiate Stroke Group.* London: College of Health and Research Unit, Royal College of Physicians.

Kesey, K. (1962). *One Flew Over the Cuckoo's Nest.* London: Methuen.

Kettles, A.M., Byrt, R., and Woods, P. (2007). Introduction. In National Forensic Nurses' Research and Development Group: Kettles, A.M.,

Woods, P., Byrt, R., Addo, M.A., Coffey, M., and Doyle, M. (eds) *Aspects of Forensic Mental Health Nursing in Acute Mental Health Settings*. London: Quay Books, MA Healthcare.

Kevan, F. (2003). Challenging behaviour and communication difficulties. *British Journal of Learning Disabilities* 31: 75–80.

Khalifa, N., and Hardie, T. (2005). Possession and jinn. *Journal of the Royal Society of Medicine* 98: 351–3.

Kilshaw, J. (1999). Can medium secure units avoid becoming total institutions? In Tarbuck, P., Topping-Morris, B. and Burnard, P. (eds) *Forensic Mental Health Nursing. Strategy and Implication*. London: Whurr Publications.

Kindell, J., and Griffiths, H. (2006). Speech and language therapy interventions for people with Alzheimer's disease. In Bryan, K., and Maxim, J. (eds) *Communication Disability in the Dementias*. London: Whurr Publishers.

King, M., Smith, G., and Bartlett, A. (2004). Treatments of homosexuality in Britain since the nineteen fifties: an oral history: the experience of professionals. *British Medical Journal* 328(7437): 429–32.

Kipping, C. (2004). The person who misuses drugs or alcohol. In Norman, I., and Ryrie, I. (eds) The Art and Science of Mental Health Nursing. A Textbook of Principles and Practice. Maidenhead: Open University Press, McGraw-Hill Education.

Kipping, C. (2009). The person with co-existing mental health and substance misuse problems. In Norman, I., and Ryrie, I. (eds) *The Art and Science of Mental Health Nursing. A Textbook of Principles and Practice*. Maidenhead: McGraw Hill Open University Press.

Kirby, S. (1997). Ward atmosphere on a medium secure long-stay ward. *Journal of Forensic Psychiatry* 8(2): 336–47.

Kirby, S. D. and Cross, D. (2002). Socially constructed narrative interventions: A foundation for therapeutic alliances. In Kettles, A.M., Woods, P., and Collins, M. (eds) *Therapeutic Interventions for Forensic Mental Health Nurses*. London: Jessica Kingsley.

Kitwood, T. (1993). Frames of reference for an understanding of dementia. In Johnson, J., and Slater, R. (eds) *Ageing and Later Life*. London: Open University/Sage.

Kitwood, T. (1997) *Dementia Reconsidered: The Person Comes First*. Buckingham: Open University Press.

Kring, A.M., and Davison, G.C. (2007). *Abnormal Psychology* (10th edn). Hoboken, New Jersey: Wiley.

Kroese, B.S., and Holmes, G. (2001). 'I've never said "no" to anything in my life': Helping people with learning disabilities who experience psychological problems. In Newnes, C., Holmes, G., and Dunn, C. (eds) *This is Madness, Too. Critical Perspectives on Mental Health Services*. Ross on Wye: PCCS Books, Ltd.

Kuipers, L., Leff, J., and Lam, D. (2002). *Family Work for Schizophrenia*. London: Gaskell.

Kulik, J., and Schweitzer, P. (2002). Making memories matter. Age exchange: a theatre of memories. *Working with Older People* 6(3): 13–15.

Kunyk, D., and Olson, J.K. (2001). Clarification of conceptualisations of empathy. *Journal of Advanced Nursing* 35(3): 317–25.

Kunz, M., Mylus, V., Scharmann, S., Schepeleman, K., and Lautenbacher, S. (2009). Influence of dementia on multiple components of pain. European *Journal of Pain* 13(3): 317–25.

Lanza, M.L., Zeiss, R., and Rierdan, J. (2006). Violence against psychiatric nurses: Sensitive research as science and intervention. *Contemporary Nurse* 21(1): 71–84.

L'Arche (2009). Website. www.larche.org.uk/ (accessed 9 February 2010).

Laurance, J. (2008). Prison study to investigate link between junk food and violence. *The Independent*, 29 January 2008. www.independent.co.uk (accessed 9 February 2010).

Lawrence, J. (2008). 'Unacceptable' levels of violence on mental health wards. *The Independent*, 23 July 2008. www.independent.co.uk (accessed 9 February 2010).

Lawson, B., and Phiri, M. (2000). Room for improvement. *Health Service Journal* 110(5688): 24–7.

Le Butt, S., and Chauhan, M. (Undated). Unpublished handout, Leicester: Arnold Lodge.

Leddy, J., and O'Connell, M. (2002). The prevalence, nature and psychological correlates of bullying in Irish prisons. *Legal and Criminological Psychology* 7(2): 131–40.

Lees, J., Manning, N., Menzies, D., and Morant, N. (eds) (2004). *A Culture of Enquiry: Research Evidence and the Therapeutic Community*. London: Jessica Kingsley.

Leff, J. (2001). Cultural influences in schizophrenia. In Lieberman, J.A., and Murray, R.M. (eds) *Comprehensive Care of Schizophrenia. A Textbook of Clinical Management*. London: Martin Dunitz.

Leiba, P.A. (1980). Management of violent patients. *Nursing Times* 76(23): 101–4.

Lester, H., and Glasby, J. (2006). *Mental Health Policy and Practice*. Basingstoke: Palgrave Macmillan.

Lim, R.F., and Bell, C.C. (2008). Cultural competence in risk assessment. In Simon, R.I., and Tardiff, K. (eds) *Textbook of Violence Assessment and Management*. Washington, DC: American Publishing, Inc.

Lin, Y., and Liu, H. (2005). The impact of workplace violence on nurses in South Taiwan. *International Journal of Nursing Studies* 42(7): 773–8.

Linsley, P. (2006). *Violence and Aggression in the Workplace: A Practical Guide to Risk Management in Mental Health*. Abingdon: Radcliffe.

Liu, J., Raine, A., Venables, P.H., and Mednick, S.A. (2004). Malnutrition at age three and externalising behavior problems at ages 8, 11 and 17 years. *American Journal of Psychiatry* 161(11): 2005–13.

Liu, J., and Wuerker, A. (2005). Biosocial bases of aggressive and violent behaviour: implications for nursing studies. *International Journal of Nursing Studies* 42: 229–41.

Livesley, W.J. (2007). An integrated approach to the treatment of personality disorder. *Journal of Mental Health* 16(1): 131–48.

Livingston, G., Johnston, K., Katona, C., Paton, J., and Lykestos, C.G. (2005). Systematic review of psychological management of neurotic symptoms of dementia. *American Journal of Psychiatry* 162: 1996–2021.

Lloyd-Williams, F., and Mair, F. (2005). The role of exercise in recovery from heart failure. In Faulkner, G.E.J., and Taylor, A.H. (eds) *Exercise, Health and Mental Health. Emerging Relationships*. London: Routledge/Taylor and Francis Group.

Long, C.G., Collins, L., MacDonald, C., Johnston, D., and Hardy, S. (2007). Staff stress and challenging behaviour on a medium secure developmental disabilities ward for women: The outcomes of organisational change, and clinical interventions. *The British Journal of Forensic Practice* 10(3): 4–10.

Lovegrove, B. (2002). Good neighbours: Help or hindrance? *Nursing Older People* 14(6): 10–13.

Lowe, T. (1992). Characteristics of effective nursing interventions in the management of challenging behaviour. *Journal of Advanced Nursing* 17: 1226–32.

Lucas, V.L., Collins, S., and Langdon, P.C. (2009). The causal attributions of teaching staff towards children with intellectual disabilities: A comparison of 'vignettes' depicting challenging behaviour with 'real' incidents of challenging behaviour. *Journal of Applied Research in Intellectual Disabilities* 22(1): 1–9.

Luckes, E. (1888). *Lectures on General Nursing. Delivered to the London Hospital Training School for Nurses* (3rd edn). London: Kegan Paul, Trench and Co, Ltd.

Lugton, J. (2002). *Communicating with Dying People and Their Relatives*. Abingdon: Radcliffe Medical Press.

Lundstrom, M., Saveman, B.-I., and Eisemann, M. (2007). Prevalence of violence and its relation to caregivers' demographics and emotional reactions: an explorative study of caregivers working in group homes for persons with learning disabilities. *Scandinavian Journal of Caring Science* 21: 84–90.

McArdle, S., and Byrt, R.(2001). Fiction, poetry and mental health: Expressive and therapeutic uses of literature. *Journal of Psychiatric and Mental Health Nursing* 8(6): 517–24.

McAuliffe, L., Nay, R., O'Donnell, M., and Featherstonhaugh, D. (2009). Pain assessment in older people with dementia: Literature review. *Journal of Advanced Nursing* 65(1): 2–10.

McCann, E. (2001). Recent developments in PSIs for people with psychosis. *Issues in Mental Health Nursing* 22: 99–107.

McChargue, D.E., Gulliver, S.B., and Hitsman, B. (2002). Would smokers with schizophrenia benefit from a more flexible approach to smoking treatment? *Addiction* 97: 785–93.

McCue, M. (2000). Behavioural interventions. In Gates, B., Gear, J., and Wray, J. (eds) *Behavioural Distress. Concepts and Strategies*. Edinburgh: Bailliere Tindall/Royal College of Nursing.

McDougall, T. (2000). Violent incidents in a forensic adolescent unit: A retrospective analysis. *NT Research* 5(2): 87–98.

McGeorge, S. (2007). Acute mental health issues. In Neno, R., Aveyard, B. and Heath, H. (eds) *Older People and Mental Health Nursing: A Handbook of Care*. Malden: Blackwell Publishing.

MacHale, R., and Carey, S. (2002). An investigation on the effects of bereavement on mental health and challenging behaviour in adults with learning disability. *British Journal of Learning Disabilities* 30(3): 113–17.

McKay, M., Rogers, P.D., and McKay, J. (2003). *When Anger Hurts. Quieting the Storm Within* (2nd edn). Oakland, CA: New Harbinger Publications, Inc.

McKenzie, B.M. (2008). Psychological approaches to longer-term patients presenting with challenging behaviours. In Beer, M.D., Pereira, S., and Paton, C. (eds) *Psychiatric Intensive Care* (2nd edn). London: Greenwich Medical Media.

McKenzie, K., Chalmers, E., Paxton, D., and Murray, G. (2003). Hitting the spot. *Learning Disability Practice* 6(3): 15–19.

McKenzie, K., Rae, H., Maclean, H., Megson, P., and Wilson, S. (2006). Difficulties faced by social care staff when managing challenging behaviour. *Learning Disability Practice* 9(2): 28–32.

Mackintosh, J. (1990). *Theories of Aggression: Principles and Practice of Forensic Psychiatry*. Edinburgh: Churchill-Livingstone.

Macleod, S. (2007). *The Psychiatry of Palliative Medicine. The Dying Mind*. Oxford: Radcliffe Publishing.

McMurran, M. (2008). Personality disorders. In Soothill, K., Rogers, P., and Dolan, M. (eds) *Handbook of Forensic Mental Health*. Uffculme, Devon: Willan Publishing.

Maeve, M.K., and Vaughn, M.S. (2001). Nursing with prisoners: The practice of caring, forensic nursing or penal harm nursing? *Advances in Nursing Science* 24(2): 47–64.

Maddern, S. (2004). Post-traumatic stress disorder in asylum seekers. *Nursing Standard* 18(18): 36–9.

Maden, T. (2007). *Treating Violence: A Guide to Risk Management in Mental Health*. Oxford: Oxford University Press.

Maffia, C. (2008). Well-being for refugees and asylum seekers through holistic practice. *Journal of Integrated Care* 16(1): 31–7.

Mandelstam, M. (2009). *Safeguarding Vulnerable Adults and the Law*. London: Jessica Kingsley.

Manos, J., and Braun, J. (2006). *Care of the Difficult Patient. A Nurse's Guide*. London: Routledge, Taylor and Francis Group.

Mansell, J., Beadle-Brown, J., Whelton, B., Beckett, C., and Hutchinson, A. (2008). Effect of care structure and organisation on staff care practices in small community homes for people with intellectual disabilities. *Journal of Applied Research in Intellectual Disabilities* 21: 398–413.

Marrington-Mir, P., and Rimmer, A. (2007). Black and minority ethnic people and mental health in Britain: A holistic approach. *Journal of Integrated Care* 15(96): 37–41.

Martin, C.A., Cook, C., Woodring, J.H., Burkhardt, G., Guenthner, G., Omar, H.A., and Kelly, T.H. (2008). Caffeine use: Association with nicotine use, aggression and other psychopathology in psychiatric and paediatric outpatient adolescents. *The Scientific World Journal* 8: 512–16.

Martin, J.P. (1984). *Hospitals in Trouble*. Blackwell: Oxford.

Mason, T., and Chandley, M. (1990). Nursing models in a special hospital: a critical analysis of efficacy. *Journal of Advanced Nursing* 15: 667–73.

Mason, T., and Chandley, M. (1999). *Managing Violence and Aggression. A Manual for Nurses and Health Care Workers*. Edinburgh: Churchill Livingstone.

Meehan, T., Vermeer, C., and Windsor, C. (2000). Patients' perceptions of seclusion: A qualitative investigation. *Journal of Advanced Nursing* 31(2): 370-7.

Meehan, T., McIntosh, W., and Bergen, H. (2006). Aggressive behavior in high-secure settings: The perceptions of patients. *Journal of Psychiatric and Mental Health Nursing* 13(1): 19–25.

Mencap (2007). *Death by Indifference*. London: Mencap.

Mental Health Foundation. (2008). *Boiling Point. Problem Anger and What We Can Do About It*. London: Mental Health Foundation. Available via: www.mentalhealth.org.uk/campaigns/anger-and-mental-health/boling-point-report/ (accessed 9 February 2010).

Mental Health Foundation and Sainsbury Centre for Mental Health (2002). *Being There in a Crisis: A Report of the Learning from Eight Mental Health Crisis Services*. London Mental Health Foundation and Sainsbury Centre for Mental Health.

Mercer, D., Mason, T., and Richman, J. (1999). Good and evil in the crusade of care. *Journal of Psychosocial Nursing and Mental Health Services* 37(9): 13–17.

Michael, Sir J. (2008). *Health Care for All: Report of the Independent Inquiry into Access to Health Care for People with Learning Disabilities*. London: Mencap.

Mistry, N. (2009). Personal communication.

Moffitt, T.E. (2008). A review of research on the taxonomy of life-course persistent versus adolescence-limited antisocial behaviour. In Flannery, D.T., Vazsonyi, A.T., and Waldman, I.D. (eds) *The Cambridge Handbook of Violent Behavior and Aggression*. New York: Cambridge University Press.

Monk-Steel, B. (2009). Unpublished student handout, School of Nursing and Midwifery, De Montfort University. Leicester: De Montfort University.

Moos, R.H. (1974). *Evaluating Treatment Environments. A Sociological Approach*. New York: John Wiley and Sons.

Morgan, S. (2001). The problems of aggression and violence for health-care staff. *Professional Nurse* 17(2): 107–10.

Morgan, S., and Wetherell, A. (2009). Working with risk. In Norman, I., and Ryrie, I. (eds) *The Art and Science of Mental Health Nursing. A Textbook of Principles and Practice*. Maidenhead: McGraw Hill Open University Press.

Morris, G. (2006). *Mental Health Issues and the Media: An Introduction for Mental Health Professionals*. London: Routledge, Taylor and Francis Group.

Morrison, E.F. (1992). A coercive interactional style as an antecedent to aggression in psychiatric patients. *Research in Nursing and Health* 15: 421–31.

Morrison, V., and Bennett, P. (2009). *An Introduction to Health Psychology* (2nd edn). Harlow: Pearson Prentice Hall.

Moss, J. (1998). Working with issues of sexual abuse. In Emerson, E., Hatton, C., Bromley, J., and Crane, A. (eds) *Clinical Psychology and People with Intellectual Disabilities*. Chichester: John Wiley and Sons.

Moyo, G. (2008). Therapeutic approaches in mental health. In Dooher, J. (ed.) *Fundamental Aspects of Mental Health Nursing*. London: Quay Books, MA Healthcare, Ltd.

Muir-Cochrane, E. (2009). The person who experiences anxiety. In Barker, P. (ed.) *Psychiatric and Mental Health Nursing: The Craft of Caring* (2nd edn). London: Arnold.

Mullan, B., and Badger, P. (2007). Aggression and violence towards staff working with older patients. *Nursing Standard* 21(27): 35–8.

Munro, V. (2002). Why do nurses neglect to report violent incidents? *Nursing Times* 98(17): 38–9.

Naldrett, T. (2007). Dilemmas in mental health nursing. In Neno, R., Aveyard, B., and Heath, H. (eds) *Older People and Mental Health Nursing: A Handbook of Care*. Malden: Blackwell Publishing.

Narayanasamy, A. (2001). *Spiritual Care: A Practical Guide for Nurses and Health Care Practitioners* (2nd edn). Dinton, Salisbury: Quay Books, Mark Allen Publishing, Ltd.

Narayanasamy, A., and White, E. (2005). A review of transcultural nursing. *Nurse Education Today* 25(2): 102–11.

National Forensic Nurses' Research and Development Group: Woods, P., Kettles, A.M., Byrt, R., Addo, M., Coffey, M., Collins, M., Doyle, M., Garman, G., and Watson, C. (eds) (2006). *Aspects of Forensic Mental Health Nursing: Interventions with People with 'Personality Disorder'*. London: Quay Books/MA.Healthcare, Ltd.

National Forensic Nurses' Research and Development Group: Kettles, A.M. Woods, P., and Byrt, R. (eds) (2008). *Forensic Mental Health Nursing: Competencies, Roles, Responsibilities*. London: Quay Books, MA Healthcare, Ltd.

National Institute for Clinical Excellence (NICE) (2005) CG25:.*Violence Guideline*. February. London: NICE., Available on: www.nice.org.uk (accessed 9 February 2010).

National Institute for Health and Clinical Excellence (NICE) (2009). *Core Interventions in the Treatment and Management of Schizophrenia in Primary and Secondary Care* (Update). March. London: NICE.

National Institute for Mental Health in England (NIMHE) (2004). *From Here to Equality. A Strategic Plan to Tackle Stigma and Discrimination on Mental Health Grounds*, 2004–2009. Leeds: Department of Health.

National Institute for Mental Health in England.and Department of Health (2004). *Personality Disorder: No Longer a Diagnosis of Exclusion*. London: Department of Health.

NPI Center (Natural and Nutritional Products Industry Center) (2008). Wellcome Trust Awards $2.6 Million to Further Research the Link

Between Diet and Antisocial Behaviour. www.npicenter/com (accessed 9 February 2010).

Needham, I. (2006). Psychological responses following exposure to violence. In Richter, D., and Whittington, R. (eds). *Violence in Mental Health Settings. Causes, Consequences, Management.* New York: Springer.

Nelson-Jones, R. (2006). *Theory and Practice of Counselling and Psychotherapy.* London: Sage.

Neno, R., Aveyard, B., and Heath, H. (eds) (2007). *Older People and Mental Health Nursing: A Handbook of Care.* Malden: Blackwell Publishing.

Neumann, C.S., Hare, R.D., and Newman, J.P. (2007). The super-ordinate nature of the psychopathy checklist – revised. *Journal of Personality Disorders* 21(3): 102–17.

News-Medical.Net (2006). Website. Advances in Treatment of Borderline Personality Disorder. 10 January. www.news-medical.net/?id=15318 (last accessed 13 January 2010).

Newnes, C., Holmes, G., and Dunn, C. (eds) (1999). *This is Madness. A Critical Look at Psychiatry and the Future of Mental Health Services.* Llangorren, Ross on Wye: PCCS Books.

Newnes, C., Holmes, G., and Dunn, C. (eds) (2001). *This is Madness Too. Critical Perspectives on Mental Health Services.* Llangarron, Ross on Wye: PCCS Books.

NHS Business Services Authority Security Management Service (2007a). *Tackling Violence Against Staff. Explanatory Notes for Reporting Procedures Introduced by Secretary of State Directions in November, 2003.* (Updated March, 2007). London: NHS Business Services Authority Security Management Service. www.nhbsa.nhs.uk/SecurityManagement.DOC (accessed 9 February 2010).

NHS Business Services Authority Security Management Service (2007b). *Violence Against NHS Survey: 2006 Report.* London: Business Services Authority/NHS Security Management Service. www.nhbsa.nhs.uk/SecurityManagement.DOC (accessed 9 February 2010).

NHS Business Services Authority Security Management Service (2009). *Not Alone. A Guide for the Better Protection of Lone Workers in the NHS.* (Revised). London: NHS Security Management Service. www.nhbsa.nhs.uk/SecurityManagement.DOC (accessed 9 February 2010).

NHS Institute for Innovation and Improvement (2009). *The Productive Mental Health Ward. Releasing Time to Care.* www.institute.nhs.uk/quality_and_value/productivity_series/the_productive_mental_health_word.html (last accessed January 2007).

NHS Patient Safety Agency (2006). *With Safety in Mind: Mental Health Services and Patient Safety. Patient Safety Observatory Report. July. Building a Memory: Preventing Harm, Reducing Risks and Improving Patient Safety.* London: National Patient Safety Agency. www.clingov.nscsha.nhs.uk (accessed 9 February 2010).

NHS Security Management Service. (2004). *Non Physical Assault Explanatory Notes.* London: NHS Security Management Service. www.nhbsa.nhs.uk/SecurityManagement.DOC (accessed 9 February 2010).

NHS Security Management Service (2005). *Promoting Safer and Therapeutic Services. Implementing the National Syllabus in Learning Disability and Mental Health Services.* London: NHS Security Management Service. www.nhbsa.nhs.uk/SecurityManagement.DOC (accessed 9 February 2010).

Niehoff, D. (1999). *The Biology of Violence. How Understanding the Brain, Behaviour and Environment Can Break the Vicious Circle of Aggression.* New York: The Free Press.

Norton, K., and Dolan, B. (1995). Acting out and the institutional response. The *Journal of Forensic Psychiatry* 6: 317–32.

Novaco, R.W. (1975). *Anger Control: Development and Evaluation of an Experimental Treatment.* Lexington KY: D.C. Heath.

Novaco, R.W. (1994). Anger as a risk factor among the mentally disordered. In Monahan, J., and Steadman, H. (eds) *Violence and Mental Disorder.* Chicago IL: University of Chicago Press.

NSPCC Inform (2006). *Key Child Protection Statistics: Bullying.* www.nspcc.org.uk/Inform/Onlineresources/Statistics/KeyCPStats/10_asp_ifeg (last accessed January 2007).

Nursing and Midwifery Council (2008). *The Code: Standards of Conduct, Performance and Ethics for Nurses and Midwives.* London: Nursing and Midwifery Council.

O'Carroll, M., and Park, A. (2007). *Essential Mental Health Nursing Skills.* Edinburgh: Mosby Elsevier.

Oddy, R. (2003). *Promoting Mobility for People with Dementia. A Problem Solving Approach* (2nd edn). London: Age Concern.

Odgers, C.L. (2009). The life-course persistent pathway of antisocial behaviour: Risks for violence and poor physical health. In Hodgins, S., Viding, E., and Plodowski, A. (eds) *The Neurological Basis of Violence: Science and Rehabilitation.* Oxford: Oxford University Press.

O'Donohue, W., and Graybar, S.R. (eds) (2008). *Handbook of Contemporary Psychotherapy: Toward an Improved Understanding of Effective Psychotherapy.* Los Angeles: Sage Publications.

Okasha, S. (2002). *Philosophy of Science: A Very Short Introduction.* Oxford: Oxford University Press.

O'Keeffee, S.T. (1999). Delirium in the elderly. *Age and Ageing* 28, Supplement 2: 5–8.

Ormerod, E. (2008). Companion animals and rehabilitation-experiences from a therapeutic community in Scotland. *Therapeutic Communities* 29(3): 285–96.

Padley, B. (2007). Prison 'increasingly dangerous as violence soars'. *The Independent on Sunday.* 5 February. www.independent.co.uk/news/uk/crime/prisons-increasingly-dangerous-as-violence-soars (accessed 24 February 2010).

Papadopoulos, R.K. (2003). Narratives of translating-interpreting with refugees: The subjugation of individual discourses. In Tribe, R., and Raval, H. (eds). *Working with Interpreters in Mental Health.* Hove: Brunner-Routledge, Taylor and Francis Group.

Parker, M. (ed.) (2007). *Dynamic Security. The Therapeutic Community in Prison.* London: Jessica Kingsley.

Parker-Hall, S. (2009). *Anger, Rage and Relationship. An Empathic Approach to Anger Management.* London: Routledge, Taylor and Francis Group.

Parish, C. (2009). Mental health services are failing people from ethnic minorities. *Mental Health Practice* 12(5): 3.

Parry-Crooke, G. (2000). *Good Girls: Surviving the System. A Consultation with Women in High and Medium Secure Settings*. London: WISH/University of North London.

Paterson, B. (2005). Thinking the unthinkable: A role for pain compliance and mechanical restraint in the management of violence? *Mental Health Practice* 8(7): 18–23.

Paterson, B., and Leadbetter, D. (1999). De-escalation in the management of aggression and violence: Towards evidence-based practice. In Turnbull, J., and Paterson, B. (eds) *Aggression and Violence. Approaches to Effective Management*. Basingstoke: Macmillan.

Paterson, B., Leadbetter, D., and McCormish, A. (1997). De-escalating aggressive behaviour. In Kidd, B. and Stark, C. (eds) *Management of Aggression and Violence in Health Care*. London: Gaskell.

Patrick, C.J., and Verona, E. (2008). The psychophysiology of aggression: Autonomic, electrocortical, and neuro-imaging findings. In: Flannery, D.T., Vazsonyi, A.T., and Waldman, I.D. (eds) *The Cambridge Handbook of Violent Behavior and Aggression*. New York: Cambridge University Press.

Patterson, G. (2005). The bully as victim? *Paediatric Nursing* 17(10): 27–30.

Peckover, S., and Chidlaw, R.G. (2007). Too frightened to care? Accounts by district nurses working with clients who misuse substances. *Health and Social Care in the Community* 15(3): 238–45.

Perkins, R., and Repper, J. (2009). Recovery and social inclusion. In Norman, I., and Ryrie, I. (eds) *The Art and Science of Mental Health Nursing. A Textbook of Principles and Practice*. Maidenhead: McGraw Hill Open University Press.

Perseius, K.- I., Ojehagen, A., Ekdahl, S., Asberg, M., and Samuelsson, M. (2003). Treatment of suicidal and deliberate self-harming patients with borderline personality disorder using dialectical behavior therapy: The patients' and the therapists' perceptions. *Archives of Psychiatric Nursing* 17(5): 218–27.

Petersen, A., and Wilkinson, I. (eds) (2008). *Health, Risk and Vulnerability*. London: Routledge, Taylor and Francis Group.

Philo, G. (2001). Media and mental illness. In Davey, B., Gray, A., and Seale, C. (eds) *Health and Disease. A Reader*. Buckingham: Open University Press.

Phoenix Futures (2009). Website. www.phoenix-futures.org.uk Last accessed 10 January 2010).

Pierce, S., and Haigh, R. (2008). Mini therapeutic communities: A new development in the United Kingdom. *Therapeutic Communities* 29(2): 111–24.

Pilgrim, D., and Rogers, A. (2005). *A Sociology of Mental Health and Illness* (3rd edn). Buckingham: Open University Press.

Piperidou, E., and Bliss, J. (2008). An exploration of exercise training effects in coronary heart disease. *British Journal of Community Nursing* 13(6): 271–7.

Pointu, A., Young, J., and Walsh, K. (2009). Improving health with acute liaison nursing. *Learning Disability Practice* 12(5): 16–20.

Porter, C. (1997). RCN to host summit on security. *Nursing Times* 93(20): 5.

Premack, D. (1959). Toward empirical behaviour laws: Positive reinforcement. *Psychological Review* 66: 219–37.

Prins, H. (Chair) (1993). *Report of the Committee of Inquiry into the Death in Broadmoor Hospital of Orville Blackwood and a Review of the Deaths of Two Other Afro-Caribbean Patients: 'Big, Black and Dangerous?'* London: Department of Health.

Prins, H. (2005). *Offenders, Deviants or Patients?* (3rd edn). London: Routledge and Francis Group.

Prochaska, J., and DiClemente, C. (1982). Transtheoretical therapy: Towards a more integrative model of change. *Psychotherapy: Theory, Research and Practice* 19(3): 276–88.

Quanbeck, C.D., and McDermott, B.E. (2008). Inpatient settings. In Simon, R.I., and Tardiff, K. (eds) *Textbook of Violence Assessment and Management*. Washington DC: American Publishing, Inc.

Quirk, A., and Lelliott, P. (2001). What do we know about life on acute psychiatric wards in the UK? A review of the research evidence. *Social Science and Medicine* 53: 1565–74.

Rabbitt, P. (ed.) (1997). Introduction: Methodologies and models in the study of executive function. In Rabbitt, P. (ed.) *Methodology of Frontal and Executive Function*. Hove: Psychology Press.

Race, D.G. (ed.) (2002). *Learning Disability. A Social Approach*. London: Routledge.

Raguram, R., Ventakeswaran, J., Ramakrishna, J., and Weiss, M.G. (2002). Traditional and community resources for mental health: a report of temple healing from India. *British Medical Journal* 325(7354): 38.

Rahkonen, T., Eloniemi-Sulkava, U., Halonen, P., Verkkoniemi, A., Niinisto, L., Notkola, I.L. and Sulkaua, R. (2001). Delirium in the non-demented oldest old in the general population: Risk factors and prognosis. *International Journal of Geriatric Psychiatry* 16: 415–21.

Ramsbotham, Sir D. (2005). *Prisongate: The Shocking State of Britain's Prisons and the Need for Visionary Change*. London: Free Press.

Rassool, G.H., and Winnington, J. (2006). Dealing with intoxication, overdose, withdrawal and detoxification: Nursing assessment and interventions. In Rassool, G.H. (ed.) *Dual Diagnosis Nursing*. Oxford: Blackwell Publishing/Addiction Press.

Ratigan, B., and Aveline, M. (1988). Interpersonal group therapy. In Aveline, M., and Dryden, W. (eds) *Group Therapy in Britain*. Milton Keynes: Open University Press.

Rawlinson, D. (1999). Group psychoanalytic ideas: Extending the group matrix to TCs. In Campling, P., and Haigh, R. (eds). *Therapeutic Communities: Past, Present and Future*. London: Jessica Kingsley.

Redfern, S.J., and Ross, F.M. (eds) (2006). *Nursing Older People*. Edinburgh: Churchill Livingstone.

Richards, D., Clark, T., and Clarke, C. (eds) (2007). *The Human Brain and Its Disorders*. Oxford: Oxford University Press.

Richards, S., and Mughal, A.F. (2009). *Working with the Mental Capacity Act, 2005* (2nd edn). North Waltham: Matrix Training Associates.

Richter, D. (2006). Nonphysical conflict management and de-escalation. In Richter, D., and Whittington, R. (eds) *Violence in Mental Health Settings. Causes, Consequences, Management*. New York: Springer.

Richter, D., and Whittington, R. (eds) (2006). *Violence in Mental Health Settings. Causes, Consequences, Management*. New York: Springer.

Richter, D., Needham, I., and Kunz, S. (2006). The effects of aggression management training for mental health care and disability care staff: A systematic review. In Richter, D., and Whittington, R. (eds) *Violence in Mental Health Settings. Causes, Consequences, Management*. New York: Springer.

Rigby, K. (2002). *New Perspectives on Bullying*. London: Jessica Kingsley.

Riner, M.E., and Flynn, B.C. (1999). Creating violence-free cities for our youth. *Holistic Nursing Practice* 14(1): 1–11.

Rippon, T.J. (2000). Aggression and violence in health care professions. *Journal of Advanced Nursing* 31(2): 452–60.

Rittermeyer, L. (2009). Community violence. In Fontaine, K.L. (ed.) *Mental Health Nursing* (6th edn). Upper Saddle River NJ: Prentice Hall.

Rogers, C. (1967). *On Becoming a Person: A Therapist's View of Psychotherapy*. London: Constable.

Rogers, C. (1990). A client-centred/person-centred approach to therapy. In Kirschbaum, H., and Henderson, V.L. (eds) *The Carl Rogers Reader*. London: Constable.

Rogers, P., and Vidgen, A. (2006). Working with people with serious mental illness who are angry. In Gamble, C., and Brennan, G. (eds) *Working with Serious Mental Illness, A Manual for Clinical Practice* (2nd edn). Edinburgh: Elsevier.

Rowden, R. (2002). Empowerment in forensic mental health. In Dooher, J., and Byrt, R. (eds.) *Empowerment and Participation: Power, Influence and Control in Contemporary Health Care*. Dinton, Salisbury: Quay Books.

Rowe, M.M., and Sherlock, H. (2005). Stress and verbal abuse in nursing: Do burned out nurses eat their young? *Journal of Nurse Management* 13(3): 242–8.

Royal College of Nursing (2008). *'Let's Talk About Restraint'. Rights, Risks and Responsibilities*. London: RCN.

Royal College of Nursing and the NHS Executive (1998). *Safe Working in the Community: A Guide for NHS Managers and Staff in Reducing the Risks of Violence and Aggression*. London: Royal College of Nursing and the NHS Executive.

Royal College of Physicians and British Geriatric Society (2006). *The Prevention, Diagnosis and Management of Delirium in Older People: National Guidelines*. London: Royal College of Physicians.

Royal College of Psychiatrists (1998). *Management of Imminent Violence. Clinical Practice Guidelines to Support Mental Health Services*. London: Royal College of Psychiatrists.

Royal College of Psychiatrists, British Psychological Society and Royal College of Speech and Language Therapists (2007). *Challenging Behaviour: A Unified Approach. Clinical and Service Guidelines for Supporting People with Learning Disabilities Who are at Risk of Receiving Abusive or Restrictive Practices*. London: Royal College of Psychiatrists.

Royal College of Psychiatrists Audit Team (2005). *The Healthcare Commission National Audit of Violence, 2003-2005*. London: The Royal College of Psychiatrists.

Royal College of Psychiatrists Centre for Quality Improvement (2007a). *Healthcare Commission National Audit of Violence, 2006-2007. Final Report. Working Age Services*. London: The Royal College of Psychiatrists.

Royal College of Psychiatrists Centre for Quality Improvement (2007b). *Healthcare Commission National Audit of Violence, 2006-2007. Final Report. Older People's Services*. London: The Royal College of Psychiatrists.

Royal College of Psychiatrists Centre for Quality Improvement (2007c). Quality Network for Medium Secure Units. *Standards for Medium Secure Units*. London: The Royal College of Psychiatrists.

Rudge, S. (2002). Age and isms: Older people and power. In Dooher, J., and Byrt, R. (eds) *Empowerment and Participation: Power, Influence and Control in Contemporary Health Care*. Dinton, Salisbury: Quay Books, Mark Allen Publishing, Ltd.

Rutter, Sir M. (2008). *Rutter's Child and Adolescent Psychiatry* (5th edn). Chichester: Wiley.

Ryan, C.J., and Bowers, L. (2005). Coercive manoeuvres in a psychiatric intensive care unit. *Journal of Psychiatric and Mental Health Nursing* 12: 695–702.

Ryan, D. (2009). The person who appears paranoid or suspicious. In Barker, P. (ed.) *Psychiatric and Mental Health Nursing: The Craft of Caring* (2nd edn). London: Arnold.

Sainsbury Centre for Mental Health (2006). *The Search for Acute Solutions. Improving the Quality of Care in Acute Psychiatric Wards*. London: Sainsbury Centre for Mental Health.

Sang, B. (2003). Patient and public participation in health systems. In Dooher, J., and Byrt, R. (eds.) *Empowerment and the Health Service User*. Dinton, Salisbury: Quay Books.

Savage, P., Long, C., Hall, C., Mackenzie, H., and Martin, L. (2009). Reaping the rewards of better fitness. *Mental Health Practice* 12(5): 32–5.

Scarpa, A., and Raine, A. (2008). Biosocial bases of violence. In Flannery, D.J., Vazsonyi, A.T., and Waldman, I.D. (eds) *The Cambridge Handbook of Violent Behavior and Aggression*. New York: Cambridge University Press.

Schafer, P. (1999). Working with Dave. Application of Peplau's interpersonal nursing theory in the correctional environment. *Journal of Psychosocial Nursing and Mental Health Services* 37(9): 18–24.

Schafer, P. (2002). Nursing interventions and future directions with patients who constantly break rules and test boundaries. In Kettles, A.M., Woods, P., and Collins, M. (eds) *Therapeutic Interventions for Forensic Mental Health Nurses*. London: Jessica Kingsley.

Schalast, N., Redies, M., Collins, M., Stacey, J., and Howells, K. (2008). EssenCES, a short questionnaire for assessing the social climate of forensic psychiatric wards. *Criminal Behaviour and Mental Health*. 18: 49–58.

Shlosberg, E. (2003). Psychological interventions. In Baldwin, R., and Murray, M. (eds) *Younger People with Dementia. A Multidisciplinary Approach*. London: Martin Dunitz, Taylor and Francis Group.

Scholl, S., Grall, G., Petzl, V., Rothier, M., Slotta-Bachmayr, L., and Kotrschal, K. (2008). Behavioural effects of goats on disabled persons. *Therapeutic Communities* 29(3): 297–309.

Secker, J., and Harding, C. (2002). African and African Caribbean users' perceptions of inpatient services. *Journal of Psychiatric and Mental Health Nursing* 9: 161–7.

Secker, J., Benson, A., Balfe, E., Lipsedge, M., Robinson, S., and Walker, J. (2004). Understanding the social context of violent and aggressive incidents on an inpatient unit. *Journal of Psychiatric and Mental Health Nursing* 11(2): 172–8.

Seddon, T. (2007). *Punishment and Madness. Governing Prisoners with Mental Health Problems*. Abingdon: Routledge and Cavendish, Taylor and Francis Group.

Selye, H. (1974). *Stress Without Distress*. New York: McGraw Hill.

Senior, J. (2005). The Development of Prison Mental Health Services Based on a Community Mental Health Model. Manchester. PhD thesis, University of Manchester.

Senior, J., and Shaw, J. (2008). Mental Healthcare in Prisons. In Soothill, K., Rogers, P., and Dolan, M. (eds) *Handbook of Forensic Mental Health*. Uffculme, Cullompton: Willan Publishing.

Sewell, H. (2009). *Working with Ethnicity, Race and Culture in Mental Health. A Handbook for Practitioners*. London: Jessica Kingsley.

Shacklady, J. (1997). Violence in the community. *Journal of Community Nursing* 3(6): 277–82.

Shepherd, J. (2001a). *Violence in Healthcare. Understanding, Preventing and Surviving Violence. A Practical Guide for Professionals* (2nd edn). Oxford: Oxford University Press.

Shepherd, J. (2001b). The future: The contribution of Accident and Emergency departments to community violence prevention. In Shepherd, J. *Violence in Healthcare. Understanding, Preventing and Surviving Violence. A Practical Guide for Professionals* (2nd edn). Oxford: Oxford University Press.

Shlosberg, E. (2003). Psychological interventions. In Baldwin, R., and Murray, M. (eds) *Younger People with Dementia. A Multidisciplinary Approach*. London: Martin Dunitz, Taylor and Francis Group.

Siddle, R., and Everitt, J. (2002). Identifying and overcoming negative symptoms. In Harris, N., Williams, S., and Bradshaw, T. (eds) *Psychosocial Interventions for People with Schizophrenia: A Practical Guide for Mental Health Workers*. Basingstoke: Palgrave Macmillan.

Sillitoe, A. (1959). *The Loneliness of the Long Distance Runner*. London: Pan Books.

Simmons, J., and Griffiths, R. (2009). *Cognitive Behavioural Therapy for Beginners*. London: Sage Publications.

Simon, R.I., and Tardiff, K. (2008). *Textbook of Violence Assessment and Management*. Washington DC: American Publishing, Inc.

Singleton, N., Meltzer, H., and Gatward, R. (1998). *Psychiatric Morbidity Among Prisoners in England and Wales*. London: Office of National Statistics.

Skinner, B.F. (1953). *Science and Human Behaviour*. London: Macmillan.

Slevin, E. (2007). Challenging behaviour. In: Gates, B. (ed.) *Learning Disabilities. Towards Inclusion*. Edinburgh: Churchill Livingstone, Elsevier.

Smail, D. (1996). *How to Survive Without Psychotherapy*. London: Constable.

Smith, E.E., Nolen-Hoeksema, S., Frederickson, B., and Loftus, G.R. (eds) (2003). *Hilgard's Introduction to Psychology* (14th edn). Fort Worth: Harcourt College Publishers.

Smith, G., Bartlett, A., and King, M. (2004). Treatments of homosexuality in Britain since the nineteen fifties: an oral history: the experience of patients. *British Medical Journal* 328(7437): 427–9.

Snyder, K.S., Wallace, C.J., Moe, K., and Liberman, R.P. (1994). Expressed emotion by residential care operators and residents' symptoms and quality of life. *Hospital and Community Psychiatry* 45(11): 1141–63.

Sofield, L., and Salmond, S.W. (2003). Workplace violence. A focus on verbal abuse and intent to leave the organisation. *Orthopaedic Nursing* 22(4): 274–83.

South, C.R., and Wood, J. (2006). Bullying in prisons: the importance of perceived social status, prisonization and moral disengagement. *Aggressive Behavior* 32(5): 490–501.

Squires, A.J., and Hastings, M.B. (2002). *Rehabilitation of the Older Person: A Handbook for the Interdisciplinary Team*. Cheltenham: Nelson Thornes.

Stern, V. (2006). *Creating Criminals. Prisons and People in a Market Society*. Halifax, Nova Scotia: Fernwood Publishing, Ltd.

Stevens, L. (2002). A practical approach to gender-based violence: A programme guide for health care providers and managers: Developed by the UN Population Fund. *International Journal of Gynaecology and Obstetrics* Supplement 1. 78: 111–17.

Stockwell, F. (1972). *The Unpopular Patient*. London: Royal College of Nursing.

Stokes, G. (2000). *Challenging Behaviour in Dementia: A Person-Centred Approach*. Bicester: Speechmark.

Stokes, G. (2002). Working with aggression: Prevention and intervention. In Stokes, G., and Gaudie, F. (eds) *The Essential Dementia Care Handbook*. Bicester: Speechmark.

Stone, L. (1971). Reflections on the psychoanalytic concept of aggression. *Matherson Psychoanalytic Quarterly* 40: 195–244.

Stuart, G.W. (2009). Therapeutic nurse-patient relationship. In Stuart, G.W. (ed.) *Principles and Practice of Psychiatric Nursing* (9th edn). St. Louis, Missouri: Mosby/Elsevier.

Stuart, G.W., and Hamolia, C.D. (2009). Preventing and managing aggressive behaviour. In Stuart, G.W. (ed.) *Principles and Practice of Psychiatric Nursing* (9th edn). St. Louis, Missouri: Mosby/Elsevier.

Swaffer, T., and Hollin, C.R. (2001). Anger and general health in the young offender. *The Journal of Forensic Psychiatry* 12: 90–103.

Sweet, A. (1998). Taking the trauma out of a crisis. *Nursing Times* 94(33): 26–8.

Swenson, R.S. (2006). *Review of Clinical and Functional Neuroscience*. Hanover, New Hampshire: Dartmouth Medical School. Accessed on: www.dartmouth.edu/~swenson/neurosci/index.html

Swinford, S., and Dowling, K. (2009). How to catch children before they go feral. *The Sunday Times* September 6, p. 12.

Taylor, D.L., and Laraia, M.T. (2009). Biological context of psychiatric nursing care. In Stuart, G.W. (ed.) *Principles and Practice of Psychiatric Nursing* (9th edn). St. Louis, Missouri: Mosby/Elsevier.

Teri, L., and Gallagher-Thompson, D. (1991). Cognitive behavioural interventions for treatment of depression in Alzheimer's patients. *Gerontologist* 31: 413–16.

Tetlie, T., Heimsnes, M.C., and Almvik, R. (2009). Using exercise to treat patients with severe mental illness. How and why? *Journal of Psychosocial Nursing* 42(2): 33–40.

Tew, J. (ed.). (2005). *Social Perspectives in Mental Health: Developing Social Models to Understand and Work with Mental Distress*. London: Jessica Kingsley.

Thampy, L., and Bhugra, D. (2004). In-patient care and ethnic minority patients. In Campling, P., Davies, S., and Farquharson, G. (eds) *From Toxic Institutions to Therapeutic Environments: Residential Settings in Mental Health Services*. London: Gaskell.

Thomas, B., Jones, M., Johns, P., and Trauer, T. (2006). PRN medication in a psychiatric high-dependency unit after the introduction of a nurse-led activity programme. *International Journal of Mental Health Nursing* 15: 266–71.

Thomas, D., and Woods, H. (2003). *Working with People with Learning Disabilities*. London: Jessica Kingsley.

Thompson, I.E., Melia, K.M., Boyd, K.M., and Horsburgh, D. (eds). (2006). *Nursing Ethics* (5th edn). Edinburgh: Churchill Livingstone/Elsevier.

Thompson, N. (2003). *Promoting Equality: Challenging Discrimination and Oppression* (2nd edn). Basingstoke: Palgrave, Macmillan.

Timko, C., and Moos, R.H. (2004). Measuring the therapeutic environment. In Campling, P., Davies, S., and Farquharson, G. (eds) *From Toxic Institutions to Therapeutic Environments: Residential Settings in Mental Health Services*. London: Gaskell.

Toch, H., and Kupers, T.A. (2007). Violence in prisons, revisited. *Journal of Offender Rehabilitation* 45(3/4): 1–28.

Torphy, D., and Hall, M. (1993). Violent incidents in a secure unit. *The Journal of Forensic Psychiatry* 4(3): 517–44.

Tribe, R., and Morrissey, J. (2003). The refugee context and the role of interpreters. In Tribe, R., and Raval, H. (eds) *Working with Interpreters in Mental Health*. Hove: Brunner-Routledge, Taylor and Francis Group.

Tribe, R., and Raval, H. (eds) (2003). *Working with Interpreters in Mental Health*. Hove: Brunner-Routledge, Taylor and Francis Group.

Turnbull, J. (1999). Theoretical approaches to violence and aggression. In Turnbull, J., and Paterson, B. (eds) *Aggression and Violence: Approaches to Effective Management*. Basingstoke: MacMillan.

Turnbull, J., and Paterson, B. (eds) (1999). *Aggression and Violence: Approaches to Effective Management*. Basingstoke: MacMillan.

Twist, S., and Montgomery, A. (2005). Promoting healthy lifestyles. In Grant, G., Goward, P., Richardson, M., and Ramcharan, P. (eds) *Learning Disability. A Life Cycle Approach to Valuing People*. Maidenhead: Open University Press.

Tynan, H., and Allen, D. (2002). The impact of service user cognitive level on carer attributions for aggressive behaviour. *Journal of Applied Research in Intellectual Disabilities* 15: 213–23.

Unison and Royal College of Nursing (2004). *Not Just a Friend: Best Practice Guidance on Health Care for Lesbian, Gay and Bisexual Service Users and Their Families*. London: UNISON.

University of Oxford (2008). Prison Study to Investigate Link Between Diet and Behaviour. 29 January 2008. www.ox.ac.uk/media_news.stories/2008/080129.html (accessed 9 February 2010).

Upson, A. (2004). *Violence at Work: Findings From the 2002/03 British Crime Survey. Home Office Report 02/04*. London: Home Office. Accessed via: www.homeoffice.gov.uk (last accessed 8 February 2010).

van Goozen, S.H.M., and Fairchild, G. (2009). The neuroendocrinology of antisocial behaviour. In Hodgins, S., Viding, E., and Plodowski, A. (eds) *The Neurological Basis of Violence: Science and Rehabilitation*. Oxford: Oxford University Press.

van Weert, J.C.M., van Dulmen, A.M., Spreeuwenberg, P.M.M., Ribbe, M.W., and Bending, J.M. (2005). Behavioural and mood effects of Snoezelen integrated into twenty four hour dementia care. *JAGS: Journal of the Geriatrics Society* 50(1): 24–33.

Viding, E., Larsson, H., and Jones, A.P. (2009). Quantitative genetic studies of antisocial behaviour. In Hodgins, S., Viding, E., and Plodowski, A. (eds) *The Neurological Basis of Violence: Science and Rehabilitation*. Oxford: Oxford University Press.

Virkkunen, M., Goldman, D., Nielsen, D.A., and Linnolia, M. (1995). Low brain serotonin turnover rate (Low CSF 5-HIAA) and impulsive violence. *Journal of Neuropsychiatry and Clinical Neurosciences* 11: 307–14.

Von Sommaruga, T. (2004). The physical environment and use of space. In Campling, P., Davies, S., and Farquharson, G. (eds) *From Toxic Institutions to Therapeutic Environments: Residential Settings in Mental Health Services*. London: Gaskell.

Walker, S. (2008). Changing spaces. *Mental Health Practice* 12(3): 14–16.

Walton, P. (2000). Psychiatric hospital care: A case of the more things change, the more they remain the same. *Journal of Mental Health* 9(1):

77–88.

Walsh, M., and Ford, P. (1989). *Nursing Rituals: Research and Rational Actions*. Oxford: Butterworth-Heinemann.

Warner, C. (1992). Responding to aggression. *Nursing Times* 88(30): 46–7.

Watkins, J. (1996). *Living with Schizophrenia: A Holistic Approach to Understanding, Prevention and Recovery*. Melbourne: Hill of Content.

Watkins, P. (2007). *Recovery. A Guide for Mental Health Practitioners*. Edinburgh: Churchill Livingstone, Elsevier.

Waugh, F. (2008). Violence against children within the family. In Fawcett, B., and Waugh, F. (eds) *Addressing Violence, Abuse and Oppression. Debates and Challenges*. London: Routledge, Taylor and Francis Group.

Weber, Z. (2008). Out of the asylum: From restraints to freedom? In Fawcett, B., and Waugh, F. (eds) *Addressing Violence, Abuse and Oppression. Debates and Challenges*. London: Routledge, Taylor and Francis Group.

Wells, J., and Bowers, L. (2002). How prevalent is violence towards nurses working in the UK? *Journal of Advanced Nursing* 39(3): 230–40.

Werbach, M. (1995). Nutritional influences on aggressive behaviour. *Journal of Orthomolecular Medicine* 7: 45–51.

West, M., and Abolins, D. (2001). Dealing with hostility. In McClelland, N., Humphreys, M., Conlon, L., and Hillis, T. (eds) *Forensic Nursing and Mental Disorder in Clinical Practice*. Oxford: Butterworth-Heinemann.

Westwood, S. (2002). *Power and the Social*. Routledge: London.

White, C., Holland, D., Marsland, D., and Oakes, P. (2003). The identification of environments and cultures that promote the abuse of people with intellectual disabilities: A review of the literature. *Journal of Applied Research in Intellectual Disabilities* 16(1): 1–9.

Whittington, R. (2000). Changing the environment in the management of aggression. In McClelland, N., Humphreys, M., Mercer, D., Mason, T., McKeown, M., and McCann, G. (eds) (2000) *Forensic Mental Health Care. A Case Study Approach*. Edinburgh: Churchill Livingstone.

Whittington, R., and Balsamo, D. (1998). Violence: Fear and power. In Mason, T., and Mercer, D. (eds) *Critical Perspectives in Forensic Care. Inside Out*. Basingstoke: Macmillan.

Whittington, R., Baskind, E., and Paterson, B. (2006). Coercive measures in the management of imminent violence: Restraint, seclusion and enhanced observation. In Richter, D., and Whittington, R. (eds) *Violence in Mental Health Settings. Causes, Consequences, Management*. New York: Springer.

Whittington, R., and Richter, D. (2006). From the individual to the interpersonal: Environment and interaction in the escalation of violence in mental health settings. In Richter, D., and Whittington, R. (eds) *Violence in Mental Health Settings. Causes, Consequences, Management*. New York: Springer.

Whittington, R., and Wykes, T. (1989). Invisible injury. *Nursing Times* 85(42): 30–2.

Whittington, R., and Wykes, T. (1996). Aversive stimulation by staff and violence by psychiatric patients. *British Journal of Clinical Psychology* 35(1) 11–20.

Wiertsema, H., and Derks, F. (1997). Residential forensic treatment. The interplay between case management and institutional management. In Van Marle, H. (ed.) *Challenges in Forensic Psychotherapy*. London: Jessica Kingsley.

Willis, B., and Gillett, J. (2003). *Maintaining Control. An Introduction to the Effective Management of Violence and Aggression*. London: Arnold.

Wilson, J.F. (2003). *Biological Foundations of Human Behaviour*. Belmont, CA: Thomson Wadsworth.

Wilson, P.A., Hansen, N.B., Tarakeshwar, N., Neufeld, S., Kochman, A., and Sikkema, K.J. (2008). Scale development of a measure to assess community-based and clinical intervention group environments. *Journal of Community Psychology* 36(3): 271–88.

Winship, G. (2009). Therapeutic communities. In Barker, P. (ed.) Psychiatric and Mental Health Nursing. The Craft of Caring (2nd edn). London: Hodder Arnold.

Wood, T. (2007). 'We need to make a football out of a goat head'. Working with young offenders in a prison therapeutic community. In Parker, M. (ed.) *Dynamic Security. The Therapeutic Community in Prison*. London: Jessica Kingsley.

Woods, P. (2006). Types of personality disorder. In National Forensic Nurses' Research and Development Group: Woods, P., Kettles, A.M., Byrt, R., Addo, M., Coffey, M., Collins, M., Doyle, M., Garman, G., and Watson, C. (eds) *Aspects of Forensic Mental Health Nursing: Interventions with People with 'Personality Disorder'*. London: Quay Books/MA Healthcare, Ltd.

Woods, P., and Kettles, A. (eds) (2009a). *Risk Assessment and Risk Management in Mental Health Nursing*. Chichester: Wiley-Blackwell.

Woods, P., and Kettles, A. (2009b). Introduction. In Woods, P., and Kettles, A. (eds) *Risk Assessment and Risk Management in Mental Health Nursing*. Chichester: Wiley-Blackwell.

Woodward, N., Williams, L., and Melia, P. (2004). Creating and maintaining a safe environment. In Kirby, S., Hart, D.A., Cross, D., and Mitchell, G. (eds) *Mental Health Nursing. Competencies for Practice*. Basingstoke: Palgrave.

Wootton, J.M., Frick, P.J., Shelton, K.K., and Silverthorn, P. (1997). Ineffective parenting and childhood conduct problems: the moderating role of callous-unemotional traits. *Journal of Consulting and Clinical Psychology* 65: 292–300.

World Health Organisation (2002). *World Report on Violence and Health. Geneva*: World Health Organisation.

World Health Organisation. (2004). *Preventing Violence. A Guide to Implementing the Recommendations of the World Report on Violence and Health*. Geneva: World Health Organisation.

World Health Organisation (WHO) and Montreal PAHO/WHO Collaborating Centre for Training in Mental Health (2007). *The WHO Atlas on Global Resources for Persons with Intellectual Disabilities: A Right to Health Perspective*. Geneva: World Health Organisation.

Wright, B. (2002). Zero Tolerance. What Does It Mean? Accident and *Emergency Nursing* 10(2): 61.

Zygmunt, A. (2002). Interventions to improve medication adherence in schizophrenia. *American Journal of Psychiatry* 159(10): 1653–64.

Index